THE
LAST ESCAPER

Peter Tunstall, portrait by John Mansel
(*see page 109*).

THE
LAST ESCAPER

by

Peter Tunstall

DUCKWORTH OVERLOOK

This paperback edition first published in the UK in 2015 by
Duckworth Overlook

LONDON
30 Calvin Street, London E1 6NW
T: 020 7490 7300
E: info@duckworth-publishers.co.uk
www.ducknet.co.uk
For bulk and special sales please contact sales@duckworth-publishers.co.uk,
or write to us at the above address.

NEW YORK
141 Wooster Street
New York, NY 10012
www.overlookpress.com
For bulk and special sales please contact sales@overlookny.com,
or write us at the above address.

A catalogue record for this book is available
from the British Library
Cataloguing-in-Publication Data is available
from the Library of Congress

Published with assistance from the
Stickles Fund for Military History, Colgate University

ISBNs
UK: 978-0-7156-5021-9

Contents

Foreword

My great friend Dick Morgan—later to be my best man—and I succeeded in escaping from Spangenberg Castle, only to be recaptured a fortnight later and sent to Colditz after a term of solitary confinement. We were marched from Colditz railway station to the *Schloss*. My first view of this ancient castle was from the bridge over the river, and there it loomed above us. It was to house us for nearly two years. To my surprise I could hear the sound of cheering and pieces of material were being waved from the windows—which, as we drew nearer, I could see were barred. The noise grew louder and by the time we entered the cobbled courtyard it had grown to pandemonium, sounding like a first-class riot.

The Germans had two tables in the yard, each placed against the wall below the windows, and German officers sat there to take our particulars, photograph us and so on. To my amazement, water bombs rained onto the tables, and then a blazing palliasse was thrown down out of an upper window. Grinning faces looked down, roaring insults at our captors. Eventually a riot squad doubled in, wearing coal-scuttle helmets and carrying weapons. The Germans pointed their rifles up at the prisoners above and the proceedings were then completed in comparative quiet. Until that time we had only seen the well-behaved officer prisoners at Westertimke, a naval officers' camp near Bremen, and at Spangenberg. Clearly, morale at Colditz was terrific and the prisoners were men to be reckoned with and respected accordingly by their captors.

Eventually the German guards left and the inmates of Oflag IVC poured down into the courtyard. "I'm Jack Keats," said a smiling officer with glasses. "Come and join our mess in the Belgian Quarters." Dick and I were taken up a spiral staircase with open doors off it through which we could see ablutions and lavatories, to a top floor and along it to an end room. This contained a number of double-tier bunks, plus some wooden tables and benches, and chairs made from Red Cross crates.

Foreword

"How do you do? I am Peter Tunstall." A well-built RAF officer with a moustache gave me a warm handshake. I learned that Peter Tunstall had just masterminded the near-riot that had only quietened down since the arrival of the armed German guards. Also that he was a fine shot with a water bomb and the result of his barrage on the tables on which the Germans had laid out the documents was chaotic and very effective.

Peter Tunstall obviously hated the Nazi system and he made this quite clear. When I got to know him better, he told me that before taking part in one of his first bombing raids, an official from the Air Ministry, who was lecturing him and his crew on how to behave if captured, told him that his first duty was to escape and his second was to be as big a bloody nuisance as possible. He was doing his best to achieve both and had already clocked up a record score of days in solitary confinement. Peter also told me that his Air Gunner, Sgt Joyce, an Irishman, was a cousin of William Joyce— Lord Haw-Haw—who was later executed for treason and whose body Sgt Joyce managed to get buried in Ireland after the war.

Peter Tunstall's book is an easy and interesting read, which certainly describes what it felt like to plan and actually carry out an escape; to be tired, hungry and thirsty in an enemy country, trying to avoid contact with the local population.

After the war Peter served in the Royal Air Force until 1958, and later settled in South Africa. A brave, charismatic and resourceful officer whose name will always be associated with Oflag IVC in Colditz Castle. This is his story.

Major-General Corran Purdon, C.B.E., M.C., C.P.M.

Introduction

"Another escaping book?" you're asking. Haven't we done all that already? Surely by this time we know everything we need to know about British escapers in the Second World War. Indeed, hasn't it become a bit of a cliché? With the theme to *The Great Escape* being played by fans at every England international football match; with the cardboard cut-out figures of the dashing POW and the dim-witted Hun having become, for the British, the nearest things to symbols of their respective nations; with the name Colditz instantly recognisable—aren't we in danger of stereotyping the Second World War, or even caricaturing it, as little more than a jolly good lark?

Well, yes—and that's the point.

I too have read a great many of these escape stories. Some are classics of war literature and their accounts of life behind the wire ring very true to me. Others, to put it kindly, tell us more about the fantasy lives of their authors. But all of them, or nearly all, were written and published at a time very close to the events they describe. Their authors were still young men, with a young man's perspective on experiences still fresh and vivid in their minds. They were also producing their accounts at a moment when readers expected a certain kind of narrative about the war: one that played up the notion of the victory having been won because of the Allies' (especially the British) superiority, rather than, as we now know, because of good fortune and the viciousness and short-sightedness of our enemies. Book-buyers weren't interested in hearing about hunger, pain, loneliness or fear. They wanted tales of excitement and adventure, of derring-do and ultimate success. And that, by and large, is what they got. It's hardly surprising that escape books became a distinct genre. Nor is it accidental that the most famous ones—Pat Reid's *The Colditz Story*, Eric Williams' *The Wooden Horse*, Airey Neave's *They Have Their Exits*—were accounts of the rare break-outs in which the protagonists made it back to Britain, rather than the more typical ones where the would-be escapers were recaptured, or their attempts were foiled after months of difficult and dangerous work, sometimes before they'd even got outside the wire.

This book is different. There are three reasons why I've written it. The first is that it is the very last of its kind that will ever appear. To the best of my knowledge, there are fewer than half a dozen of us still alive who were in Colditz during the Second World War. The book you hold in your hands is the final testimony that will ever be given by those who experienced these things for themselves.

The second is that this is not a Boy's Own Story. The subject matter is too serious for that. It's often forgotten that for us, the war was not a game. At the age of twenty, a time when the most that young people usually have to worry about is their exams, or what to do at the weekend, my friends and I were thrown into a grim battle for national survival, under circumstances that made it all but certain that we ourselves would not survive.

The figures tell their own story. For every one hundred bomber airmen who flew on operations during the war, fifty-one died in action, nine were killed in flying accidents, twelve became prisoners of war. Others were seriously injured and never flew again. Less than a quarter survived undamaged, physically at least, to see the end of the war. For those like me, who were in it from the very beginning, the odds were far worse. To put it another way, the number of officers from Bomber Command killed during the Second World War was higher than the *total* number of officers in the British Army killed during the First.

If we didn't see the war as a lark, still less did we consider our captivity in that light. The experience of becoming a POW was a devastating one, especially for those captured at the early stages of their operational career who felt they hadn't had a good swipe at the enemy. There were a lot of people in that category: forty percent of all losses occurred during a bomber crew's first five missions. Rightly or wrongly, many who were captured believed they'd failed in some way. We felt our sense of duty very strongly in those days, and one of the things that drove hard-core escapers forward was an overwhelming sense of urgency to get back in the fight. For just the chance to do so, we paid a high price. Escaping was a dangerous business. We were constantly warned that we could be shot while trying to get out of Germany, and some were. For my seven escape attempts, I was court-martialled by the Germans five times; spent a grand total of 415 days in solitary confinement (an all-comers' record among British POWs); and was placed by my captors on the exclusive list of *Deutschfeindlich* (irredeemably anti-German) prisoners. Rumour had it that if Germany lost the war, the people whose names appeared on that list would not be permitted to survive. When fifty recaptured British prisoners were murdered after the Great Escape of spring 1944, that rumour seemed a great deal more credible.

But the third, and most important, reason for this book is that it's the product of a lifetime of reflection. Had I written it fifty or sixty years ago, it would, perhaps, have had the immediacy and fine detail of recent memory and experience. But it could not have included the sense of perspective or quality of judgment that only comes with age and distance from the events of one's own life. What you're reading, then, is not just a reminiscence of vanished youth. For whatever reason, it appears that I am, quite literally, the last man standing from an entire generation who lived and experienced these things. In the pages that follow, you will find his final report, containing the information about his times that he hopes will be of most value to the generations that follow.

Chapter One

Mission impossible

I'm not psychic, so I can't say that I knew on that summer evening, as the aircraft lifted above the boundary fence and began a climbing turn toward Germany, that none of us would be coming back. But I wouldn't have bet against it.

August 1940 was not a good time to be a bomber pilot. France had fallen. It looked very much as though Great Britain was next. Most of the British Army had been pulled off the beaches at Dunkirk, but they had had to leave nearly all their weapons and equipment behind. The losses would take years to replace and we simply didn't have that long. The Germans were massing on the Channel coast to follow up their conquest of France with a quick invasion of Britain. If they got across, it was hard to see what could stop them. Our troops had little more than small arms with which to defend themselves, and not much more than haystacks to shelter behind. Every morning and afternoon immense swarms of German bombers roamed across the southeast of England, seeking out airfields, factories and ports, clearing a way for the ground forces that were to follow. RAF fighters were desperately fending them off, but God alone knew for how long that could go on.

In all this darkness there was only one faint gleam of hope. The British bomber force still remained, the only weapon that could directly affect Germany's war-making capacity. We knew that Germany had few natural resources of her own. In particular she was highly dependent on imported oil. She must already have used up most of her existing stocks in the campaign against France and the Low Countries. If bombing could destroy Germany's remaining oil plants, her entire intricate war machine might grind to a halt. That, of course, couldn't win the war for us. No doubt she would respond by building new refineries in places we couldn't easily hit. But it would buy us precious time, at least until the autumn gales set in and made a sea-borne invasion an impossibility until the following spring.

Such, at any rate, was the theory. In reality my comrades and I were being handed a Mission Impossible. We had begun the war believing that we would be able to fly into Germany in daylight, and that formations of bombers would be able to defend themselves against fighter attacks. Our first few raids disabused us of that notion. Loss rates approached fifty percent, with the survivors being so badly mauled that they had little or no chance of hitting their targets. So we turned to night attacks. The darkness gave us some prospect of living long enough to be able to reach our objectives. But it also increased the difficulty of the task exponentially. For one thing, none of us knew very much about flying after dark. When I began my operational career, I had precisely two hours and ten minutes' worth of experience as a pilot in command of a bomber at night.

Nor was that all. A bomber aircraft faces three challenges: navigation, target identification, and bomb aiming. With the miserably inadequate technology available at the time, all three largely defeated us. Unable to see the ground in the dark and lacking any radio-navigational aids, we found our way by what was officially known as dead reckoning (more honestly described as "by guess and by God"), that is, flying a compass course for a specified time and hoping that we would somehow wind up in the same province as our intended destination. The best of us navigated in much the same manner as Columbus had done when sailing to America in 1492—by using a mariner's sextant to sight the moon or stars and measuring their altitude above the horizon. A skilled navigator using these methods could tell you, to within a radius of around twenty miles, where you had been fifteen minutes ago. That assumes, of course, that high clouds didn't make it impossible to see the sky clearly. But this wouldn't have been of any help to my crew. None of us had had any training in astral navigation.

Even if one did find the target area, identifying a black building against a black landscape was usually impossible. Often, the only time we knew we were in the vicinity of something valuable to the enemy was when his anti-aircraft guns started shooting at us. Our bomb-sighting equipment was also primitive, producing errors of hundreds of yards even in skilled hands. And the bombs themselves were too small, carried too weak a charge of explosive, and in a shockingly high proportion of cases failed to go off.

Lastly, there were innumerable problems with our new aircraft, the Handley Page Hampden. This was a twin-engine bomber with a crew of four. It was about the same size as one of the smaller commuter turboprops used today for short hops between regional airports and the big hubs. But in 1940 it represented the last word in British bomber technology. Although it was quite a robust aircraft and pleasant to fly, many of the technical issues had not been worked out when we started using it in operations against Germany. The mechanics, no less than the aircrews, were learning on the job, and breakdowns were frequent. Hardly a single flight took place without some critical component—engines, compasses, radios—giving up the ghost. But in a world war, it's not possible to spend months or years in testing and development, especially when the war is going as badly as ours was. So we were simply thrown in at the deep end and left to figure out a way to cope with all these challenges by ourselves. Those who didn't manage, never came back. It was as simple and as brutal as that.

These sombre reflections were much in my mind when, on the afternoon of 26 August, we were called to the briefing room to be told the details of that night's mission. Our target was the Leuna synthetic oil plant at Merseburg near Leipzig. It was a hell of a long way away from our base at Hemswell in Lincolnshire, much further than any of us had ever been before. The round trip would take at least eight hours if the weather stayed kind, and longer if it didn't. The target was difficult to see, and, as we knew from an unsuccessful attack by another squadron ten days earlier, heavily defended.

As was usual in 1940, we were briefed to choose our own individual routes to the target. The idea of a concentrated bomber stream which sought to overwhelm the defences, allowing most of the aircraft to slip through while the Germans were preoccupied with just one or two of the leaders, had not yet been conceived. We bumbled along singly, getting everything that could be tossed up by the enemy all to ourselves, like driven pheasants coming stupidly out of cover—only one at a time.

This formidable assignment was received with the usual apparent nonchalance, but left a distinctly heavy feeling in the stomach. It was especially discouraging as the Met forecast was the usual story of fronts and cloud systems along the way with "perhaps" some clearance in the target area. The last item of guesswork, no doubt intended to help morale, was quite unconvincing, and we knew only too well how unreliable the forecast winds could be.

After briefing, we went for a quick meal to the mess. When our flight commander, Charles Kydd, who had personal service transport, shouted, "Who's for flights?" there was an undignified rush to scramble aboard his little Hillman van rather than walk the quarter of a mile down to the hangars. There in the locker rooms, dimly lit with windows already blacked out for the night as an air raid precaution, we put on thick woollen sweaters under our uniform tunics. Mine was a white one, which Ann had knitted for me with RAF colours in the V-neck. Then, over our tunics, we pulled on the harsh Sidcot flying suits, which in August would be warm enough without the detachable lining. Finally, we tied on our Mae West life jackets and began to feel like Michelin Men, cumbersome with clothing and equipment. Next came a last quick check of gear: topographical maps, code books, target maps, briefing instructions, and in my breast pocket, the usual six snapshots of Ann and—sentimental little boy that I was—the receipt from the Imperial Hotel, Llandudno, for the dinner dance on our last evening together.

Leaving the dim locker room in the hangar, with parachutes slung over our shoulders and leather helmets in our hands, it was odd to hit daylight again, like coming out of a cinema matinée. A watery sun was setting, giving a pink underglow to the ragged broken clouds scudding across the sky. The tarmac apron outside the hangar glinted with puddles from a recent downpour, and the tyres of the canvas-topped lorries sang in the wet as they sped towards us and stopped.

We clambered aboard the high three-tonners bound for the aircraft dispersal points, handing up to each other parachutes, navigation bags, ration packs and thermos flasks. It was going to be a long haul to Leipzig and back and a lonely night. As our lorry started to roll, somebody called from the hangar: "Good luck, chaps, see you in the 'Snake Pit' for a pint tomorrow night." Somebody always did it and I rather wished they

8

The bomber pilot's "office"—the cockpit of Peter Tunstall (PDT)'s Hampden.

wouldn't. Everyone knew the casualty rate well enough. The odds were against finishing a first tour of thirty sorties, and the jovialities always seemed a bit like tempting fate. This was by far the most trying part of any bomber sortie and I much preferred to be airborne.

We dropped out of the lorry at our own Hampden, which we had flight-tested that afternoon and found serviceable except for a minor instrument snag. Now the ground crew had her fully re-fuelled and our middle-aged corporal in charge of the ground crew assured me that everything was on top line, instruments all okay, bombed up and ready to go. I made a quick routine inspection round the aircraft, took a look into the open bomb bay to check that all safety pins had been removed from the bombs, and it was time to climb aboard. I noticed that one of my crew always gave the ground a ritual pat before he climbed into his battle station.

Parachute and helmet on and up the ladder to waddle across the wing with the pilot-type parachute bumping at the back of my thighs. One step up into the cockpit and I sank down into the metal seat with the 'chute and its sorbo-rubber pad forming the only cushion. Our corporal handed the safety harness over my shoulders and I buckled the straps to the ones coming up from the floor. Plug in the intercom for speaking to the rest of the crew; plug in oxygen and a nod to the corporal who gave me two pats on the shoulder (better than words) before disappearing down the ladder and removing it. I hoped nobody ever saw me trace the letters A N N for luck on the windscreen with my right forefinger.

Having run through the long list of routine checks, I shouted out, "Starting Port" and pressed the button to turn that engine while the lad underneath was priming fuel into the cylinders. With ignition switches on, the big three-bladed prop turned twice slowly, then jerked and, with a shuddering belch of blue smoke and a flash of flame from the exhaust, the eighteen-cylinder Bristol engine started. Now that we were committed, the tensions always eased. Starboard engine started, bomb doors closed, time now to wriggle a bit more comfortably down on that sorbo pad and tighten the shoulder straps.

Clear of dispersal, we were on our way and taxiing towards the caravan where "Paraffin Pete", a junior aircrew officer, was in charge of the flare path laid out on the all-grass airfield. It was still bright enough, however, for us to be able to take off without illumination. Pete flashed us a green with his Aldis signalling lamp. Once in line with the avenue of unlit paraffin goose-neck flares, like a row of old black watering-cans with a fat wick sticking out of each spout, I completed the take-off checks and pushed the two throttles all the way forward.

With an almighty bellow, the Hampden heaved herself forward over the grass and began to accelerate. On she bounded towards that far hedge, which had already been breached by a Hampden or two in the past. Then a gentle backward pressure on the control column, followed by a bit more, and we unstuck from Mother Earth. At about 100 feet from the ground I brought in the wing flaps and began a climbing turn onto our first course and we were bound for Leipzig, nearly four hours and, by the route we were taking, somewhat more than 600 miles away.

Looking down through broken cloud in the failing light we could see Englishmen carrying on their normal lives, going home for a peaceful evening or on the way to the village pub. My Irish rear-gunner, Sergeant Joyce, said: "Wouldn't mind changing places with them, sir, would you?" I thought it was a somewhat demoralising remark and I made some daft reply about how lucky we were to be able to travel so widely at government expense.

Soon after we crossed the English coast, the sea horizon merged with the sky as darkness fell and the cloud began to thicken. We were flying into the night and towards dirty weather. When I asked the navigator, Sergeant Murdock, what he could see below, I got the familiar answer, "Nothing, sir. It's black as a witch's tit down there."

It is a pity we caught no glimpse of the enemy coast, for had we seen it, probably before the expected time, we might have become aware that the winds we had been given for navigation purposes were inaccurate in speed and direction. In retrospect, it's clear that we were being blown faster and deeper into enemy territory than we expected and somewhat off track to the north.

We probed around for sight of a landmark but finally abandoned hope and climbed to a more comfortable height between cloud layers, trusting that we would later find the promised clearance in the weather that would enable us to make another effort at fixing our position visually. On the matter of finding the target I had come to a personal resolve. Too many of our previous missions had been failures—no more than the squadron average, perhaps, but failures nonetheless. Tonight we were going to extend ourselves to the utter limit or, as we used to say at the time, "shit or bust!"

As we forged on across Europe, the enemy would occasionally engage, their searchlight beams reaching up through low cloud, the heavy flak bok-bokking away, and sometimes getting a bit too close when we neglected to weave around and confuse their sound detectors.

Eventually, by our time calculations we should have been nearing the target area. It was now necessary to descend through the cloud and try, once again, to establish our position visually once we had broken out into the clear. Ordinarily, no pilot would ever dream of doing this. If the cloud extends all the way down to ground level, as it often does, the first you'll know of it is when you find yourself being quizzed by St Peter at the pearly gates. But these are risks that must be taken in wartime. If we were to find our target, there was simply no alternative.

More than seventy years later, my blood still runs cold at the memory of this descent. We sank into the blackness through the dense layer of cloud, throttles back, fretting about the higher ground we knew lay to the south of Leipzig, and trying to contrive that we erred in our navigation only in a northerly direction, if at all. As the altimeter unwound, my crew had their eyes straining for first sight of the ground while I concentrated on the instruments to keep the Hampden on an even keel.

The mind races quickly in these situations. The altimeter was showing 1,500 feet above sea level, but that was based on what the air pressure had been when we took off from Hemswell. Now, hours later, we might already be at ground level. 1,200 feet. Most hills that height are too low even to have names. 1,000 feet. This was getting ridiculous. We were going to fly into the ground and be killed instantly, without even having seen it. 900 feet. Two voices called over the intercom simultaneously:

"There's the ground!"

"I can see the deck!"

For the first time, I lifted my eyes from the instruments and, sure enough, there were a few scattered lights below. The Germans appeared to be a bit careless about blackout regulations this far to the east and perhaps over-confident about an air attack on account of the foul weather. We scudded along the base of the cloud with the altimeter reading a perilously low 800 to 900 feet, twisting and turning in an effort to find the target and still petrified about invisible hills, factory chimneys or radio antennae. Our chances of identifying the refinery were hopeless and I knew it, but we continued to try.

Down below the natives were obviously hostile, opening up on us with some light flak. As the tracer flitted up, we reckoned there must be something worth defending, and we managed to discern the reflected glint of some railway lines. These led into an array of buildings that looked like enormous sheds or workshops, so we turned back and bombed them.

Murdock the navigator, who admittedly had a better view of things than any other crew member, and whose job it was to find and identify the target and then aim the bombs, always maintained that we were indeed over the Leuna oil refinery. Furthermore, he thinks he saw another Hampden over the target area. I cannot vouch for either of these assertions and, on reconstructing the operation over and over again, have always been of the opinion that we must have been much further to the east than we believed. I sincerely hope we didn't bomb Russia.

Anyway, with the bombs gone among the buildings and railway lines, we were thankful that, with a clear conscience at having done our very best, we could pour on the power and start climbing, away from the terror of flying low and blind in unknown terrain, and away from the flak. As the altimeter wound up to a much safer reading, we were conscious only of our own deliverance from the acute anxiety of the past half-hour. Now there was a renewed chance of sharing eggs and bacon with Mike and Andy in the Mess, and a peaceful pint or two tomorrow night. We had done our best, inadequate though it was, and it was a relief to know that the rest of our efforts that night could be honourably devoted to our own salvation.

We found a comfortable level between layers of cloud, and sped homeward with no more than the usual interference from blind-firing flak, until the time approached for an essential navigation check as we crossed the enemy coast. We again descended to feel for the cloud base, but still found identification of ground features extremely difficult in the dark and dirty weather. We all knew that the only critical object was to see that coastline, for there was little hope of pinpointing our position exactly. Once clear of the European continent, we could send a radio message and get a course to steer from the ground stations tracking our transmissions. What mattered was to find England, any part of it from the Thames to the Humber.

Some minutes before his estimated time of arrival at the enemy coast, Sergeant Murdock, and soon after him, Sergeant Joyce, called over the intercom: "There it is, sir—enemy coast!" I banked the Hampden for a better view and saw dimly what certainly looked more or less like a coastline. Then the downward visibility was again obscured. We were heartened by the knowledge that all the signs on the way out had pointed to a probable weather clearance at base, so that we should not experience too much difficulty locating ourselves over England, provided another front had not swept in behind. Right now we were still in the cloud and I was becoming anxious about fuel. The gauges were reading uncomfortably low and I wondered whether we were losing any fuel due to flak hits, despite our self-sealing tanks. We had been airborne for nearly nine hours and had not seen a single thing that could verify our position after leaving our own coast. The situation was becoming really worrying. All now depended on getting those headings by radio from base.

It was time for the wireless operator, Sergeant Brock, to start passing me information. I asked him how things were going. He replied that he was having trouble with the radio. The engine-driven generator, which had packed up umpteen times on previous flights, seemed to have broken down yet again, and the main battery appeared to be flat. In an anxious tone of voice, Brock said he would try the emergency battery. I was concerned; not only was the fuel situation rapidly becoming critical but so was my personal pain threshold. These early Hampdens made no concessions at all to the pilot's comfort. He was supposed to perch for the entire flight on a rock-hard parachute pack, with only a thin layer of foam rubber to ease the pressure. This was adequate, just, on relatively short flights of four hours or so. After seven or eight hours it became completely unendurable. We were now approaching the nine-hour mark. I wriggled and squirmed to try to relieve the intense stabbing pain in my spine and bum, but nothing seemed to help.

In the midst of all this, Brock called me and I thought he sounded almost tearful: "I don't think we're transmitting, sir. I can't get any reply and all I hear is some European station like Hilversum playing gramophone records." He patched it through on the intercom so that we could all hear it. Of all things it was that dear old African-American singer, Paul Robeson, performing "Deep River". To this day that song gives me the creeps. Right then I was more concerned about the deep bloody sea.

It was long past our estimated time of arrival for the English coast. We could still see nothing and Brock had given up battling with the radio. Then came the most amazing remark of the whole episode. It was becoming a trifle lighter and clearer when Sergeant Joyce said,

"There's a coastline and land behind us, sir, and we are heading out to sea again!"

Brock left his useless radio and joined in: "It looks like one, but it could be low cloud or something. We already saw the coast anyway, so it can't be, and, anyway, it's pretty clear we are still over the sea."

This was mystifying, so I turned the aircraft to look for myself. There it was, a thin dark line on the sea, way back, not very distinct, but certainly something. It looked as if we were just leaving a land mass.

"What do you make of that, navigator?"

"Doesn't make sense, sir. It can't be a coastline of land *behind* us. There should be one *ahead* of us. We're already well overdue to cross our own coast inwards."

"Well, if that's a coastline and if we are just heading out to sea, we've made a hell of a cock-up somewhere. I'm turning back on course; check through everything. And Brock, for God's sake, keep trying for a bearing."

"I've been trying, sir, for the last twenty minutes. Can't get a bloody thing. I think our transmitter has packed up."

"Well, keep trying. And Navigator, when you've checked through everything, pass the maps and your log up here. If that was the enemy coast and we went back to check up in this light, the Luftwaffe would have us for breakfast."

A lone Hampden in daylight would indeed have been dead meat. On further consideration, we all felt sure that what we had just seen could not have been a coastline, but rather a trick of the dawning light on the sea and a bank of low cloud. By now I was really anxious about fuel, for there was still a minimum of thirty-five minutes' flying to do before we could be seeing base—longer if we had a head wind, or if I throttled back and flew for maximum range or endurance.

We had now been airborne for more than nine hours and, no matter how I wriggled or eased a foot momentarily off the rudder bar, the bones in my backside ached so agonisingly that it was a struggle to keep my mind on what really mattered. By this time the fuel gauge needles were hardly flickering above zero.

Then a ghastly thought began to form and gradually fixed itself in everyone's mind. Was it possible that we had overflown some narrow bit of England and were heading out into the Atlantic where we would eventually run out of fuel and nobody would ever look for us? We knew of so many strange things that had happened when crews had become as uncertain of their position as we were. Wally Sheen's crew had landed in Ireland with his navigator not sure whether they were over the North Sea or the Atlantic. A Whitley bomber crew had mistakenly bombed an RAF airfield in England thinking they were over Germany. A good crew, whom I later got to know, were said to have thought they were crash-landing near some Scottish woodlands that turned out to be the Black Forest in Germany. All these stories came to mind.

A few lucky crews had been rescued from their rubber dinghies after ditching in the sea, but usually after they had been able to transmit an SOS and a position report. Many more had perished in those dinghies, and the bodies of RAF aircrew, supported by their Mae West lifejackets, were often washed up on the shores of western Europe.

Murdock passed his maps, instruments and navigation log up to the cockpit and, with the automatic pilot engaged, I checked through all the calculations as best I could. I could spot no obvious error but having been over the sea for well over an hour and with that pain in my spine, I was ready to believe almost anything. I had to imagine the British Isles and assume distances and Eastern Atlantic coastlines as best I could. How much gap was there between the Cumberland coast and the north coast of Ireland? I simply did not know that bit of the country intimately and now found it hard to visualise a map as accurately as I needed.

Oh for a simple school atlas at that crucial moment! It would have made all the difference. Joyce swore we were heading out into the Atlantic. If we had been in the grip of strong enough tailwinds, almost anything was possible. Murdock the navigator could suggest nothing either way and by this time poor young Brock was almost reduced to tears of frustration by his bloody radio.

Fuel gauges were flickering almost dead on the stops where I had never seen them before. How much leeway this allowed I did not know. Our situation was utterly desperate and inexplicable. A major decision was needed at once, otherwise I was going to be responsible for the tragically stupid loss of four lives.

As I saw it at that moment, the decision seemed a straightforward one. We were either east or west of England. If we were east, still in the North Sea and our fuel held out, we might reach our coast and, with a bit of luck, pull off a crash landing of the kind I had already experienced in my operational career. But if we had already crossed England and were now in the North Atlantic (next stop America) and stayed on a westerly heading, my crew would suffer a lingering death in a rubber dinghy where nobody would look for it.

On the other hand, if we reversed course onto an easterly heading, the prospects seemed brighter. Assuming we were already in the Atlantic, we would run up against the western coast of Britain or Ireland, and make a safe landing. At worst, if it should transpire that we hadn't yet reached England, we would either ditch in the North Sea with at least some chance of being picked up by our own people, or we would reach the French or Dutch coast where there were allies and friends who could help us. The very worst-case scenario was that we would become prisoners of war.

Put like that there seemed only one reasonable choice. I turned around on to a course of about 120° magnetic, heading back for the coastline we all thought we had so very recently seen. My course was intended to hit, I hoped, the northwestern coast of Britain, or possibly Land's End, if the hazy maps in my mind's eye were about right.

Much too late for it to do us any good, we learned that the Hampden flies for quite a while with the fuel gauges registering empty. Meanwhile, we prepared ourselves as best we knew for ditching in the sea. Unlike the properly trained crews that would follow us, we had done no ditching drills or dinghy drills in a swimming pool, or even sailing drills in case we were lucky enough to have an airborne lifeboat dropped to us from a rescue aircraft. Brock jettisoned his two Vickers K machine guns, to make it easier for him and Joyce to escape the ditched Hampden through the rear upper hatch after releasing the self-inflating rubber dinghy, and that was about it.

It seemed like nearly half an hour before Murdock spotted the real

17

coast ahead, by which time I had come to the sickening conclusion that I had probably made a wrong decision. After that, to turn westward yet again with virtually empty fuel tanks would have meant a certain lingering death for all of us. Then the starboard engine shuddered twice and cut—obviously out of fuel. By now we were almost over a coast. I turned to line up with a long firm-looking stretch of wet sandy beach and made a good wheels-down landing as the port engine also cut out. We had been airborne for over ten hours.

My nether regions had passed the painful stage and were almost numb so that my crew had to lift me out of the cockpit and help me down to the ground, but I still could not stand up quite straight. Sergeant Joyce was ecstatic: "'Tis Ireland, sir, 'tis Ireland! I'd know it anywhere!"

I had a sick feeling he was talking utter crap. There was no sign of life so I told Brock and Murdock, who knew what was what among our documents on board, to gather together any confidential material, make an inflammable heap of it inside the aircraft, and stand by to set fire to it. I told them to augment this with any residual petrol they might be able to drain from the fuel tanks. Meanwhile, I would take Joyce with me towards a hut on the sand dunes about 200 yards away. I took the Very signal pistol and a red cartridge with me and told the others to set fire to the confidential stuff, and, hopefully, the whole aircraft if I fired off the flare. Then Joyce and I set off. I found even walking rather painful at the bottom of my spine and could not quite straighten my back. I felt a bit bent, like an old man and not a very heroic one.

The hut was deserted and locked up. I peered through a window and saw a magazine with a headline in a language that was not English. I pointed it out to Joyce and asked him, "Is that Irish?"

He took a look through the window and said in a lugubrious voice, "No, sir, 'tis not."

I replied, "No! It's bloody Dutch!" And I fired off the red cartridge into the air.

Joyce and I started to run back to the Hampden and I was glad to see a wisp of smoke curling up from within. We were halfway back to the others when the sand kicked up in front of us and we heard a burst of machine-gun fire. Then we saw the German soldiers, five or six of them with sub-machine guns, walking towards us in an open line abreast from the sand dunes. There was nowhere for us to take cover. We were all unarmed and it was obvious that we were about to become prisoners.

The German troops, having fought their way across France, were obviously well practised in taking prisoners and had all the clichés ready.

"England kaput."

"Ve shall be in London for Christmas."

"For you, ze vore iss ofer."

They were wrong on all three counts.

Those Germans were cock-a-hoop after their successful Blitzkrieg. They were really enjoying our plight and it made me angry. I thought of photographs I had seen at various times of miserable-looking, newly-captured prisoners and decided they were not going to have the satisfaction of seeing us like that. So I laughed at them and their boastfulness and told the others to do the same. I remember saying to the Germans, "The British may lose a few battles but they always win the last one."

I had many occasions to think of that remark during the next four years and eight months.

Chapter Two

"Do you really fly?"

The hand on my shoulder squeezed gently as a warning and, as it pressed downwards, I sank slowly on to my belly and hoped I had disappeared into the tangled undergrowth. My companion's larger frame had also melted silently from view and lay close beside me. It was he who had first taught me the technique of stalking.

"Lie flat and dead still. Remember, it is the twitching of an ear that betrays a buck to the eyes of a hunter—no fidgeting, no peeping. Cease to exist, and if an animal is sniffing around, try to relax. They can smell fear or panic."

I had not spotted the reason for my companion's alarm and could only guess at the danger. Then I heard the scratch of clothing pushing through bushes. Disaster would be upon us within the next few seconds. The earthy scent of leaf mould and pungent weeds, so long associated with a sense of freedom in these woods, became a fearsome stench. My thumping heart defied control and I was ashamed that I could not conform to the relaxed survival drill. Then, self-discipline slipped further. Very slowly I raised my nose off the ground and with eyes straining upwards peered through the lace of tangled autumn stems. Along the narrow woodland path I saw the man approaching. The gun lying comfortably across the crook of his left arm was gripped at the small of the stock with his right hand. I knew he could throw that weapon up and shoot accurately in one swift easy movement. At his heel was a black Labrador, eyes alert and eager for his master's bidding. I let my face sink back on to the ground. A breath of wind stirred my hair like a flag to betray our presence. Now the stealthy footsteps were almost upon us and I could hear the dog panting. Man and dog passed almost within spitting distance and continued on their way.

After a cautious interval my father slowly rose to his feet and brushed off dead brown leaves and twigs. He looked down at the pallor in my face and his eyes crinkled as he smiled. "That was a close one, old lad."

A "close one" seemed to me an understatement. We village boys held all the squire's gamekeepers in some awe, but Head Keeper Compton was an ogre! His purple veined face, fierce white upturned moustache, bushy eyebrows and thunderous bellow held all trespassers in abject terror.

"Dad, I thought the dog would scent us—why didn't the dog…?"

"The wind. We were lucky. Just as they came up to us a breeze took our scent away. He keeps that dog very close to heel. Come on, time we got home for tea or we'll be in trouble."

Thirteen years later at the age of twenty-one, I was to experience a similar situation under truly perilous conditions near a German prison camp and I would remember the lessons learned that day.

My father and fellow poacher had grown up far from our village of Orsett in rural Essex, east of London. As the son of a stern God-fearing Cumberland miner, young Joseph Tunstall grew up with an acute awareness of the social disparities of those times. This permanently coloured his political outlook so that he grew into a committed champion of the underdog. A scholarly lad, he won a place at Durham University but, caught up in the surge of patriotism, left shortly before graduation to join the Durham Light Infantry to fight in the Boer War. Even then he had a soft spot not only for the underdog native Africans but also the wily Boers.

After the war my father became a schoolmaster and married a schoolmistress, Maude Carpenter, who gave him my first sister, Mary, then brother Geoff followed by sister Lucy. All too soon my father was away to another war, fighting the Turks in the bitter campaigns of Gallipoli, the Dardanelles, Palestine and Egypt. After his final home leave from the war he did not return again until some months after the Armistice and after I had become his second son, born on 1 December 1918.

As I came into the world, the mass slaughter of the war had stopped, but the scourge of another killer, influenza, now swept Europe. This claimed my mother thirteen days after my birth. Several months later, my father returned from the Middle East to deal with the problem of raising a motherless family. It was suggested to him that somebody's distant cousin, a Miss Edith Attrill, had just broken off an engagement and might be enlisted as housekeeper and nanny. "Edie" agreed and to me she was "mummy" until I was about three years old when I learned differently with a jolt.

Possessed of a dominant spirit coupled with native wit and impudence, the handsome Edie soon established herself as the mistress of the house, now called Grasmere. With the forging of a powerful bond between her and me, she considered her position unassailable, and it began to take on a permanence that my father had not anticipated. He, undoubtedly starved of intellectual companionship at home, was strongly discouraged from having any women friends for fear, I suppose, that another might oust the ruling mistress and, worse, deprive her of her foster baby. She became utterly and passionately devoted to me—in an age before child psychology was really understood.

One distressing eruption and its immediate sequel is the earliest clear-cut memory of my life and every detail remains indelibly printed. This particular melodrama climaxed with my father declaring that Edie must go and that I should be sent to live with his relatives in Cumberland. Edie swept me up possessively into her arms and we were both tearful. I remember the smell of tears. Pa delivered a final blast and swept off to his study. Edie set me down and retreated wailing to the scullery. I trailed after her tugging at her skirts and crying, "mummy, mummy". She turned on me in exasperation:

"Don't call me mummy. I'm not your mother. Your mother is dead!"

My brother and two sisters, considerably my seniors, soon fled. Mary was something of a prodigy and at sixteen her headmistress reckoned it was pointless keeping her at school any longer. She was accepted by London University and soon had a first class honours degree. Geoff, full of derring-do, was packed off to the wilds of Canada at sixteen, and dear Lucy entered a London business house, progressed well and later married a local farmer.

After the war, my father took up a position as headmaster of the Training Ship *Exmouth*, which was anchored fore and aft in the River Thames off Grays, just four miles from our home in Orsett. This imposing vessel was a black and white steel monster built for her purpose on the lines of Nelson's *Victory* with mizzen, main, foremast and bowsprit. Administered by a charity and later by the London County Council, she trained a complement of 600 boys mostly for careers at sea in the Royal Navy or the Merchant Service. All personnel wore naval uniform on which my father's Military Cross looked incongruous and caused comment from more observant visitors.

At nine years old, bursting with enthusiasm, I entered Palmer's Endowed School for Boys, a minor public school at Grays in Essex. Because of the school's proximity to home I was, like some others, enrolled as a day boy and not a boarder. This marked a new and somewhat chequered chapter in my life.

Palmer's was academically a highly successful school with its counterpart, Palmer's School for Girls, a couple of miles away. My two sisters had been educated there and my brother Geoff had left the Boys' School some years before. Unfortunately, he had not hit it off with the Headmaster, the Reverend H.A. Aldridge Abbott, M.A., better known as "Bunny". My induction by Bunny dampened my enthusiasm slightly. He was not an attractive man, having rather fleshy lips, discoloured teeth and thick-lensed glasses. The rest of the teaching staff varied in popularity but none was really unlikable. Many of them I remember with respect and affection. "Dickie" Freestone, the gym master, taught me to swim by the simple expedient of dangling me from a pole in a canvas belt while I went through the prescribed motions. He gradually lessened the support, and told me I was swimming, whereupon I sank. Dickie then hauled me out, whacked my backside and said he would do it again every time I went under. I soon swam! Mr Jolly's Shakespeare classes were vivid and delightful; enormously tall Frank Hughes could put anything over simply because he was such a thorough gentleman in every best sense of the word; and we enjoyed the savagery of Scottish Benson's maths:

"Get ootside the door, boy, before ye feel ma boot on yer backside."

Bunny's teaching of Latin, on the other hand, did nothing to resurrect the dead language, but only buried it deeper. He made us chant loudly in chorus: "Amo amas amat, amamus amatis amant. Hic haec hoc, hunc hanc hoc," all the while beating time with loud whacks of a ruler on the front desk. Over and over we had to do it until, by the time we came to the Gallic Wars, all of us except for a few creeping swots hated Bunny, Caesar, Virgil and all.

I enjoyed my part in the School Cadet Corps, as it was then called, and despite the fact that Bunny chose to run the band, I progressed. This must have been because my bugle noises were not as horrible as those of most of the other chaps. We marched and countermarched every Tuesday and Thursday blowing our guts out to the thunder of drums. For the local inhabitants the noise must have been appalling. We had four tunes to play, only two of which had the distinction of lyrics, and these were of limited inspiration. One went, "If your trousers do fall down, tie 'em up with string, tie 'em up with string," and the other, "I asked Old Brown to tea, and all his family, and if he don't come I'll tickle his bum with a piece of celery." It was hardly enough to keep a chap's enthusiasm going for seven years.

Bunny appeared to have two principal roles at Palmer's. One was to whack his ruler fanatically to "Amo amas amat" and the other was to whack little boys' bums with a cane. I must admit he did this with an element of artistry. Any morning or afternoon, defaulters could be seen outside his office forming a subdued and apprehensive queue. Eventually he would emerge, a transformed character, not his usual dour self but in a kind of ecstasy which I ought not to have begrudged to such a miserable creature. He would rub his hands together in a washing motion, bare his yellow teeth in what was intended to be a smile and even put an arm around my shoulder as if we were buddies at last: "Well, well, well, so you're here again—now I wonder what I can do for you! Just run along to my office and bring me a cane."

In his office there was a drainpipe standing on its big end, and out of the top sprouted an array of canes. The thing was to select the most kindly looking one and hand it hopefully to the Reverend Headmaster. He would take it and make a few swishing passes at the air to see if it suited his current mood just as, I imagine, Titian would have selected a brush. "No," he would say, "I think I'll have another." So back one crept to his armoury for the next least unkindly cane. Sooner or later he would be satisfied. A formalised crouch then had to be adopted, head very low, knees bent so as to protrude a properly presented target. Next Bunny would conduct an examination of the nicely rounded bum to ensure that nothing had been heinously inserted as protection between trousers and flesh. This gloating examination by feel was prolonged and conscientious; it would have exposed even a layer of tissue paper.

Then he would take up his expert stance like a top-flight golfer addressing the ball and at last the smile would fade and his face take on a dark flush of concentration. The cane would be laid lightly three or four times upon the target before he drew back for the cut. It came in a loud vicious swoosh preceding the sharp crack of impact. Although the pain was sometimes blinding, there was an etiquette to be observed at this stage. First, it was a matter of pride not to let Bunny know how much he had hurt. Second, if the victim involuntarily straightened up at the shock, even very slightly, Bunny purred that such indiscipline would entail an extra cut. Having taken two or four or six, as Bunny thought just, the offender was dismissed. Honour was thus satisfied and men were supposed to be forged. As for the psychosexual imperatives that underlay my headmaster's magically transformed demeanour on these occasions, the nature of which suggested themselves to me only in retrospect, the less said the better.

There came a day when a worm turned and Bunny got his comeuppance. He administered six to a particularly recalcitrant youth and having told him to get up, could not resist another final cut just as the chap was unbending. The recipient saw red, snatched the cane out of Bunny's hand and used it to give him a stinger across the face—for which deed he was expelled. Expulsion was a dreadful thing in those days, calculated to set a young man well on the road to ruin. In this case, however, the villain rose to the top of a most honourable profession, was knighted and became one of the Palmer's legends.

To the disappointment of my scholarly father, my academic prowess at school faltered. I played all the sports and ran quite fast but never became a star at anything. Father began to preach to me only of study and success while I loathed school more and more. I employed every conceivable device to dodge my stint of homework. As in most unhappy circumstances there were compensations and I became a bit of a loner, escaping often to the fen. There I found a new outlet that was fascinating and different even if it did earn me some opprobrium as "that nasty boy who keeps snakes".

I redeemed myself to some extent when a Scout Troop was inaugurated in Orsett to widespread enthusiasm. Then, as now, the worth of a Scout

Group depended on three main factors: the attitude of the boys, the cooperation of their parents, and the calibre of the scoutmaster. In the early Thirties there was little problem about the first, especially in a more or less feudal village where everyone respected the squire, Sir Francis Whitmore; patriotism was still a virtue, we were proud of the Empire and its builders, and one could still speak openly of duty and honour without embarrassment. As our scoutmaster we were fortunate to have a pillar among men. Mr Hills, or "the old man" as he was affectionately called, was a martinet who bristled with all the military virtues and was utterly dedicated to doing all he could for his lads. In no time we were the smartest, most efficient unit for miles around and extremely proud of it. Since then I have encountered a fair share of testing experiences in life, and of one thing I am absolutely certain. When the chips were down I coped with them far better than I would have done without Scout training in those formative years.

My early boyish leisure reading concentrated upon adventure books, like F.S. Brereton's *A Boy of the Dominion*, and I often fancied myself in a similar role, braving the menace of ferocious animals, the wilds and cruel savages. White men were all decent chaps and the other lesser beings could also be acceptable provided their behaviour was "civilised" and they had a proper respect for the King, the Empire and the white administrators who were doing their best to uplift them from their primitive ways. I saw that stirring film *Sanders of the River*, about a wise and heroic British District Commissioner in Africa in which there was an enlightened negro played by Paul Robeson. He could sing too. No doubt about it, not all black men were savages, some were okay.

The Great Empire Exhibition at Wembley confirmed to me that the subject races loved us and were grateful, and I was touched by the loyalty of native troops. Always an impressionable lad, these things together with the National Anthem, pipe bands, "Rule Britannia" and "Land of Hope and Glory", never failed to bring a lump to my throat and a surge of pride. My attitudes were idealistic and the blemishes of the Empire were not then apparent to me.

One day a barnstorming character lobbed into a cow pasture near my home in an old Avro 504 biplane offering joy rides for five shillings a head.

This aeroplane was a "kite" in the true sense. The whole contraption was supported on a leggy undercarriage with huge wire wheels fitted with narrow tyres. Between these a skid projected forwards like a huge ski to discourage the aircraft from doing somersaults after landing. I managed to scrape up five bob from somewhere and was soon thrilled beyond description to see Orsett looking like a clutch of little model houses. The pilot was at one stage alarmed at the strange noises coming from my cockpit until he realised I was laughing and cheering. I was hooked for good and all.

With more maturity, my leisure reading focused upon aviation and I doubt if there was an aircraft flying that I could not identify at a glance. My heroes were the great aerial fighters of the First World War—Mannock, Ball, Richthofen and Boelke—and I avidly awaited each new edition of the magazines *Flight*, *The Aeroplane* and, best of all, *Popular Flying*. I admired the German aces as much as our own and respected many of the national characteristics of the German military.

Fanning my growing ambition to be a pilot in the Royal Air Force was the proximity of my home to 74 and 54 Fighter Squadrons at RAF Hornchurch. They had Bristol Bulldogs and Hawker Demons, later replaced by Gloucester Gauntlets and then Gladiators. To gaze up at those silver flashes over the Thames Estuary as they flew in immaculate formations, or twisted, turned, rolled and looped in practice dog fights, filled me with a painful pride and longing.

Meanwhile, school continued a dreary necessity. Scout activities sublimated endeavour while tentative experiments with the comely lasses of the village became increasingly interesting. The house next to ours, half a mile away, was the home of the district surgeon, his wife and their only child, Ann. Although she was two years younger than me, she and I soon became friends. Ann was special, different, sensible. She never squealed with alarm at my snakes and was unafraid to handle them or tickle them under the chin. Snakes enjoy that. She had a pony and we enjoyed similar country pursuits. I had a respect for her that was a little tinged with awe. I always felt on my best behaviour and took no liberties, forgetting all the down-sides of life, school, Bunny Abbott, home tensions. It was nice and I was really happy. I did not realise what was gently, imperceptibly happening to me—not for some time to come.

Miles away in Germany and in a secretly loaned Russian base, a dedicated band of militarists disguised as civilians had long ago given birth to and nurtured the carefully planned German Luftwaffe which was soon to sweep the skies of Europe and help smash nations into subjection. I was not really interested in politics or international affairs at the time. It seemed to me that Hitler was a bit of a nutcase and needed to be brought down a peg or two, but the rumoured excesses of Nazi oppression were less of a reality to me than Bing Crosby's latest gramophone record. Even the Luftwaffe's role in the Spanish Civil War did not perturb me—or my contemporary potential cannon fodder—as perhaps it should have done. The young were very ingenuous.

At home, another clash was becoming imminent between my father and me. His ambition for me equalled my own but did not run parallel. His own academic fulfilment had been sacrificed to war. My elder sister had been an incredibly brilliant success and my father's sights were set rigidly upon a similar performance by his younger son. The only role he saw for me was as a scholar following the path of learning trodden by him, my mother and my elder sister. His ambition was also fired by my headmaster's repeated accusations that I had the capability but refused to apply myself. He was outraged by Bunny's submission to him of some of my Latin examination papers when I first failed matriculation. I had answered none of the dreary questions but, perhaps in a gesture of defiance, had decorated my answer paper with a sketch of Bulldog fighters swooping in to attack a lumbering Handley Page Heyford bomber. Oh, what a scene there was about that!

When the shouting was over it was obvious that we must come to terms. I convinced my father that only the RAF would do for me but he was appalled when my impatience to join up crystallised into a demand to do so forthwith as a boy apprentice.

"You couldn't even pass the entrance exam," he roared.

"Let me try, then," was the obvious rejoinder.

I was interviewed soon afterwards by a beady-eyed recruiting officer at Chelmsford who concluded the ordeal by opening a drawer behind his desk, at the same time watching me like a ferret sizing up a rabbit.

"Here. Catch!" From his hand shot a small object which flew high and off to my right. My arm reached out to full length and with a satisfying smack the missile was taken in my hand. It was a toffee. Only once on the Palmer's cricket field had I ever managed such an immaculate performance. The inquisitor's face softened; I had passed the interview. I wondered afterwards if the Air Ministry made a special stores issue of toffees to recruiting officers and how many careers must have been stillborn by a fumbled catch!

When I sat the examination I wrote upon the answer papers with reverence, for they had printed upon them the hallowed cipher, "Royal Air Force". Would this be the first and last time I would be privileged to use its stationery? I romped through the examination with inspired success, and now poor old father had another problem. Although he flatly refused to allow me to go further, my bargaining position had improved immeasurably. No matter what, I was to remain at school for a further two years.

Compensation for my continued schooling arrived one day in the form of an impecunious, bearded aviator named "Dixie" Gerrans. In a rough little hayfield, four miles from home at West Horndon, he had erected a tattered First World War canvas hangar within which was installed a rather decrepit two-seater wooden glider, a battered old Chrysler motor car for towing it off, and a dual-controlled, radial-engined biplane called a Redwing. He was anxiously looking for pupils. This was it! I promised my father to apply myself more seriously at school if I could learn to fly. It was agreed and we stuck to our bargain. I passed matriculation well enough and he stumped up for flying lessons as best he could.

The first time we hauled the glider out of the hangar, with the assistance of a couple of equally poverty-stricken enthusiasts, there was an interesting rustling noise at the back end of the fuselage. Once we had evicted the nest of rats, we were ready to fly. The Chrysler roared down the field pulling, by a length of frayed cable, the glider which rattled its progress across the rough field. Abruptly the noise ceased except for an exhilarating swoosh of airflow and we were soaring upwards. Dixie heaved on the lever that released the cable and we were in free flight. I cannot remember what I learned from these sorties because Dixie was a taciturn fellow and had none of the patter that I later discovered was an essential part of flying instruction. He just let me have a go.

Flights in the Redwing were exciting but not very productive. I remember one day saying to Dixie: "I've hit upon a great idea to keep the thing level, Dixie. All I have to do is line it up on the horizon and keep it there."

"Jolly good wheeze, old boy," was his breezy reply.

(The more formalised instructional patter, of course, thumps this message home in lesson one.)

Dixie's enterprise inevitably failed, but eventually he joined forces with a newly formed flying club at Maylands aerodrome near Romford and I followed him. The charges here were a bit steep. Two pounds an hour for dual instruction and thirty bob for solo meant that I could seldom afford a lesson of more than thirty minutes' duration. The aeroplane was a Cirrus Moth G-EBTG, known as "faithful TG"; it was indeed a faithful old thing and bits hardly ever fell off it. When TG was not available there might be an Avian, and I flew twice in a really modern sophisticated monoplane called a Puss Moth.

There were three factors militating against my first solo—money (synonymous with training continuity); the airy-fairy instruction; and a field that was unlicensed for first solos. Little wonder since it was perched on the side of a hill! As long as the club management was making money, nobody cared except me.

When sister Lucy had married her farmer I found a way to augment my budget for flying fees. A part of the farm abounded with destructive rabbits. Occasionally I managed to shoot one with my air rifle, but this entailed the most painstaking stalk to very close range and hitting the thing slap in the eye. Then I had my big break. Brother-in-law Willy's head horseman offered me an astonishingly decrepit, double-barrelled, twelve-bore shotgun at a price I was able to afford. It had innumerable defects, and would hardly have graced Sir Francis's gunroom at Orsett Hall, but one couldn't expect a Purdy in good condition for one pound.

From then on I frequently slept at the farm, got up at dawn and slaughtered rabbits. By breakfast time I had them all skinned, jointed and wrapped in greaseproof paper. I then sold them to local housewives for sixpence a pound. At about sixteen or so rabbits to the flying hour my first solo was imminent. Perhaps I should say my first solos, at flying and the other most enjoyable activity known to man!

31

With the blood money jingling in my pocket I was able to be more demanding that things come to a head more quickly. My instructors had agreed I was more than ready for my first solo, so late one afternoon I borrowed the family Ford Eight and drove over to the club. There I suggested forcibly that they had better do something about it or else! A one-legged character by the name of Paddy Flynn was telephoned there and then. He ran a little flying club at Aybridge, a nearby aerodrome fully licensed for instruction. Paddy was an ex-Imperial Airways captain who had lost his leg in a crash, a qualified flying instructor and an official observer of the Royal Aero Club, which meant he could authorise my solo and later test me for my Pilot's "A" Licence. Everything was fixed and the club bar was already open so, feeling eight feet tall, I decided to swagger a bit.

That evening the bar was quiet. The regular barmaid had not yet arrived and—let us call her Jenny—the club proprietor's secretary was standing in for her. Jenny was in her early twenties and gorgeous. She wore a close fitting jumper that did nothing to hide some very exciting equipment. A broad patent leather belt contained her tiny waist and a filmy smooth black skirt caressed a lovely firm roundness. Her legs were long, slender and sensational. She had shoulder-length raven-black hair, a flawless complexion and a smile which sparkled and inflamed urges.

For some time I had been jealous of the older, more confident chaps who were on easy terms with her, but I was only just eighteen and I knew she wouldn't look twice at me. I ordered myself half a pint of ginger beer shandy with the casual air of a hardened drinker. As Jenny served it she looked at her wristwatch with a frown and said:

"Oh, I do wish Freddie Banks would show up."

A pang of jealousy shot through me. Freddie's hair was receding at the temples.

"What's so special about Freddie Banks?"

"Oh nothing, but he did promise to give me a lift home."

"Where do you live, Jenny?"

"Waltham Abbey. You don't go that way do you, Peter?"

My pulse rate increased slightly.

"Well, I don't, Jenny, but I'll run you up there if you like. It's no trouble."

"Do you really fly?"

"Oh Peter, you darling. I wish I could kiss you now—I'll have to do it later."

Jenny had turned to the bottles behind the bar and presented her firm little bottom. My racing pulse was now having serious physical effects and I stammered some sort of reply.

"Jenny, I look forward... I would... I'd like that."

She paused in her work, half turning so that the sweater was more stretched and a proud nipple was clear to see. For seconds she looked at me solemnly through those limpid dark eyes and long sweeping lashes as if she had just realised something. She spoke very softly:

"Is that all you'd like, Peter?"

When I tried to answer, my voice had gone slightly husky and I think I slopped some shandy down my sleeve. I forget what I croaked to her but it must have been something of a plea and it was quite obviously granted. There was time for me to consume two more half pints and each time I re-ordered I made some ingenuous query as to whether she really meant it. She laughed at my anxiety.

"Of course I do, you silly boy."

I couldn't believe it!

When we set off in the tiny Ford Eight, filled with her fragrance, it was raining and I had no idea how or where things might be accomplished but I felt I was in good hands. Jenny happened to know a cosy little entrance into Epping Forest and the car squelched into it. She gave me the promised kiss and it was nothing at all like the dry three-second efforts of the village girls. It was quivering and moist and my senses reeled. She then suggested we would probably be more comfortable in the back of the car. Although it was horribly cramped, she was quite right. We were.

When normal breathing was restored and we were watching the little rivulets run down the steamy car windows I eventually found voice:

"Is that all there is to it?"

Jenny sounded surprised.

"What do you mean, Peter?"

"Well I didn't think it was all *that* marvellous."

Dear forgiving Jenny broke into peals of laughter, hugged me close again and kissed me.

"Oh Peter, you *are* funny!"

I still had a lot to learn, and Jenny helped me to progress. There was no love involved in my short, sweet but undeniably exciting relationship with her. Any love notions I had were still very subdued and beamed unwaveringly in the same single direction. But Jenny had opened up a new dimension in my life, one that I accepted with enthusiasm.

Before the war, pilots were not as common as they have since become and still enjoyed some of the aura left over by those magnificent men in their flying machines. With eyes sparkling, sweet young things would ask:

"Do you really fly?"

"Yes, I do a bit," (absently looking at the fingernails with calculated modesty).

"Have you ever looped the loop?" (eyes now widening in admiration).

(With a tolerant manly chuckle) "Oh yes. Do it quite often actually. Damn good sport."

That alone was often worth the equivalent of dinner and a bottle of wine on the way down the primrose path, and it was a lot cheaper. It was a delicious time for which I was to become very grateful, for on 1 July 1939 it ended. For the next five years and ten months I led a celibate existence—at first by choice and then with no option.

Paddy Flynn was as offhand as all the other people I met in flying-club circles. I lost count of the times I journeyed to Aybridge before my solo, only to find he was not there as arranged, or had forgotten the booking and someone else had the Gipsy Moth, or it was unserviceable, or the field was. I was becoming slightly fed up with old Paddy's manner. At last I got in a couple of check flights with him and off I went solo one glorious day in April 1937. Once airborne I started singing above the chitter of the Gipsy engine. There was no real tune but the words were: "I'm solo, I'm solo, I'm bloody well solo!" As the slipstream caught my open mouth it inflated my cheeks and a drip of saliva was whipped across my face, which I wiped away with a gloved hand. I felt like throwing my leather helmet and goggles away to let the wind truly baptise me. I later discovered that, in those carefree open-cockpit days, many chaps on their first solo reacted in much the same way.

After my first solo I had to fly a requisite number of hours at Aybridge under Paddy's surveillance before I could take my test. This consisted of, among other things, carrying a barograph on board which registered my height keeping and steadiness of climbs and descents during prescribed manoeuvres. The frustrations with old Paddy continued until I had a stand-up row with him. I told him that I would not pay my bill for the last few hours if I did not attempt my test without fail next time, as arranged. When I turned up to take it he greeted me with a beaming face:

"Congratulations, old boy. You passed your test."

"What the hell are you talking about, Paddy? I haven't taken it!"

"Yes, you have. I did it for you and you passed. Can I have some money please, old chap?"

I was shocked, furious and felt cheated, but what could I do? It was unthinkable to shop poor old Paddy Flynn, so I just had to let it pass. I like to think it was a most unusual event.

My licence and my Royal Aero Club Aviator's Certificate arrived home by post in mid-April 1937. Each document bore a photograph of a very serious chap trying to look tough. In actual fact he looked more like a rather sulky eighteen-year-old schoolboy.

Life had taken a tremendous upswing in all directions. At school there were only three of us in our particular section of the sixth form so that lessons were more like casual discussions with rather friendlier masters. Taffy Jones would entrance us with impish discourses on entirely irrelevant subjects such as the mating antics of salmon, and Bunny kept out of my way. One or two of the younger masters knew that if they behaved themselves I might take them up for a flight, and I drove to school in the Ford Eight.

My application was in for a four-year Short Service Commission as a pilot in the RAF and I had attended all the necessary interviews and medical examinations. I awaited the result in a fever of expectation. The flying club occasionally allowed me to ferry aircraft around and I now drank bitter instead of shandy, a pint rather than a measly half. I saw very little of my real heartthrob because she was away at finishing school and spent most of her holidays abroad polishing up languages. The little I did see of her slowly fixed the idea that, ultimately, she would be "the one".

Empire Air Day at Hornchurch and the Hendon Air Display had me in raptures of hopeful anticipation. Once or twice I managed to get near enough to Service aircraft to discover that, on top of everything else, they had an intoxicating smell of high octane fuel and fabric dope which was all their own and as heady as Jenny's perfume.

One day a Gladiator, flown by a sergeant pilot from Hornchurch, did an unauthorised beat-up of the club followed by an extremely exciting display of low-level aerobatics. Unfortunately, during the finale the poor fellow misjudged his height for pulling out of a loop and smeared the aeroplane and himself across Maylands aerodrome. For a while afterwards, aerodrome staff were picking up tiny pieces of pilot indicated by concentrations of flies. It was grisly but not at all discouraging. If anything, it added a spice of dangerous reality to the dream.

In retrospect it seems significant to recall how, as a youngster, one developed a singularly callous attitude to these tragic events. It was not intended unkindly, nor was there a lack of proper sympathy, but it was almost as though a shell was forming which subsequently became even more necessary for self-protection as so many friends and acquaintances—before, during and after the war—"got the chop".

My first experience of night flying was quite fortuitous. A chap named Henderson landed a profitable little contract to fly his Avian around as a practice target for the local Territorial Army Searchlight Units and invited me along. It was my only flight in an aeroplane exposed by our searchlights, although a similar experience was to be frequently repeated three years later with unfriendly Germans at the other end of the beams. The dazzle was quite stupefying, but it was fascinating to look out at the lower mainplanes of the old Avian to see the spars and ribs silhouetted black through the doped linen fabric made translucent by the hard white light.

While I was waiting for a response from the RAF, my father had secured a place for me at Southampton University, and towards the end of my last term at Palmer's I was required to go to a local mixed school as a student teacher. The novelty was amusing and became positively fascinating when, due to a regular teacher's illness, I was instructed to take the senior school leavers for biology. They were about my own age, just eighteen, and my teaching was gravely affected by one very attractive young lady who insisted upon sitting in the front row and fluttering her eyelashes throughout the lesson. Flesh and blood can stand only so much and eventually we contrived to give greater breadth to our practical biological experiments after school with a friendly frolic in Hangman's Wood. Bad for discipline, excellent for morale!

My schoolboy flying resulted in a couple of brushes with the law. The first occurred when, by arrangement, I landed the Cirrus Moth in a newly mown hayfield on Lucy's farm, picked her up and gave her a flip. When we returned to land, the village constable had appeared on his bicycle with his blue-black cape folded over the handlebars. As Lucy climbed out of the front cockpit he motioned imperiously that he would have words with me and, bicycle and all, approached the cockpit while I kept the engine ticking over. Most British bobbies are first-class chaps and I have always had the highest regard for them, but this one was obviously looking for trouble.

"This 'ere is not an aerodrome," he declared with an air of intense outrage.

Knowing I was legally in the clear, I was no doubt unnecessarily truculent.

"That's a profound observation," I agreed. "It looks more like a hayfield, doesn't it!"

"You can't land 'ere then."

"That's not such a clever observation. I've just done it."

"I'll 'ave to take your partikklers."

"Go ahead," I said, "but if you knew the law you wouldn't be wasting your time."

He laboriously took my particulars and then intoned darkly, "You'll hear more about this."

"I still say you're wasting your time, old chap," I told him and eased open the throttle causing him to beat a hasty retreat from the blast of the slipstream. I then swung the tail straight at him with malice aforethought and opened the throttle wide. The slipstream caught a haycock which showered upon him a cloud of hay. He clutched at his helmet so that his bike fell over and his cape took off, careering across the field like an enormous black bat. Lucy was biting her knuckles to control the giggles and I was gone. I heard no more about it.

The second incident occurred on a beautiful warm July day when friends invited my father and me to join them on an excursion to The Chase at Ingatestone. This was a country club at which they intended to spend the afternoon by the swimming pool. Having accumulated enough cash to buy myself an hour's flying I declined to join them but dropped off en route at the Flying Club to hire "faithful TG". Knowing that I should have an appreciative audience at The Chase I then decided to commit the youthful pilot's inevitable sin of showing off.

My father and friends were relaxing by the pool when the roar of a low-flying aircraft suddenly shattered the tranquillity. The aeroplane dived and passed over, barely missing the nearby tree tops. I am told people ducked and there was the odd scream of fright as I pulled up into a steep climb, stall turned, and came back at them like a fighter-bomber intent upon their destruction. A few ran aimlessly hither and thither while one heroic fellow tried to allay panic by shouting, "Keep calm, he's only taking photographs!" The Moth executed a series of steep turns centred upon the pool, wing tips just missing the taller trees, while the pilot beamed upon the outraged throng from such a low level that several declared they would be confident of identifying him in court. Some, with that intention, noted the registration letters on the wings. The aircraft then returned to Maylands Aerodrome where the young pilot landed, extremely pleased with himself and anticipating the adulation of those he must have so thoroughly impressed.

That evening my father's wrath was something to behold and he threatened to withdraw his sanction of my plans for joining the RAF. This was bad enough, but paled in comparison with the next turn of events. I was at home when the police officer banged on the front door and asked to see Mr Peter Tunstall. The clammy grip of impending doom closed upon my vitals and I stood before him in no doubt as to what was coming. He pulled a fat notebook from his top pocket where it resided with his police whistle on its silver chain.

"Are you Peter David Tunstall?" he asked.

I tried to say "yes" but only croaked. I cleared my throat and told him that I was.

"I warn you that anything you say may be taken down and used in evidence against you."

That was it! My world and hopes began to crumble. The RAF would obviously turn its righteous back upon a flagrant perpetrator of the cardinal sin—unauthorised low flying.

"On the twenty-fifth of July 1937 at 3.15 p.m. were you the pilot of an aeroplane G-EBTG?"

I had to admit it all and my confessions were ponderously written down in that dreadful black book.

My father, who doubtless could have turned the situation to his own ends of steering me into the teaching profession, turned up trumps. A county Justice of the Peace, he went to see the Chief Constable of Essex and presented an honest plea for his consideration. This was not in order to pervert the course of justice, but to prevent the termination of so long cherished an ambition and the possible blighting of a career. No doubt some reference was made to the rousting I had already received from him, the immediate need for pilots in the desperate expansion of the Air Force, and the worsening international situation. The dear old boy pulled it off and I was served with an official caution threatening dire penalties in the event of a repetition. I was suitably chastened—for a while.

In the same month the postman delivered an envelope marked, "On His Majesty's Service". I ripped it open with trembling fingers. It contained a railway warrant and a letter instructing me to report to the famous civilian flying school at Hamble for *ab initio* flying training on 21 September. There was also a form to be signed and returned accepting the offer of one year's continuous service in the Reserve of Air Force Officers. What was this? My spirits sank as I learned that a new scheme was being introduced to increase the throughput of pilots quickly and then to hold them in reserve. Half a loaf being better than no bread, I resolved that if I ever got my foot in the door, the RAF would never get me out.

Chapter Three

Never say die

The flying training syllabus for Short Service and Reserve Officers in the RAF of 1937 consisted firstly of two months at a civilian flying school for the *ab initio* (literally, from the beginning) stage. The main object of our *ab initio* training was to sift out those unfortunates lacking natural aptitude for flying before wasting hours of more costly training on powerful service aircraft. At all stages of their RAF training, pilots battled for survival in the face of Flying Training Command's slogan: "If in doubt, chuck him out." Ability to fly was not the sole criterion; equal consideration was given to "officer qualities". As one CO put it, "If you don't measure up as officers you will be out, and I don't give a damn if you've sprouted feathers." In 1937 there were very few *ab initio* pilots who, like me, had already qualified for a civilian pilot's licence and these were at no advantage. The RAF had its own flying standards and we were as vulnerable to the service axe as anyone else.

All those who succeeded in surviving this stage, plus the *ab initio* trainees from other civilian schools, formed the intake at the Royal Air Force Depot, Uxbridge. To an Air Force man Uxbridge conjures up a picture of vast tarmac drill squares, everything either polished or whitewashed, immaculate strutting drill instructors, clarion parade-ground voices, and an unwritten law: "If it doesn't move, paint it white; if it does move, salute it!"

At Uxbridge, pilots acquired their first uniform, opened a bank account with one of the accredited service agents, were issued with camp kits suitable for campaigning in the outposts of Empire, lectured by a medical officer about how to avoid sunstroke and STDs, and appointed to the precarious rank of Temporary Acting Pilot Officers on Probation, or "bograts", as they were invariably known. Embryo pilots who had the physical and mental stamina (or cunning) to survive the depot passed on to one of several Flying Training Schools dotted around the British Isles. Here the training aircraft was the Hawker Hart, a shining silver biplane with a Rolls-Royce Kestrel engine, an open cockpit and fixed undercarriage. There was a basic dual-controlled trainer version, or one of its operational variants in which the rear cockpit had been equipped for a wireless operator/air gunner, known as a "Wop/AG", who also did the bomb aiming.

But first I had to complete my eight-month stint at the Flying Training School at Hamble. Here I was instructed in improving basic flying techniques and skills, and given a superficial introduction to formation flying, reconnaissance, target finding and identification. Ground school covered aeronautical subjects as well as administration, RAF history, law and suchlike. In the later stages, young pilots learned how to use the aircraft as a weapon of war: to dog-fight using the front camera gun, and also how to crew the rear cockpit of a Hawker Audax as bomb aimer, photographer and defensive rear-gunner. The programme ended at an Armament Training Camp where student pilots exercised in earnest with live ammunition aimed at drogues (targets towed far behind other aircraft) or on ground targets. They also dropped practice smoke bombs.

On completion of armament training, the lads were then considered operational pilots and were posted to front-line squadrons, still with the precarious rank of acting pilot officer but without the "on probation" bit.

Service pilots who trained in wartime will note the absence of what later became known as Operational Training Units, at which training took place that prepared aircrew for specific types of front-line aircraft and brought them to combat readiness. This omission was deliberate. Bombers, it was staunchly maintained by our political leaders, were for bombing, not for training. This omission in training and the unreasonable demands imposed upon some inexperienced aircrew were subsequently to be emphasised by my own woeful experience.

Another gap in training specifically affected reservists destined for bomber squadrons. On completion of our skimpy operational flying training, we (unlike our colleagues destined for immediate induction into the service) were not sent on a two-month course at a Navigation School.

Thus when Bomber Command was converted into a night-flying force, we were not only half-baked bomber pilots but less than half-baked navigators as well, neither fish nor fowl.

Until I began to know the other chaps on my course at Hamble I had considered myself quite a man of the world. I could fly an aeroplane (after a fashion); I could drive a car (but did not own one); I knew all about women (or so I thought); I shaved every day (though it wasn't really necessary); and I could down my pints (though not nearly as many as the others). I soon realised that I had quite a way to go to catch up with the men, to whom I must have appeared gauche, naïve, boyishly over-enthusiastic and, when it came to ground school work, an unmitigated young swot.

Outside the hangars at Hamble were our aircraft: two well-dressed lines of Avro Cadet biplanes with uncowled Genet radial engines and wooden propellers. It all looked so business-like after the rather tin-pot flying clubs to which I had been accustomed, and there among the Cadets was a Hawker Hart on a visit from Training Command. It dwarfed the Cadets with its mighty Rolls-Royce engine cowled in polished metal that ran in graceful lines through the airscrew to the painted spinner on its boss. To me the aeroplane appeared almost disdainful to be in the humble company of Avro Cadets, and it had "the smell". No time was wasted before getting airborne and my flying instructor, Sergeant Kirkland, had me off solo in an Avro Cadet after a couple of hours spent on spinning and forced landings. My flying club training had been relatively sketchy in these respects.

The Avro Cadet was a particularly suitable aircraft for aerobatic training because its engine, unlike most, would not cut out when upside down. This permitted prolonged inverted flight, bunt manoeuvres—looping with the pilot on the outside of the loop instead of the inside—and inverted spinning. To the inexperienced, like myself, a spin was impressive enough but inverted spins were hideous. However, one gets used to anything and I enjoyed the aerobatics more than any other part of our training.

Ground School, which occupied one or the other half of each day, taught navigation, meteorology, airmanship, engines, airframes, instruments, compasses and the rudiments of Air Force law. All these subjects I absorbed with avid interest, took copious notes, drew meticulous diagrams and spent hours in the evening converting them into fair copies that were minor works of art. I had little time for trivialities and was dissatisfied if I scored less than ninety percent on any test. Bunny Abbott would have been flabbergasted to see my transformation. I was gloriously happy despite good-humoured ribbing from some of the other chaps who were taking life less seriously.

Our course was supposed to be thirty-two strong, though one student did not show up for several days. He was apparently an ex-army officer, and we were told he would become the course commander both by virtue of his commissioned army status and because he was considerably older than the rest of us, being in his early thirties. He was rumoured to be "quite somebody" whose influential father had pulled strings with the Secretary of State for Air, a personal friend, to slip his son onto the course several years over the normal age limit. A few days after the course began the "quite somebody" arrived. Most of us were very properly impressed. He was a tough, crisp military type and took charge of us like a veteran commander of men. He was immediately on easy, hob-nobbing terms with the instructional staff whom the rest of us held in awe. He had a little handle to his name by virtue of his father's very big handle, and everybody tended to laugh unnecessarily loudly at his jokes. I felt positively insubordinate in calling him by his first name, Jock, but it was the done thing. Anyway, I had very little to do with him except in his capacity as course commander when I took his instructions passed down from the school hierarchy. If he spoke to me gratuitously, I felt quite honoured.

My flying instructor and I had excellent rapport, which is always a great blessing, and by the time the course was halfway through I was confident that I would make the grade with ease. I was being assessed "above average" on flying, often scored top marks on written tests, and was keeping my nose clean—what more could be expected?

Even the "quite somebody" was taking some friendly notice. He was beginning to be chatty and seemed graciously pleased to invite me to have a drink or two in his company before dinner. Things were really looking up. One afternoon, I was surprised by his friendly concern for my wellbeing when he told me he thought I was working too hard and suggested I should let up at least for an evening. "Leave your bloody books in the lecture room

44

for once and let's bash into Southampton and see what's doing." "I know a couple of good spots," he added with a wink. It sounded interesting and feeling greatly honoured by the invitation, I agreed.

The idea was to change immediately after tea and crack off to the bright lights in his very superior car. After tea, my distinguished friend suggested that we have a couple for the road, which was a bit disappointing especially when this stretched into three or four, and time was ticking by. But I was hardly in a position to bitch about it and fell in with his plan. It was even more disappointing when he suggested that we might just as well have a quick bite in the mess before leaving and I protested that by the time we hit town most of the action would be fizzling out.

"You don't know the places I know, laddie," he assured me and we sat down to a quick meal at which he ordered up some wine.

"At this rate," I told him, "I'll be half seas over before we start hitting the action."

"Rubbish," he said. "Drink up and let's go. I can make town in less than twenty minutes."

We drank up and walked to his car, by which stage I was treading carefully so as to avoid weaving. Once in the car we drove surprisingly slowly up the road towards the various digs and he started cursing. "Damn it, I've got a bloody awful headache. Do you mind much if we don't go after all?"

I did mind, and somewhat ungraciously said my piece about wasting an evening that I had intended to spend working. He was most apologetic and so decent about the whole thing that I felt a bit of a toad for complaining. Then he came up with a reasonable idea.

"Tell you what we can do. I have my books in my room. We can use them and you could run over some of the stuff on compasses with me if you like. All this business about turning error and acceleration error has got me foxed. Could you go through it with me? I'd be grateful."

It was not a lot to ask and flattering to think he had such confidence in my grasp of a subject which, in fact, I did know inside out. His room was a much better one than mine, but there was only one chair and it was cluttered up with clothing.

"Kick your shoes off—we can sit on the bed."

He tossed some books on to the bed and we sat there propped up against the bed head while I flicked through the pages of his notes to find the appropriate section on compasses. He turned towards me and in the most natural accidental manner his hand fell on my thigh. I felt a bit embarrassed about this but still no alarm bells rang. The next moment his hand began to move upwards and a slow shock began to run through me which I did not immediately know how to handle. Then things moved fast. Very suddenly my flies were open and his hand was moving inside. Bloody Hell! The bastard was up to some funny business. Trying to mess me about!

I suppose the situation, even at that stage, could have been handled wisely, but I panicked, knocked his hand away furiously and tried to get off the bed. He grabbed my arm which I wrenched free and was up and out of the door and into the road with no shoes on. I padded back to my digs confused and feeling sick—both physically and mentally—because I realised instinctively that an impossible situation was bound to follow. And it did!

The incident was never discussed between us and I never saw those shoes again. I avoided contact with the man and when we had to speak to each other it was on surly clipped terms. I felt a need to discuss the situation with somebody but couldn't decide in whom to confide. I assumed that some of the shame of it all was bound to rub off on me if I did and, anyway, I doubted whether anyone would believe me— especially as the course commander was regarded as such a hell of a great chap and was growing from strength to strength in popularity with the staff. I resolved to try to let the whole thing blow over until a friend one day gave me a warning.

"Look out for him, he's gunning for you."

Then surely, little by little, I began to be picked out by him for niggling disciplinary matters, each one so ridiculously petty it was insignificant, and many clearly engineered from nothing. The cumulative effect was insidious and began to be frightening. At last I confided the whole business to the "schoolmaster" who was a somewhat ineffectual character and as much at a loss as to what to do as I was. We agreed it was too late to make a fuss and that I would just have to weather the situation as best I could. At least my flying and ground work continued at a good standard, but I began to collect the occasional official reprimand for trivial matters, reported and exaggerated by my persecutor. I fearfully assumed that poison was being dripped into influential ears. I felt I was on a slippery slope, and my new life, so recently consisting of endless halcyon days, was becoming an anxious misery, a fight against odds too great to handle on my own and with no hope of raising an effective ally.

The Hamble course ended, and after a long weekend we reported to the Royal Air Force Depot Uxbridge where we met up with the *ab initio* courses from other civilian schools. From the moment of arrival we were, at last, really a part of the RAF. We were left in no doubt of this from the moment the trumpeters sounded the Air Force reveille until the time we flopped exhausted into our beds. It was all go at a cracking pace with a great deal to be absorbed. The main accent was on smartness and discipline. This was largely inculcated during hours of drilling on the enormous Uxbridge "squares", from the cream of the RAF drill instructors. They were mostly elderly be-medalled fire-eaters, many of whom had transferred to the Royal Flying Corps during the First World War from Army Regiments in which ceremonial was a cult.

We were paid eleven shillings a day, from which we had to meet our messing expenses and buy our uniforms for which there had been a small inadequate initial grant. There was little left over to encourage mischief and most of our two weeks was spent marching, marching, marching, stamping, turning, saluting to the front by numbers, and forming fours under the outraged eyes of the NCOs. They bristled with disgust and skilfully injected utter contempt into the word "sir". We were encouraged to do better with such exhortations as:

"That gentleman in the front rank of the third file. You are supposed to be marching, not scratching around like a crippled hen on a dust heap. SIR!"

Nobody resented these verbal lashings which were accepted with good humour. We knew what we wanted to be and these men were forcing us into the mould. Nobody complained.

There were more relaxed moments when we were lectured on the history and traditions of the service and introduced in greater detail to Air Force law, which is faithfully based upon the humanity of British jurisprudence. The medical officer, who assumed that ninety-nine percent of us would become (if we were not already) rumbustious young lechers, impressed us with cautionary tales. The officers' mess, with its sombre atmosphere of a London club, set off with deep heavy leather armchairs, splendid silver, venerable portraits and apparently devoted servants, introduced the majority of us youngsters to an entirely new way of life. At a single stroke we were being elevated to a position in a special society, one it was incumbent upon us to earn and maintain.

Some respite from the rigours of this harsh training was afforded by our several visits to the London tailor to whom we had been allocated for the fitting of our first uniforms. There was a small approved handful of these who specialised in supplying uniforms, accoutrements and tropical kit: firms like Gieves, Alkit, Hector Powe and Moss Bros.

On one of these visits, a couple of Canadians and I became involved in some good-humoured banter with them suggesting that we English were unable to man our own air force and that they had of necessity come over to save the day. To which my equally good-humoured repartee was along the lines that they probably couldn't get a job in Canada anyway, and should be mighty grateful that the British government was prepared to keep them off the breadline, especially with so much unemployment about.

Two days before leaving Uxbridge, I received an awesome summons to the office of the depot commandant. It had been reported by our course commander that I had been overheard making remarks resentful of the presence of Dominion officers in the RAF and criticising the government's policy of allowing them commissions in this country. The commandant informed me that an extremely serious view was taken of such insubordinate and disruptive behaviour and the question of my continued service would come under review! I was flabbergasted and requested the presence of the Canadians who were duly called in. They too expressed amazement at such a turn of events. As one of them said to the commandant, "Aw gee, sir, we were only joshing each other."

This apparently had little impact on the great man who perused the petty niggles on my record from Hamble and decided that further action would have to be contemplated and a report forwarded to my next station.

So the vendetta was still on! I had carelessly lapsed into a false sense of security. Something had to be done. The day before we departed from Uxbridge I requested an interview with the senior chaplain, Wing Commander Hughes, and told him the whole story. Once again the problem was dropped back on to my own plate.

"What would you like to do about it?" he asked. "It's rather late to make a fuss."

Eventually the wing commander assured me that the fact of our interview would be recorded, but he advised that I had better do my best to soldier on. We moved to our flying training school; two *ab initio* courses combined together under our Hamble course commander, and in a state of desperation I knew I would be lucky to survive much longer.

Our flying training school was a legacy from the First World War. It consisted of a grass airfield—runways were still unheard of—a scattering of dreary creosoted huts and a few hangars. Some were wooden and some of the canvas Bessenot type, such as Dixie Gerrans had used to house his rat-ridden glider. It was December and the overall scene would have been depressing but for the immaculate line-ups of those beautiful Hawker Harts, Audaxes and Furies. In uniform at last, we had a true sense of belonging. We were about to fly behind those snarling Rolls-Royce engines, strapped into shining silver machines with RAF roundels on the wings, and "the smell". This would indeed have been my idea of heaven but for the sense of impending disaster. No matter which way I turned I felt powerless to avoid it.

Each flying instructor was allocated four pupil pilots and he dealt with two of them in the morning and the other two in the afternoon as we alternated between ground school and flights. My instructor had joined the RAF as a boy apprentice, had become a sergeant pilot and was now a pilot officer. He had achieved precisely what had been my own aim two years previously when I had no idea how rarely it was attained. Pilot Officer John Marshall was a man of the highest calibre, as his record proclaimed. I very quickly decided I was extremely lucky to be under his wing. As was usual in those days of stricter protocol, there was never a suggestion of familiarity between us, even though we both wore the same thin stripe of a pilot officer's rank on our sleeve. I was a bograt and he almost a god. In spite of this there was a rapport which gave me new hope that here, perhaps, would be the ally I so desperately needed. Even so, it was unthinkable that I should kick off by sicking up all my misery to him.

My tormentor now had an added weapon in his armoury. Our RAF station lay only twelve miles from the family seat from which his aristocratic father ran their vast estates. For those who enjoyed a taste of high society, a mansion as a change from the officers' mess, or an excellent day's shooting or fishing, it was all there to be graciously offered by the young lordling. He easily and immediately ingratiated himself with the station's hierarchy.

The new tactic in his campaign was, whenever possible, to roar a reprimand at me by name in incensed tones provided, of course, that there was somebody within earshot who mattered, such as the commandant, adjutant, chief flying instructor or the chief ground instructor. It worked to create an overall impression of my unsuitability and I guessed the end must be near. My only defence was to go on scoring high marks in both ground and air work, and with John Marshall as my flying instructor the latter was no problem.

The Hart was a delight to fly and an excellent trainer, not because she was foolproof as modern trainers tend to be, but because she would bite the unwary and insist that her pilot remain on the ball, especially when landing. She had a narrow undercarriage, which was also fairly high to allow for the enormous wooden prop. If one did not land precisely into wind as indicated by the windsock, she would touch down with sideways drift. This could collapse one leg causing a wing tip to graunch into the ground and slew the aircraft drunkenly round to face the way she had come. When the wind was blustery she would touch down and, as a strong gust hit her, tend to become airborne again and start porpoising. This could quite easily end up in a spectacular somersault.

Luckily I had no embarrassing incidents with the Harts, and John Marshall seemed well satisfied with our progress. It was therefore something of a surprise when we climbed down from our cockpits after a dual instructional flight and he said:

"Tunstall, I want to have a talk with you."

Instead of walking back into the busy flight offices as usual, he said we should stroll along the tarmac. Having handed our cumbersome parachutes to the ground crew we proceeded to stroll. In my present state of prolonged anxiety it was ominous and I wondered what trouble I was in for next.

"What's the matter with you, Tunstall?"

"I don't know what you mean, sir."

"I think you do know what I mean. Your flying is pretty good. I hear excellent reports from Ground School. You are obviously as keen as mustard and yet you don't seem to be able to keep yourself out of trouble. And you're miserable as hell. Why?"

Marshall was being a model flying instructor, playing a role important to any man who is responsible for the efficiency of aircrew. He must be on the lookout for a disturbed state of mind which might affect concentration and cause accidents.

"It surprises me, sir, that nobody realises all my troubles originate from the same source."

"I wouldn't be so sure that nobody has noticed. I have for one and there are others. But make no error, you are heading for the chop, fast! What has this chap got against you?"

"It's a long story, sir, and not a very pleasant one."

"I've got plenty of time. Tell me about it."

The flood of relief nearly choked me up and I had to take a few deep breaths before I could embark on the miserable saga. I told him everything, including how each little incident had been exaggerated or fabricated into a "black". At the end of the story Marshall was silent for a while and then spoke quietly and thoughtfully.

"I knew damn well there was more behind it than met the eye. The thing is, what do we do now? I suppose you don't want to submit a report?"

"No, sir, it's far too late for that and I don't think most people would believe me. I would probably be accused of inventing an unlikely story against such a fine fellow just to get myself out of trouble."

Marshall agreed. There was another long silence, then he asked:

"Would you be prepared to leave this to me and let me handle it my own way?"

I could think of nothing I would like better and told him so.

"All right then," he said. "Now let's see you cheer up a bit and start enjoying yourself."

His last remark was entirely superfluous for I felt like a man reprieved. I could begin to hope again for the career that meant so much to me and the zest I had first felt at Hamble began to surge back to send my spirits soaring.

A few days later, while I was away on a long weekend leave, Pilot Officer Marshall was suddenly posted away to a station at the other end of the kingdom. A week after that I was detailed to carry out some inventory checks at station HQ and was informed that this chore would take all day. It was a warm morning for January so I reported for the job without my greatcoat. This was quite in order since I was on my own and not marching about the place with the rest of the course when, for the sake of uniformity, greatcoats for all was the current rule. Once into the job I decided I might be able to get it finished in time to attend the afternoon's lectures and by working on though lunchtime I just made it. I was now in a slight dilemma. I could make the fifteen minutes' walk to my quarters and back to get my greatcoat, thereby missing some of the lecture, or go direct to the lecture room with no greatcoat but miss none of the instruction. To my mind, and with my usual lack of shrewdness, the latter seemed the lesser of two evils. After the lecture we were fallen in by the course commander to be marched back to the mess.

"Tunstall, where is your greatcoat?"

I tried to explain but the upshot was that I should report to the station adjutant at 08.30 hours the following morning. From the adjutant I was passed to the commandant where my course commander waited, poker faced, to lay his complaint of further indiscipline. The riot act was read. My record was recited with emphasis upon the Canadian episode and I was finally told that I was to be suspended from all duties pending the termination of my commission. I could imagine the outraged innocence of the course commander's denial if I dared to make an allegation against such a lionised pillar of society, so I held my peace. I knew that to remonstrate could achieve nothing but added unpleasantness.

The adjutant gave me a clearance certificate which I was to have signed by all sections as I handed in kit, gas mask, flying clothing, parachute and so on. He told me my uniform was personal property—for what use it was—and he made out a railway warrant for my return home to Orsett. I went through the clearance routine in a numb state of shock and misery and arrived home, utterly desolate, thirty-six hours later.

"But why didn't you tell what was going on?" my father asked for at least the fourth time.

"Considering how it all started I didn't think I'd better. Do you remember one day when we were walking on the fen? I was quite small and I asked what the dogs were doing when they were mating. Do you remember? Do you remember what the answer was? You gave me a thick ear!"

I saw the look of hurt on the old boy's face and was sorry I had said it. I hastened to add:

"It wasn't just that, dad. You know how I feel about the service. I didn't want to admit to you that I could run into that kind of trouble. It was, well, it would have been like letting the service down, especially as you were so anti at one stage."

"Well I'm not anti now. I want you to write a full report on the whole thing, as if you were writing it just for me and as if I knew absolutely nothing about it. Do you understand?"

"Yes, dad."

"And don't look so woebegone. Come on now. Never say die."

It took several days to get the whole thing down on paper without whinging, and after he had read it my father made no more mention of the matter for a while and would not even discuss it. Then one afternoon he told me to polish my uniform buttons.

"Whatever for?" I asked him. "I'm out of the service. I can't wear uniform."

"You are not out of the service yet, and tomorrow you are making an official visit to the Lord Lieutenant of Essex. He has read your report and wants to see you."

"Do you really think we should involve him in this?"

"He already IS involved. He wrote a personal reference for you, didn't he? That involves him then. He thinks so, anyway."

I had not thought of it that way and it made me realise what a responsibility is accepted when one writes a reference and furthermore what a responsibility there is in ignoring one.

Colonel Sir Francis Whitmore asked me a number of searching questions and seemed satisfied on all points. He complimented me on my good sense in confiding my problems to the senior chaplain at Uxbridge. He rounded off the interview with an aside to my father.

"He is not the first youngster to go through something like this nor will he be the last. Give me some time. I particularly want to know why that feller left a damn fine regiment like the Gordon Highlanders after several years' service. Funny thing to do!"

And so it was left while the anxious days dragged by. The only hopeful sign was that no letter arrived from the Air Ministry confirming the termination of my commission. When a letter did arrive nearly a month later it simply ordered me to report to No. 3 Flying Training School at RAF South Cerney for the continuation of service. My father beamed.

"I told you, boy, never say die."

I reported to South Cerney, near Cirencester, and was ushered in to the station commander's office. As befitted his name, Group Captain Iron was one of the toughest-looking men I had ever seen and the impression was confirmed by the array of First World War ribbons on his chest. As I was announced he looked up from his desk and smiled.

"Hullo Tunstall," he said. "There isn't very much to say except that I think you'll find some old friends here and I hope you enjoy your training. Oh yes, one thing you might like to know. You've got an absolutely clean record. Good luck to you!"

It was lunchtime and I went straight to the mess where I found, to my delight, that I was joining the course with most of the overseas chaps on it. There were boisterous welcomes and slaps on the back. In the afternoon I was told to report to B flight commander of the Elementary Training Squadron. He gave me the usual sort of introductory welcome and as he finished he said, "You'd better report to your instructor now. I think he's next door."

"Thank you, sir." I saluted, turned about and made my way next door.

The man who looked up from a desk with a big grin on his face was my old flying instructor from Montrose, John Marshall, now promoted to flying officer. It was the first of some of the happiest days of my life.

Never again did I have a whiff of that kind of problem arising in the RAF, or even in prison camps, until years after the war when I was appointed as a member of a court martial. We had to try a case against a senior officer, an engineer, who had many years' service from the age of fifteen as an RAF boy apprentice. He was charged with making sexual advances to two young batmen (officers' personal servants). It was a tragedy for all concerned. The accused was found guilty and was cashiered. That meant he was kicked out of the service in disgrace with loss of all benefits such as pension rights.

Chapter Four

Bomber pilot

South Cerney aerodrome was one of the many being built to a pattern in the feverish expansion of the RAF during the late 1930s. The hangars and essential technical buildings were complete but the domestic buildings, like the officers' mess, were still creosoted huts, capped with roofing felt. The station swarmed with building contractors and where roadways were incomplete was under churned mud. Our uniform included knee-length, air force blue webbing, gaiters and boots.

The shambles detracted little from the quality of a lively social life and we lived like fighting cocks. Every lunch and dinner offered a choice of hot meat dishes, a spread of cold meats, cheeses, including the inevitable Stilton suitably marinated with port, and apart from a couple of choices of cooked dessert, bowls of luscious strawberries in season, with thick cream.

For so many of those youngsters it was to be a short life, but it was certainly a merry one. Of my course of thirty-two pilots, only six or seven survived the war. It was a way of life that encouraged enthusiastic drinking. Work hard and play hard was the order of the day, and the interests of most of the chaps outside their flying and swotting, like those of young men of any generation, did not extend far beyond rugby, boozing and wenching. By accident or design it bred a pretty swashbuckling, rumbustious type for whom readjustment in later years, if they lived to have any, was not always easy.

Once a week we had a ceremonial "dining-in night" which for students and a few junior officer instructors was a compulsory parade in mess kit with "bum freezer" monkey jackets, starched shirt, black tie and those near-skin-tight trousers called "overalls" which reach above the navel and strap under calf-length patent-leather mess "wellingtons". Once a month the evening was devoted to even sterner protocol under the misnomer of "guest night". There were seldom any outside guests, but all officers on the station were obliged to attend, from the station commander—irreverently referred to as the "stationmaster" —downwards. Stiffly formal though these occasions were, as soon as the meal had been concluded with the loyal toast, the rigid protocol was relaxed. Cigars could be lit and banter was free, but always with the mess taboos about mentioning religion, politics, ladies' names and flying. The hangar doors had to remain firmly closed.

Soon everyone would adjourn to the large anteroom with its hefty leather armchairs of the traditional club type. The room was cleared for action and mess games began to the accompaniment of bawdy songs, especially those bewailing the sad lot of the poor airman in sandy outposts of Empire. This was when the serious drinking began, usually involving the swilling of innumerable pints of bitter from pewter mugs. The games that ensued were, by and large, downright ferocious and were generally contests between the junior and senior terms with the staff officers blandly taking a few tots on neutral ground round the fireplace. This was the occasion for the juniors to pay off scores against the almighty seniors, and with games like Hi-cock-a-lorum and mess rugby, which were organised excuses for a roughhouse, the opportunities were plentiful and used to maximum effect. It has been said that the peacetime intake of officer casualties to RAF hospitals due to guest night injuries outnumbered all their other accident causes put together, including flying accidents and proper rugby matches.

As the night wore on the challenges became increasingly hairy. Relay races were performed over room-length obstacles of tables and chairs—some back-to-back or front-to-front so that negotiating them entailed a headlong charge followed by a series of dives, jumps, skids, somersaults and flying leaps which only the very young and fairly inebriated could possibly survive unscathed. Then a tottering pyramid of furniture would be erected to see who could be first to imprint the blackened soles of his feet on the ceiling—resulting in the occasional splintering crash and another casualty among the debris, the target of ribald comment and peals of derisive laughter. On one occasion in another mess, a salutary lesson was taught a particularly resented senior by a most ingenious plot. A rotund pony belonging to the station commander's daughter was smuggled into

Formation flying in Hawker Furies at South Cerney.

the victim's bedroom where it was fed copious oats and a bucket of water, after which the door was locked and the key thrown into the shrubbery.

It was juvenile stuff but no doubt fostered the reckless spirit which later sent small sections of Spitfires and Hurricanes diving, regardless of odds, into the Luftwaffe armadas over the Thames Estuary. The results of these capers were all taken in good part, legends were created, sore heads soon cleared, collar bones mended and everyone paid up cheerfully the increment on their mess bills to make good the damage to public property. The mess waiters maintained their urbane Jeeves-like aloofness and the serious business of air exercises and ground school forged an air force with a morale second to none, even though our current equipment was far behind that of the Luftwaffe, and the training syllabus was archaic and had tragic shortcomings.

A great occasion for showing off to the public was the annual Empire Air Day when family and friends turned up in force. On that day nearly every RAF station was thrown open to the public and each one mounted its own show. At South Cerney this consisted mainly of a flying display in which all participated to a greater or lesser degree. Large formations of Harts and Audaxes deafened the crowd with their crackling Rolls-Royce Kestrel engines; a mock-up fort of recalcitrant tribesmen was bombed into proper respect for the Raj; and a wrecked Hart was pieced together, stuffed with oil and petrol, manned by a dummy and set ablaze for our gallant firemen to quench and effect a rescue. For these displays we were seldom short of a wreck. One day while I was duty pilot under instruction manning the Watch Office (forerunner of Air Traffic Control), a squall hit the airfield and as a string of recalled Harts came in to land I watched three of them touch down and somersault on to their backs within five minutes. The Hart types always did this very gracefully and usually without physical injury to the pilot. Only his pride suffered. Even the aeroplane was often repairable. There was always something to laugh about!

At last we had our wings and were assigned to either fighter or bomber duties. Normally this appointment was made on the basis of the pilot's temperament, with reckless individualists being steered onto fighters and the steadier, more team-oriented types reserved for bomber duties. In our case, however, the entire course was marked for Bomber Command, perhaps because there were few differences between the Audaxes on which we had been trained and the Hawker Hind biplanes still being used by some bomber squadrons. Whatever the reason, I was bitterly disappointed because I thoroughly enjoyed aerobatics, was good at tail chases and had been a crack shot since a nipper—all of which were the ideal attributes of fighter pilots.

We now progressed to advanced training. The bomber pilots were paired off and alternated between flying the aircraft, usually an Audax, and doing the observer's work in the back seat. This involved bomb-aiming, extremely basic map-reading navigation, photography, and handling the First World War Lewis gun on its rotating Scarfe ring. My designated mate was a joyful devil-may-care character, Dennis Baker, and what an endless adventure flying with him turned out to be!

The chap in the back wore a parachute harness with a separate clip-on pack, which resided on a rack until needed. At the bottom of the harness was a metal ring and on to this was clipped, like a dog lead, a flexible wire cable which was anchored to the floor. This cable, which we called "the monkey chain", could be shortened or lengthened by a sliding catch. When it was shortened right down, with the knees very slightly bent, the observer's feet were held firmly down to the floor, or, when the aircraft was upside down, up to the floor! He was then literally "hanging by his ring".

When the observer lengthened his monkey chain he was able to squirm his way underneath the pilot's seat and lie on his belly at an open hatch and peer through the old course-setting bomb sight while he breathed hot oil fumes. Or he could crawl aft to a circular hatch in which was mounted the "vertical" camera. In normal level flight the custom was to loosen the monkey chain and hang over the pilot's shoulder to enjoy the protection of his small windscreen, otherwise the slipstream battered the observer's cheeks despite his helmet, goggles and all the intrepid birdman paraphernalia. Communication was maintained by shouting down a flexible pipe called a Gosport tube. There was no radio or intercom.

It was a new thrill to take off facing backwards and in the shuddering roar watch the tail come up, the ground streaking away behind, and feel the lurching aircraft responding to the minute but observable movements of the elevators and rudder. It was even more exciting to be in the hands of another pupil pilot—especially Dennis Baker's. Sometimes it was just as stimulating flying the Audax with him in the back because he was full of jolly pranks, like reaching over me from the rear cockpit and, screaming with mirth, putting his hands over my goggles for a few seconds immediately after take-off. It was his perverted expression of *joie de vivre* and very wearing.

We managed to survive the rest of the course at South Cerney and off we went with our aircraft to Armament Training Camp at RAF Woodsford on the south coast. Here we were to drop practice bombs on the nearby range and to do our air firing with live ammunition. This was to be the greatest fun of all, shooting with our fixed front gun, like a fighter, at ground targets or at a cloth drogue towed at a safe distance behind another aircraft over the sea.

PDT (right) plans his flight at No. 3 Flying Training School,
South Cerney, 1937.

One day I was in the back doing a bombing exercise. It was a lengthy rigmarole and Dennis had been bored, poor fellow. He slung the Audax into a spirited wing-over and down we dived at full lick. Suddenly his eye lit on a train innocently puffing its way through a large wood and he had one of his awful flashes of inspiration.

"Let's put the wind up the engine driver!"

Like a goshawk after a field mouse Dennis swooped on the train. The trouble came when, at a terrifyingly low altitude, he tried to pull up. Simply snatching the control column back doesn't result in the aircraft instantly going back up again. If you do it too abruptly, the nose will certainly point upward but for a few brief moments the entire machine will continue to descend. These so-called high-speed stalls were not emphasised in our flying training, but Dennis managed to verify the principle quite adequately. When he yanked back on the stick, just a few feet above the train, we went on rushing downwards. There came a swooshing crashing noise as we careered through the adjacent tree tops. The camera hatch lid hit me up the backside and there were leaves inside the fuselage as the aircraft staggered into a reluctant climb.

There were two certain ways in those days for an officer to get himself kicked out of the RAF. One was to bounce a cheque, the other was to be caught doing unauthorised low flying. Leaves and twigs inside a fuselage are evidence of the latter that even the dimmest investigator could not miss. So, muttering obscene imprecations, I got down on hands and knees, gathered all foliage within reach and heaved it overboard. I also prayed the undercarriage had suffered no serious damage for the sake of both our necks on landing, and Dennis's neck on the disciplinary block.

The Audax was not very noticeably scarred, heaven knows why, and nothing was said. We were both shaken up and I fervently hoped that the incident had at least cooled the lunatic's ardour. It had a bit, but not for long.

A week or so later I was flying the Audax and this time Dennis was bomb aiming. The exercise completed, he reached over my shoulders, pinched my nose and put his other hand over my mouth. I'd had enough. I knew his monkey chain must be slacked right off so I gave the stick a healthy prod forward. The aircraft shot nose-down into an outside loop and out the blighter went with his feet well off the floor. Then I hauled back sharply and sent him crashing back into his cockpit again. He was a game boy, our Dennis, and still came up for more. He put his hands round my throat and gleefully started to shake and throttle me. When he let go I feigned unconsciousness and, slumping forward in my straps, hauled the stick back again and kicked on full rudder. Away the Audax went into a spin. Still slumped I kept one eye on the unwinding altimeter and let Dennis sweat.

"Pete, Pete," he yelled, shaking my shoulder. "Pete—wake up, Pete! For Christ's sake wake up!"

I let her spin. I was a bit worried that he might bale out in which case there would have been an awful lot of explaining to do. When I judged the situation was nearly critical I kicked on opposite rudder and eased the stick forward to bring her out of the spin. We landed back at base, still good friends, but I had no more nonsense from Dennis Baker.

These stories have an unhappy sequel. Shortly after we left Flying Training School to go our separate ways I stood sadly at the cemetery while a firing party sent their volleys over his grave. Dennis had been killed in a low-flying accident.

When the bombing exercises were completed we next did our air firing with the First World War type Vickers fixed front gun. This was mounted so that the bullets flew through the arc of the spinning propeller. To prevent them from hitting the prop an interruptor gear sent a hydraulic pulse to the gun so that it fired only when the blades were out of its line. That was the theory and it usually worked very well. When it didn't the pilot shot his own propeller off.

Our aircraft were fitted with two types of front gunsight. One was the crude ring and bead and the other was the much more accurate Aldis sight, similar to a magnifying telescopic sight on a hunting rifle. The Aldis was supposed to be used only for air-to-air shooting at a drogue and never for air-to-ground targets; leather caps were placed over the sight to ensure that this restriction was observed. A and B Flights, though, were keenly competing for the best bombing results and for the highest air-firing scores. The word was out that by the dangerous process of releasing their safety harness and their parachute harness, then standing up in the cockpit, control column held between the knees, one or two of the A Flight monkeys had leaned over the windscreen; removed the caps; and used the Aldis on the ground target, thereby scoring extremely well. Very enterprising indeed! All is fair in love and war was the general feeling.

The ground targets were set up on shingly Chesil Bank just off the coast near Weymouth. The range officer, a junior lad, supervised the exercise, seeing that the targets were renewed and that nobody did anything outrageously dangerous. When new targets were set up and the range party safely sheltered, he would fire a green flare and the next young hero commenced his firing. Each pilot was supposed to pull out of each dive at about 200 feet. If the range officer thought he came too low, a white flare was fired. This meant "You were too low. If you do that again I will fire a red, and you must return to base." Each pilot had exactly 100 rounds and would fire these off in four or five dives at the target.

I was on the last detail for air-to-ground firing. My flight commander called me in.

"It's up to you, Tunstall," he said. "A Flight are ahead of us. You go out there and get a bloody good score. See?"

He did not say "or else" but I knew what he meant. So I became airborne and, feeling pretty damn scared, unstrapped myself; stood on the seat and gingerly removed the caps from the Aldis; strapped myself into the cockpit again; arrived at the range and got my green. First pass I held my fire until the lowest legal limit and, dissatisfied with my angle, let go about two rounds. For two more passes I did the same thing, which meant only about six rounds had gone. Next pass I held the dive so that the target grew larger and larger on the crosswires of the telescopic sight and I gave it a long sustained burst and pulled out far too low. Up sailed a white "warning" flare. One more pass to go for which I knew very well I would get a red, so it was imperative to get all the remaining rounds fired off. Again I held that target until it loomed horribly large in the Aldis sight and then belted it until the ammunition ran out. As I looked away from the telescopic sight I pulled out immediately, aghast at the closeness of the ground. The result was a slight crump and a jolt. I had bounced my wheels off the shingle of Chesil Bank.

An outraged range officer fired off a red and, amazed I was still airborne or, for that matter, alive, I returned to base anticipating a "bollocking". I had very nearly killed myself as so many young pilots did in those days. Before I landed, the hotline from the range to base had been busy and, as I had expected, my flight commander was waiting for me. He treated me to one of the longest strings of highly descriptive invective I have ever heard—all apparently without drawing breath in, and ending up with:

"Jolly good show, old chap, you got 87. We've beaten A Flight."

As if that was not enough, as I came out of the flight commander's office the technical flight sergeant came up to me with a grave face.

"Come and 'ave a look at yer prop, sir."

One of the wooden blades had two bullet holes through it and a nasty nick on the trailing edge. Luckily it had not disintegrated and caused the unbalanced vibration to tear the engine out of its mountings. The fault lay with the old Constantinesco gear which had gone on the blink. I'd had enough air-to-ground for one day!

We all flew back to South Cerney, our final exams behind us, and having duly qualified as fully operational pilots we were feeling pretty cock-a-hoop and ready to enjoy the last highlight of our course. This was the annual Hunt Ball at Cheltenham, to which a small contingent of us were invited. It was our first public appearance in those dashing mess kits which, resplendent with gold braid and wings, mingled with the hunting pink. How the lovely young county debutantes purred around us like slinky little pussy cats! How the cup of gilded youth brimmed to overflowing and what spoilt brats we were. Of course, we were on our very best behaviour and, anyway, one or two of our senior officers were very sensibly keeping a sharp eye open.

The ball concluded, I received notification that my operational assignment was to 49 Bomber Squadron at RAF Scampton, just north of Lincoln, flying Hawker Hinds. The only cloud on the horizon was that I would have only two months to serve before my precious year with the RAF would be up. It didn't bear thinking about.

In July 1938, Scampton was being built to the same pattern as South Cerney and was at a similar stage of incompletion. The officers' mess and quarters were still creosoted huts and last on the list of priorities. 49 Squadron shared the Station with 83 Squadron, also equipped with Hawker Hinds. In the mess we were as one, but on guest nights the two squadrons joyfully tried to break each other's necks at the usual boisterous games. My squadron commander was Squadron Leader Willie Watt who had flown with the High Speed Flight at Calshot. The CO of No. 83 was Squadron Leader Willie Snaith who, by coincidence, had done the same thing.

Willie Watt allotted me to B Flight and off I went to report to my flight commander, Flying Officer George Lerwill, the son of a retired air commodore. George turned out to be another of the "characters" and to some extent an influence in my life. Very tall, somewhat gangly, with a slow drawl and a wisp of downy moustache, he was pure P.G. Wodehouse. Regardless, I snapped him an impeccable salute.

"Good morning, sir, Acting Pilot Officer Tunstall reporting."

"All right, Stall Turn, relax."

"Yes, sir."

"You can call me 'sir' first thing in the morning, the rest of the day it's 'George'. You're on a squadron now, laddie."

"Yes, sir."

"George."

"Yes, George."

"Can you fly, Tunstall?"

"I hope so, sir, er, George."

"All right, we'll see."

He indicated another pilot officer and introduced us.

"That's Mister Forsyth. He's known around here as 'Skin.'"

He pointed to three Hinds on the tarmac outside his window.

"We three will now strap those flying machines to our backsides and do a spot of formation flying and then we'll have a tail chase. If you lose us you can do an extra stint of orderly officer. Let's get airborne."

For the beginner, formation flying is a nerve-racking, muscle-tensing, sweat-producing ordeal of over-anxiety and over-reaction. The first essential is to learn to relax. I had just about achieved this fairly elementary standard when I joined 49 Squadron.

George briefed us for a formation take-off, which was a bit challenging at my stage in the game, but I coped—more or less. Then we tucked in on him, myself thankfully on his right because for most people it is easier to fly in formation looking out to one's left; don't ask me why. I was doing well, I thought. I even spared a second to look at George himself. He wore a mirthless, almost sadistic smile on his face and his gloved forefinger was beckoning to me. He wanted me in closer!

"Oh God," I thought, "he's trying to kill us all."

I edged in a little bit, but he still beckoned. Tension began to screw up my muscles and I repeatedly had to command myself to relax. George smiled and beckoned again. In the end I was reduced to the state of a sweaty beginner with moist hands and my shirt clammy on my back.

After the sortie George remarked dryly:

"In 49 Squadron we fly in formation. We do not occupy adjacent areas of the sky flying at approximately the same height in roughly the same direction!"

The tail chase went no better for me. When George signalled with his hand for us to break formation, Skin and I peeled away and re-formed in a line with myself at the rear as briefed. Then George started to try to shake us off as if we were fighters peppering his tail. First he barrel-rolled, which was easy to follow, the nose of each Hind describing a circle as it rolled round the horizon. He held the bottom of the roll into a steep dive then pulled straight up into a vertical climb.

So far so good. I had them both in front of me but as yet had been unable to hold either steady in my gunsight. Then George flick-rolled and suddenly passed close by me going downwards—so close that I flinched. Skin went past hard on his tail. I was almost out of airspeed so that my flying machine had become a huge chunk of uncontrollable metal and taut fabric hanging in the sky. I tried to rudder her over into a stall turn but must have been clumsy for she flicked on to her back and started to spin. It took only a couple of turns for me to recognise the problem, take proper recovery action, stop the spin and ease out of the dive.

Now where the hell were George and Skin? I searched the sky for them but they were gone. As a final afterthought I twisted round in the cockpit to look behind, and there they were, both of them sitting on my tail where they could have gunned me to ribbons. I had thought I was an operational pilot but learned in the space of thirty minutes that I had a long long way to go. What a wonderful exciting life this was!

My comrades at Scampton were a remarkable bunch. In 83 Squadron there was young Gibson, who we knew in those days as "Gibbo" or "Hoot", after Hoot Gibson the cowboy hero of early Hollywood movies. I never heard of him referred to as Guy Gibson until after he received his Victoria Cross as the leader of 617 "Dambuster" Squadron—in fact, not until long after the lad was killed.

In my own squadron we had another up-and-coming VC in bluff, good-hearted Babe Learoyd. Was it Babe or another who, dead to the world towards the end of a riotous mess party, was laid out serenely in a wardrobe, carried by a gang of irresponsible giggling pall bearers to the shore and launched on to the waters of Cromarty Firth? It was not until breakfast that his presence was missed. In sudden hung-over panic at the fatal possibilities, there was a rush down to the shore where the wardrobe-coffin was found mercifully beached and the occupant still in peaceful slumber, unaware of his seafaring adventure.

Our two future VCs were not the only great men at Scampton. In my estimation another of them was Aircraftsman Keating. To our young eyes, Keating was an old man. He had iron-grey hair and a row of First World War medal ribbons, having transferred from the cavalry to the Royal Flying Corps. Keating also played rugby for the station and died young at heart.

Before the days when all aircrew were promoted at least to the rank of Sergeant, Keating was a wireless operator/air gunner, or "Wop/AG" as we called them. Volunteers all, most were still not particularly partial to aerobatics on the end of a monkey chain in an open cockpit. Dear old Keating was an exception. The pilot did not exist who could wipe the grin off his weathered face and I think he enjoyed being upside down, standing in the back, as much as we enjoyed being firmly strapped down into our seat in the front cockpit by a Sutton harness.

If Lord Trenchard was the "father of the RAF", Keating was the father of 49 Squadron. He took a kindly but sometimes stern interest in the welfare of the younger officers and I am sure he had more direct access to the squadron commander than we had. If one of us had misbehaved ourselves at a party, or otherwise, it was not such a dreadful ordeal to stand on George's mat or even Willie Watt's. Anyway, there were few rowdy parties in which George wasn't involved. After having your ears burned off by them you could always take the attitude: "If I can't take a joke, I shouldn't have joined up." But when an airman came up, saluted smartly and said, "Excuse me, sir, but AC Keating would like to have a word with you," you knew you were in for a quiet fatherly dressing-down that would really hit home.

"Now that's not the way to go on, sir, is it now?"

"No, Keating."

"I mean, we'll never really get on in the service if we do silly things like that, will we, sir?"

"Yes, Keating—I mean, no, Keating."

"Very well then, we'll have to pull our socks up, won't we, sir?"

And so it was with the pilot officer looking sorrowfully at his shoes in the august presence of the old Wop/AG.

Keating and I flew together often. One day as we were walking in from the tarmac he asked:

"Excuse me, sir, but wot's up? You're not yerself."

"Keating, I've got exactly two more weeks in the service."

"Ah!— I thought that was it! You love the service don't you, sir!"

I tried to sound casual.

"Hell, it's all I've ever wanted. How long have you been in, Keating?"

"Twenty-four years, sir, counting the Army. Me and my brother was in the same cavalry regiment. I was there when he was killed. That's when I transferred to the Royal Flying Corps. I wanted to belt them bloody Huns and the cavalry wasn't much good any more was it, sir! 'Ave you applied for a Short Service Commission, sir?"

"Yes, Keating. I did that in the first place but this is all I got."

"Well why don'cher apply again, sir?"

"They know I want one, so what's the point?"

"Don't ask, don't get, I always say, sir. Why don'cher bung in another application? I'll see if I can't 'ave a word with somebody."

So I dutifully bunged in another application.

A fortnight later on my last flying day in the RAF, I sought out Keating for a final flight together.

"I want to do everything in the book, Keating. What about it?"

"Course you can, sir. You know me!"

We climbed to 7,000 feet, checked our harnesses were tight and nothing loose in the cockpit, no other aircraft around and away we went into my best sequences. As we looped, rolled, barrel rolled, looped again and rolled off the top, stall turned and looped again, I occasionally twisted round to see how old Keating was taking it. That cheerful grin was always there and he gave me a thumbs-up whenever I turned to look. I decided to finish off the last sequence with a spin—a long one to throw away all our height.

I was almost over Lincoln, which was naughty, but nothing mattered so much any more. With stick hard back and the airspeed needle fluttering around 55 mph, I kicked on full left rudder so that the Hind immediately lurched into a sharp spin to the left, which tightened up progressively. The countryside was whirling beneath the nose of the aircraft as if it were mounted on a giant turntable. The huge wooden propeller flicked round to the tick-over of the Kestrel engine. It was a long spin and I suppose the engine grew cold. In the light of more experience I would probably have given the engine a burst or two to warm it up, or I might have noticed the almost imperceptible slowing of the propeller. I was about to initiate recovery action when the worst happened. The prop slowed, almost stopped, flicked back half a compression, and stood stock still. Calamity!

The surge of guilt-flavoured adrenaline was horrible. What now? How do I get out of this? Ignominy and shame—Keating in the back—so close to Lincoln—King's Regulations—squadron commander—Keating's censure. Personal physical danger came a long last. We would survive somehow, but what a way to end a short Air Force career. A Hind pranged in a forced landing in an impossibly small field on the outskirts of a town! This all in a flash as I took immediate recovery action. Lacking, as these primitive aircraft did, any kind of starter—the engine was fired up on the ground using an external device that was wheeled away afterwards—there was only one possible way of getting under way again: diving steeply until the airflow was fast enough to force the propeller to begin turning again. Wasn't I already too low for this? But I must! Spinning stopped, keep the stick forward, plunge straight down. The ground now coming up faster, prop still unmoving, airspeed building. "Turn over, damn you, please for God's sake turn over. Can't dive much longer. Ground too close." A jerk from the prop. Trees growing larger. Prop turning over, throttle open a bit, prop spinning and a roar from the engine. Relief but almost too late. "Pull out, pull out," and there we were, horribly close to the treetops, engine bellowing full bore and climbing away. Straight back to Scampton a few minutes away and a landing—heart still thumping a bit, mouth still dry.

I climbed out of the cockpit on jellied knees fearful to look Keating in the face which I knew would convey his stern disapproval. When I turned to him he was still standing in the rear cockpit arms folded, head on one side with his usual grin and a knowing look in his eyes. Almost contemptuously he said:

"You can't put the wind up me, sir!"

I left it at that.

I was at home, a miserable civilian, for only two weeks before a letter came from the Air Ministry advising that I had been granted a Short Service Commission and a further four glorious years of active service. Dear old Keating must have "'ad a word" with "Boom" Trenchard.

Thomas Alexander Keating, promoted to Corporal, was killed at the age of 46 on 23 November 1939 when a Hampden, flown by his squadron commander with five Wop/AGs on board, crashed into a hangar. The crew of six all died and so did some ground crew working in the hangar. In foul weather they were experimenting with a new-fangled instrument landing system called ZZ which apparently did not work all that well. I can still hear old Keating saying, "You can't put the wind up me, sir." He is buried in the graveyard of St John the Baptist Church, only a mile or so from the aerodrome at Scampton. He will forever be one of my heroes and, in my opinion, a model of a great Englishman.

One reason for my own and others' immediate recall to the colours in September 1938 was the worsening international political scene, with Hitler's truculent forces threatening and rampaging in Europe. With might proving right, 49 Squadron was not the only one still armed with open-cockpit biplanes whose adversaries at any moment might be the sleek monoplane cannon-firing Messerschmitt 109s of the Luftwaffe. At the time of the *Anschluss*, when Germany walked into Austria, what easy meat we would have been! Hitler was playing poker with the statesmen of Europe who, fearful of their weak hands, would not call his bluff. With their fatal policy of appeasement they played for time, which was running out fast.

My return to the squadron coincided with the news that we would soon be the first to be rearmed with the new Handley Page Hampden medium bomber. With the gradual disposal of our Hinds an era was ending in the annals of the Royal Air Force. It had been a joyful, carefree and perhaps somewhat irresponsible service with the atmosphere of a superb flying club. Everybody knew nearly everybody else. There was a happy informality about the way one could, for example, scrounge a few circuits in a visiting chap's aircraft and notch up a new type. "Weekend aircraft" were easy to come by with pilots buzzing off to all corners of the kingdom for parties and romantic rendezvous. To be sure, it was all good cross-country navigation practice. Perhaps there was a somewhat greater "press on regardless of weather" factor on Fridays than on Monday's return flights. This, it was noted, imposed a grim Friday blip on the accident rate graph, as more aircraft tended to fly into hills shrouded in the low cloud of filthy weather. Damn bad luck!

Our 49 Squadron had its fair share of the peacetime "prangs", both with Hinds and then with the new Hampdens. Quite a few mishaps were due to night flying, which was never taken very seriously. We were not, after all, one of the very few specially designated "night bomber squadrons". The rest, like us, very occasionally laid out on the grass the old paraffin goose-neck flares and had a go at it for a bit of fun—if the weather was calm and the moon was bright. It was not really much different from day flying and very enjoyable. We did no night bombing or navigation or instrument flying or anything serious like that. Mostly the senior chaps would do five or six take-offs and landings—"circuits and bumps"—and then have a few beers in the mess to round off the rare occasion. We junior "bograts" seldom got even that much.

I have a favourite old photograph of George Lerwill and Skin Forsyth posing cheerfully in front of one of the latter's broken night-flying Hinds, and another taken when George overshot the paraffin flarepath with a Hampden which straddled the public highway alongside the airfield. I understand George pranged another Hampden after that, on return from a nasty bombing operation on Germany. He fortunately survived two tours of bomber operations, which was extremely lucky and no mean feat, and for this he was awarded a Distinguished Flying Cross. But considering all our pre-war prangs, it's no wonder some ground staff engineers erected a colourful coat of arms outside their technical repair hangar, with the cod Latin motto "Ubendum Wemendum."

It is remarkable to note from my official RAF logbook that, as a pilot whose imminent war operations were to be nearly all at night, I did not once fly in the dark between April 1938 at Flying Training School and November 1939. It was then that I managed to sneak one hour of night flying on an Anson which, so far as we were concerned, was not even an operational type. Moreover, it was in brilliant moonlight; not really much different from flying in broad daylight, except that it was jolly to see some pretty twinkling lights down below and made a youngster like me feel a bit of a master aviator.

On my twentieth birthday, 1 December 1938, I flew the last Hind from 49 Squadron down to its graveyard at Hatfield, and was flown back as a passenger by George in a new Hampden. For me it was the last of those really carefree flying days of the RAF. Only the more experienced senior squadron pilots were allowed to fly the new type with all its new-fangled gadgets. Even squadron "elders" like George and Skin had no conventional conversion course on this new wonder plane—not even any lectures. They just read the pilot's notes, then got in and flew 'em!

The rest of us disgruntled juniors became dogsbodies. For some months we flew only as passengers, serving no other purpose than ballast on development trials for this new Hampden type. The purpose of this seemed to be to find out what was likely to go wrong with them first and most often, before any other squadrons were equipped with them. We, like our seniors, had no ground school instruction on them and we became rusty, testy and dejected.

Some weeks after we lost the last Hind, three of us were sent rejoicing up the road to RAF Hemswell where 61 Squadron had some Bristol Blenheim bombers. We were to receive three hours "twin engine conversion training" on these operational bombers by ordinary squadron pilots who were not even flying instructors. This was deemed all that was necessary to qualify us as Hampden pilots. By now I had a total of 152 hours solo flying by day and one hour twenty minutes by night, all on single-engined, open cockpit, fabric biplanes with fixed undercarriages, with another hour in bright moonlight in a twin-engined Anson. We now took the air for three hours dual instruction on hefty all-metal Blenheims with these new-fangled flap things, retractable undercarriages, two 840 hp Bristol Mercury VIII radial

"All Vehicles Will Be Towed." George Lerwill (left) and PDT (centre) survey
the remains of Lerwill's Hampden after overshooting at Scampton.

air-cooled engines and the equally new-fangled variable-pitch propellers.
An additional two hours training on these aircraft completed our so-called
"course". We were then considered fully converted twin-engined pilots fit
to fly the even bigger and more sophisticated Hampdens.

Nowadays, people get more training before they're allowed to drive a
moped.

After another month cooling my heels on the ground, a Hampden was
finally made available to me for a first solo. No dual instruction could be
given because it had a fighter-type cockpit with no room for an instructor.
We just had to get in and fly the thing. We were delighted to do so; absolutely
cock-a-hoop. It's a great thing to feel you are the bee's knees, when in reality
you are the untrained, pathetic lamb ready for the slaughter.

All the same, we soon came to appreciate the Hampden's merits.
Streamlined and relatively large, it had a wingspan of seventy feet. It was
probably the biggest aircraft ever to have a single-seat fighter-type cockpit,

affording the pilot a completely uncluttered view. We could really feel as one with the machine. Although it had a wheel-type control column, as opposed to the spade-grip "stick" usual in fighters, the manoeuvrability of the Hampden was superb so that she was a joy to fly. It was particularly exhilarating to slide back the canopy in flight and to feel that some of the *joie de vivre* still remained even flying a modern heavy aircraft. She was fast for her day, but I'm doubtful about a top speed of 265 mph quoted in some popular publications.

In addition to the pilot, there were three other crew members. Behind him, in the very narrow but deep forward fuselage, a dorsal gun was manned as required by the wireless operator; on top and beneath there was a ventral gun position where reposed the observer. These two characters gazed rearwards at the long thin after-fuselage—little more than a hollow boom permitting the tail assembly to shudder and twist as though it would break off at any moment. This was a little daunting at first, but, as I heard one positive-thinking rear-gunner say, "At least there ain't much of it for the bloody flak to hit." Up front, ahead of and beneath the pilot, the navigator-cum-bomb aimer sat in a narrow, largely perspex, nose with a truly glorious view. There seemed very little between him and the whole world but a bit of glass and sometimes not even that, as the perspex canopy had a bad habit of peeling off from the aircraft and plummeting away when the speed built up too much.

Underneath was the Hampden's bomb bay. It was enormous by the standards of the day and could carry either 2,000 lbs of ordinary bombs or the new cylindrical anti-shipping mines. These had to be dropped from a mere 200 feet, an exciting low level in a well-defended enemy harbour or estuary. With additional external racks under the wings, the Hampden could carry an even larger bomb load but only with a reduced fuel load.

With a lighter load and at economical cruising the Hampden had a range of nearly 2,000 miles and could stay aloft for more than ten hours. Therein lay a problem. The crew was cramped, there was no room to walk about, and the pilot could not even get out of his seat. This meant that the carriage of a so-called "second pilot" was pointless and wasteful. The only concession to crew comfort was an Elsan chemical lavatory just aft of the main spar of the wing, but I never knew of anyone using it, and the pilot couldn't possibly get to it anyway. He was stuck in his seat for the duration of the flight—however long! There was not even any kind of an emergency bottle as far as I knew.

Having gone solo in a Hampden with no crew, one was immediately deemed to be "qualified on type" and, presumably, ready for war. This was a tremendous ego booster and little else. What purpose it served I do not know, but from then on whenever we junior pilots flew in a Hampden, in any crew position, the time had to be logged as "second pilot". This was complete nonsense. Unless one sat in the pilot's seat, it wasn't possible even to see the instruments. No doubt it looked good for somebody's statistics, but it added nothing to our experience or confidence in this new aircraft as we prepared for night operations in all weathers against a formidable enemy.

On a strict seniority basis the older pilots flew all the exercises while we juniors had to be content with map reading (by no stretch of the imagination could you really call it "navigating") and bomb aiming. We occasionally snatched a few, very few, minutes without a crew, piloting here and there on a ferry flight or errand that none of the seniors wanted to do. George, my flight commander, assigned me to his own crew and I greatly appreciated his gesture of confidence. I forgive him for one heinous accusation against me. One morning, after a good boozy party the night before, he accused me of farting in the navigator's position down in the nose. He claimed it wafted up to the pilot's position. He threatened that if I did it again he would put me under arrest. And he did. He never released me from arrest so I suppose, technically, more than seventy years later, I still am! It eases my conscience to admit he was quite right.

As for myself, whatever shortcomings life might have on the professional front, it was suddenly compensated by the fulfilment of a longing I had only half recognised. Since leaving school two years previously I had seen nothing of my neighbour Ann who was never home at Orsett when I was on leave. She was either away at school or abroad at a finishing school or polishing a language somewhere. Our early teenage friendship, during which I thought it best, for fear of rebuff or ridicule, to repress my callow feelings about her, seemed an age away. Now she was home for good and we met again during one of my weekend leaves which I normally spent quite happily roistering on or in the vicinity of RAF Scampton. Could this lovely, physically mature young woman, with her poise and charm, her flair for dress, her gay laughter, all delivering a stunning blow to my senses every time she glanced my way—could this really be that same girl, that child? I just gaped at her like a dumbstruck ninny and when she greeted me warmly I could only croak an awkward reply. I was henceforth a poor, smitten creature!

From that day, whenever the opportunity arose, I tore myself away from Scampton to be home by hook or by crook—crewing George's "weekend aircraft", driving my own ancient banger of a car, or in somebody else's. What long impatient drives south they were down that old tortuous Great North Road. What tedious reluctant drives back north again. Swimming, dancing, tennis parties, film shows, all such things in life had but one basic object—to be near Ann, and the misery about the lack of "hands-on" flying was slightly assuaged. Very slightly!

Among our young company there were few who did not seize most opportunities to satisfy their youthful libido and those few were generally regarded as oddities or "lilywhites", apart from exceptional chaps I remember, like Jamie Pitcairn-Hill who was religious and moral in all respects. He was grudgingly admired by most concupiscent rapscallions and later proved his valour in war until his death in September 1940. I became one of the oddities, chaffed by the others, especially my erstwhile wenching companions. I enjoyed our drinking together as before, but to be in another woman's company was a twist of the knife. Separation was indeed sweet sorrow. Perhaps I was living on a euphoric plane of immature rapture. Or perhaps the chemistry was indeed exceptionally powerful. Who dares to say?

In June 1939 Scampton's permanent buildings were completed and the officers moved into the imposing new officers' mess. A flourish was given to the opening of the mess with a Grand Summer Ball and to my joy Ann's parents consented to her coming with my elder brother, Geoff, and his very highly respected fiancée as chaperones. They were to stay the night, or what was left of it after the ball, at the old Saracen's Head Hotel in Lincoln, below the twin-towered cathedral on its hilltop.

The ball was a colourful affair with more than the usual number of senior

"Air Rank" officers attending the inaugural occasion. There, in the midst of it, I was resplendent in my dashing blue and gold mess kit among my fellow fighting cocks but with eyes only for Ann, radiant in a simple white full-length backless gown which set off her smooth golden tan, tiny waist and the rest of a very exciting figure. It was with smug satisfaction that I saw many a head turn her way. There was, of course, protocol to be satisfied, a string of introductions, payment of respects and woe betide the young officer who neglected to request the pleasure of a dance with the wives of at least his own close hierarchy. It was strict protocol. Understanding souls that they were, most of the seniors' ladies excused themselves.

By midnight the formalities were over and I found the chance to lead Ann into the freshly laid-out rose gardens, and there, as best I could, I said the things a young fellow should say as he pledged his love. My spirits soared when she said she only wondered why I had taken so long about it and that I was an ass if I didn't know she felt the same way. I was scared lest the glittering occasion had launched this nineteen-year-old girl into an unrealistic romantic spin, but only time would tell that. I, at any rate, was sure beyond any possible doubt. The rest of the night was a whirling heady dream and when, in the small hours, my three guests departed for the Saracen's Head I snatched a few hours sleep, high on champagne but mostly on euphoria.

In August I was given some leave. The talk was all of war with Germany. My own thoughts were all for Ann, but our joy was short-lived. Hitler threatened to invade Poland and the British Prime Minister, Neville Chamberlain, gave a guarantee that if Hitler did so, Britain would go to war with Germany. We were on the brink and I received a telegram ordering me to return to my squadron immediately.

Chapter Five

Temporarily unsure of our position

When a telegram ordered me to return to my squadron at the double, there were stiff upper lips and over-fond farewells—which all seemed a bit over the top when one was secretly delighted at the prospect of some live action and the end of the present unsatisfactory status quo. Now they would need us all, not just those senior chaps who were hogging all the hands-on flying.

The thought of death hardly arose. Anyway, it was quick in the air. We had all seen *Hell's Angels* and *Dawn Patrol* at the cinema—the oil-spattered goggles; the clutch at the breast; a dribble of blood from the corner of the mouth; the slump into the cockpit; spinning in; wires screaming and CRUNCH—Oblivion! All over very quickly. Nothing to get steamed up about and, anyway, it couldn't happen to me. That, I think, summed it up for most of us silly young idiots.

I hated the prospect that I might see less of Ann, but no doubt we would devise a plan. Our relationship had flared into a passionate white heat, disciplined by the "nice girl" ethics of that distant age. Though we were both frustrated to the point of agony, it was unthinkable that such pure love could be consummated other than in marriage and I did not even contemplate an attempt at seduction. With her, it was quite unthinkable.

As for marriage, it had been made quite clear that there was little hope of parental consent for a couple of years or so. The service also took a jaundiced view of young marriages and there were no married quarters or even marriage allowance for officers of my tender age. But love, we felt quite sure, would find a way.

A few days after my return to the squadron, the armies of the Third Reich marched into Poland. Britain, honouring her guarantee, declared war on Germany on 3 September 1939.

At Scampton dark green hedges were painted across the all-grass airfield; huge camouflage nets were rigged over the hangars; the aircraft, when not in use, were dispersed in local fields or flown to nearby "scatter" non-operational airfields, so as to be less vulnerable to a sneak raid by the Luftwaffe. The Waddington Squadrons, 50 and 44, were delighted to be scattered to Nottingham civil airfield, which was close by the big city with all its nice pubs and flighty young women.

All leave was stopped and we had to wear uniform all the time, even for visits to the "Snake Pit". Apart from that, there was little change, and the senior pilots still hogged all the operational-type flying, dammit. My only hands-on flying in the Hampdens consisted of little hops from Scampton to RAF Newton, a nearby scatter airfield. This took place at the end of the day's flying and back again in the morning, all in broad daylight and with no crew. I felt like an utter dogsbody getting nowhere fast.

Analysis of my log book shows that between March and the declaration of war in September, I had averaged only three hours and forty minutes' actual Hampden flying per month—about one tenth of a normal squadron pilot's monthly total. Nonetheless, we were ordered to log all airborne time with the seniors as "second pilot" even though we were never anywhere near the cockpit and could not have taken over from the pilot even if he had thrown a fit. I suppose it looked better for the record when we few untrained, inexperienced lads were thrown into the deep end a little later on.

I became more and more frustrated. I *knew* I could drop into the seat of a fighter aircraft and do a good job right away. I loved aerobatics and had been a crack shot since boyhood. I had proved it at Flying Training School, but now here I was stuck with bombers and not even allowed to fly those. Nobody would listen to my pleas for a posting. Bomber Command said they could not afford to lose anybody. I was becoming more and more disillusioned, angry and, I am sorry to admit, bloody-minded and undisciplined.

Getting on for mid-November 1939, I had suffered enough of this frustration. Everybody knew in those days that one sure way to get posted was to do something really naughty. So with two other young gentlemen, who I promised would always remain nameless, after fortifying ourselves with a few beers, I accepted a challenge that I could not get the new Scampton station commander out of bed to test the rumour that he wore an old-fashioned Dickensian nightshirt while sleeping.

Taking my father's ancient Colt .45 revolver, with the other two rascals sniggering in the background, I made my way down to the officers' married quarters. Outside the station commander's house, I banged off two shots safely down into a flowerbed and shouted that I had just chased a pair of intruders away. This excuse was all part of the fun because of crazy rumours going around about local fascist sympathisers (including an inoffensive parish parson) who were supposedly using kids' fireworks to identify our airfield at night for the benefit of enemy bombers. Even my flight commander, George Lerwill, was, at one stage, caught up in all that crazy nonsense.

My desperate ruse worked like a dream. There was a kerfuffle to which I played dumb, and it was reckoned to have been an alcoholic prank, which wasn't far wrong. I was to be punished with a posting under a cloud away from Scampton. Splendid, I thought. Best of all, I was posted to 185 Hampden Squadron at RAF Cottesmore which, under a new scheme, was intended to take on the role of a Hampden Operational Training Unit (OTU). I thought it was about the best outcome I could expect other than an escape from Bomber Command to a fighter squadron.

Alas, this very new OTU had not yet got its act together. Instead of the more than 100 hours that I ought to have received (half of them at night), I was given only thirteen hours day flying on Hampdens with no crew, and only one hour at night on an Anson, which was irrelevant. Two months later, in January 1940, I was posted to 61 Squadron at Hemswell.

Things didn't get better. I had flown my first war operational flight on Christmas Day 1939, during which I sat for several hours in the nose of a Hampden, nominally as navigator/bomb aimer, doing absolutely nothing while we swept the North Sea looking for the elusive German fleet. An equally fruitless sweep took place in January. There followed the magnificent total of one hour's flying in February; none at all in March; and an hour at the controls in April on a moonlit night so bright that I might as well have been flying in daylight.

It was a sickening situation that confounded all my boyhood ambitions of becoming an active pilot in the RAF. My idealistic dreams about love and war were both becoming nightmares of frustration. It was utterly despairing for a few of us very junior pilots, who seemed to be caught in a demoralising trap of inactivity and boredom.

If I had only realised it, I wasn't missing much. The Hampdens of Bomber Command's No. 5 Group were engaged at this time in what were considered to be serious operations, but in retrospect have an irresistibly comic aspect. When not dropping useless propaganda leaflets that, as Air Vice-Marshal Harris said, merely "supplied the continent's requirement for toilet paper for the five long years of war", they were busily shovelling overboard tiny bits of wet phosphorus attached to little squares of celluloid, the whole contraption being known as a "razzle". These things were dropped in their tens of thousands over ripe grain crops or forests in the expectation that when the phosphorus dried out it would flare, set fire to the celluloid and start a merry blaze to confound the wicked Germans.

The most startling conflagration I ever heard told about these razzles occurred when an RAF station commander was first shown one of these devilish new weapons in its damp state during an initial introductory briefing of his Hampden crews. The CO was examining the thing, when an intelligence officer interrupted him. The poor CO absent-mindedly put the little thing in his trouser pocket where it quickly dried off and ignited to the wicked amusement of the assembled bomber crews. It was a cracking good story even if it was far too good to be true.

My purgatory of underemployment was not to last for ever. In mid-April I was sent for a five-week course at the RAF School of Air Navigation at St Athan in Wales. Upon its completion, I returned to Hemswell where I joined the crew of Pilot Officer Alec Webster. My temporary rôle was as a navigator/bomb aimer. Sergeant Bob Jones was the wireless operator/air gunner and his fellow sergeant, Bill Bissett, the air observer. At last I was to have a chance to get really stuck into the enemy. My enthusiasm at this prospect overshadowed the fact that in place of the four-month course at an OTU, in which we were supposed to learn how to work together as a team, we were allotted just four days for the purpose.

As it transpired, Bomber Command could barely wait that long. The day before we completed our training, the last British ship steamed out of Dunkirk carrying the battered remnants of the British Expeditionary Force. There seemed to be little to stop the Germans from pressing their advantage and sweeping across the Channel. Whether we were ready or not, there was no more time. As a result, just two nights later, we were despatched to bomb an oil refinery near Hanover. Remarkably, we found our way to the target without incident and dropped four 500 lb general purpose bombs and some incendiaries on the refinery, to the satisfaction of everyone on board, and headed for home.

All went well until the time came to send a radio transmission to obtain a course to steer towards base. We were then informed by Bob Jones that he could not transmit because, apparently, the engine-driven generator which powered the radio had packed up and he was unable to make contact with RAF Hemswell or anywhere else—what a familiar story that was to become. So now it was all up to me. When I calculated we should be seeing the English coast, there was nothing whatsoever ahead of us in the early morning light but a solid blanket of thick white fog covering everything as far as the distant horizon! To make matters worse, Alec Webster then informed us that, for whatever reason, we were running short of fuel. He said we could not waste time waiting for the fog to clear. He considered the situation an emergency and ordered us to prepare to abandon the aircraft.

Next he demanded of me, as the navigator, absolute assurance that we were over land and not the North Sea. I could only tell him that, according to my calculations, we should have just crossed the coast and now be over land. He replied, "Well, you'd better be right because we have no option but to bale out of this thing." We clipped on our parachute packs and were preparing to jump into the unknown when Webster said, "Hold it! I think I can see a hole in the fog." He was right. It was a small murky tear in that solid white blanket, and beneath it there appeared to be a small patch of Mother Earth with no buildings visible. Webster ordered us to take up crash positions in the Hampden and said he was going to duck through the hole and crash-land with the wheels still retracted up under the engine nacelles.

Oh Hell! Crash landings could be successful or a flaming funeral pyre depending upon what you hit when you made contact with the ground. It was all up to the pilot's skill and, under circumstances like this, more luck than anything else. It was a brave decision, though, because there was no knowing where an abandoned aircraft would eventually crash. It could be in the middle of a built-up area causing immense damage and terrible casualties among unsuspecting civilians. Alec Webster could have ordered his crew to bale out and tried to make the crash landing as the sole occupant of the aircraft, but he did not suggest this alternative and nobody questioned his decision. He very sensibly switched off everything that might ignite the remaining fuel in the tanks and, at the last moment, as he approached the small hole in the fog blanket, he cut both engines as well. The relative quiet was, to say the least, bloody frightening.

I had pressed myself, curled up as much as possible, against the back of the armour plating behind the pilot's seat and waited for the crunch. As we hit the ground at approximately 100 mph the noise and the violent thumping and bumping were terrifying. The Hampden careened its way across a rough grass field, hurdled a ditch and smashed through a hedge into a ploughed field. It came to rest with a blessed silence except for a faint hissing and gurgling noise which we all knew could be the remaining fuel about to burst into flame with an almighty Whoompf! We were all out of that wreck like a bunch of scalded cats. The Hampden was a write-off.

Our next concern was for the reaction of the newly formed Home Guard, consisting mainly of elderly gentlemen with shotguns and ancient rifles, who were famously over-keen to "do their bit" against the expected German invasion. What was especially worrying was that the Hampden's slender fuselage was so often mistaken by the uninitiated for a German Dornier. I suggested we should all sing at the top of our voices the new popular song, "There'll Always Be an England" but my joke didn't go down all that well. Everyone's sense of humour was running a mite short at that moment.

Then some soldiers suddenly appeared out of the fog and tensions were eased. We were greeted by the troops who put a guard on the wreckage of our Hampden and conducted us to the local "stately home" which was quite nearby. The Army had taken it over as a District Headquarters. There we were entertained royally while a signal was sent to RAF Hemswell to come and get us. Transport did not arrive until midday on the morrow, and found us contentedly floating on our backs in a decorative pond among the lily pads, glasses of good cheer nearby, and with enormous goldfish resenting our intrusion. It was a strange finale to our crew's first night bomber operation.

In time of war there are no opportunities to brood over harrowing experiences. Two nights later we were again on Ops, but apart from bombing the target and being shot at by flak, which was a normal occupational hazard, the sortie was uneventful. I have often wondered, though, if Alec Webster didn't resolve to make up for it with the next one—which he did with a vengeance three nights later on 13 June.

Until briefed an hour or two before take-off, bomber crews only knew what they were going to drop after it had been loaded on the bomb racks of the aircraft, but not where or when. The target we were finally given at briefing was a main road running east and west through the French city of Rheims. What remained of the French Army was still fighting valiantly, and we were going to give them all the support we could. Germans were said to be pouring along this main road and the desperate plan was to block it with craters and rubble to slow them down. At briefing, the intelligence officer gave us the last known disposition of the Germans and told us, "You need have little concern about flak defences near Rheims as the Germans are only just approaching there and have not yet had time to bring them up." Not being a Guy Gibson or a Babe Learoyd, I found this bit of information particularly agreeable and Webster and I decided we would take advantage of the situation by going in relatively low and making a really good job of it. We were soon to learn that intelligence officers sometimes did not know as much as they thought they did.

The weather was reasonable and we found Rheims without difficulty after a tranquil flight. We identified our target and were running in for the attack when a searchlight started to comb the sky ahead. It looked as if the beam was going to swing one way ahead of us and would swing back behind us. Webster was pulling all the tricks—weaving the aircraft to the left and right and de-synchronising the engines to cause the heavy "wow, wow, wow" heterodyning noise reckoned to confuse sound detectors guiding searchlights and guns. But the Germans down there were good at their job. As the searchlight was sweeping harmlessly in front of our nose, they suddenly seemed to spread the beam so that we were picked up on the fringe, illuminated and then focused upon. Almost immediately, two other searchlights exposed and we were "coned". Then the light flak (which, apparently, "the Germans had not yet had time to bring up") started to pour tracer at us, snaking up slowly from the ground until it seemed suddenly to accelerate and flash past in vicious streaks of light. It is strange how death on its way up can look so harmless and pretty.

True to form, the audacious Alec Webster decided that the best way to get out of this situation was to do a "stall turn". This is a nice aerobatic manoeuvre—for aircraft designed for aerobatics, in daylight, at a safe height, with no bomb load and without the utterly dazzling confusion of several searchlights. Alec did not warn us of his intention. The first thing I knew at the navigator/bomb aimer's position was that the nose swung up to point almost vertically at the black sky. With a shocking rush of adrenalin, I assumed that our pilot must have been hit and the aircraft was out of control. We learned from him later how, at that moment, Alec realised that he had bitten off more than he could chew. He said he had become completely disorientated by the dazzle and had lost control so he ordered the crew to abandon aircraft. The last I heard from him was a frantic, "Bale out! Bale out!"

At that moment I sailed off from the floor of the Hampden and momentarily seemed to float like an astronaut amid a shower of other loose objects, including an ammunition pan, my maps, a packet of sandwiches, a thermos flask and a banana. Then I was pinned against the roof of the aircraft with a thump. The intercom plug came adrift from my helmet and now I was alone with only the noise of rushing air and the rattle of light flak, some of which sounded as if it was hitting us. Alec later described how he was in quite a predicament at this stage. He said he had slid back his hood, unstrapping himself in order to jump out; stood up on his seat; and was halfway out of the aircraft when the hood decided to slam forward again and pin him by the guts so that he was waving his arms about in the airstream with his feet still on his seat. And there he was trapped while the aircraft did its own thing. It had the bit between its teeth and now decided to show him what it could do of its own accord, starting with an exhibition of inverted flight. This was what had slammed me onto the roof so that the searchlights appeared to be shining down at me from the sky. Then as the aircraft completed its uncontrolled loop, gravity reasserted itself so that I was hurled back onto the floor with one hell of a thump and, at the same time, became aware of a stabbing pain in my ankle, which I thought must be a bullet wound. A few feet away, in its rack, I could see my observer-type parachute pack. I tried to reach out for it in order to clip it onto my harness before trying to jump through the escape hatch in the floor. By now the G force was so powerful that I could not push my hands out against it and was pinned, helpless, against the deck by that tremendous invisible force. Knowing that the whole performance had started at little over 1,500 feet, I knew that we must now be very near the ground and could only resign myself to the final crunch that would mean instant oblivion. I felt utterly helpless and, strangely enough, not so much frightened as sad because it flashed through my mind that I would never see Ann again and that the "missing in action" telegrams were going to cause my family grief. Then the G seemed to ease off a bit and I saw roofs skimming past just under the bomb aimer's perspex panel.

Alec Webster later described how at some stage during these aerobatics, his hood had obligingly slid open again so that he dropped back into the cockpit, grabbed the controls and, by pulling hard, had managed to stop the Hampden from diving straight into the ground. He then called to the crew over the intercom, "Is there anyone there? Is there anyone there?" Because my intercom plug had disconnected itself, Bill Bissett was the only one who answered. Webster said he concluded that he and Bisset were the only two crew members still in the aircraft. By this time my navigation compartment had become an utter shambles. The floor was littered with all sorts of loose equipment and there was an unusual smell which seemed quite out of place. I managed to find my intercom lead and plugged it in again.

The good news was that, because of our wild gyrations, the searchlight crews had lost us, no doubt thinking we had crashed. But the aircraft still worked and we had a full load of bombs. Accordingly, I directed the pilot round for an extremely low bombing run and we dropped our bombs on target. I then gave Webster an approximate course for home and started to sort out the mess so as to be able properly to resume my duties as navigator. In the dim light, I rummaged among the litter of loose objects, rations, code books and Very cartridges and found my navigation instruments and maps, which were wet with a dark liquid. I assumed at first it must be blood from the wound in my ankle which was now extremely painful.

My next anxiety was to realise that the strange smell came from the dark liquid, so it couldn't be blood so what the hell was it? Oil? I rubbed some between my fingers and somehow it didn't feel right for oil. Then I assumed it could only be hydraulic fluid. Having disposed of this problem, I tried to compose myself, gather together my navigation gear and my wits and begin to find our way home. I was about to settle down to navigation when I noticed in the semi-darkness, on the floor behind me, a strange metal cylinder. The thing looked to me like a small edition of those naval depth charges they roll off the stern of destroyers to clobber enemy submarines. We had all heard rumours of "Hitler's secret weapons" and the last of my adrenalin gave another surge. I wasted no time trying to figure out how they had shot the thing up or lodged it in the aircraft. All I cared about at that panicky moment was how to chuck the infernal thing out before it went off! I wrenched open the escape hatch and clutched the device with both hands. Then, in the dim light of the navigator's station I managed to read the inscription on the side of that infernal canister. It read "ELSAN CHEMICAL LAVATORY". For two pins I think I could have kissed the horrible thing. I had never used it and seldom even looked at it. The pungent-smelling liquid on my maps and things was its disinfectant, Elsanol.

This funny story has a sad coda which I did not hear about until after the war when it was told to me by our erstwhile wireless operator, Bob Jones, who was still in Alec Webster's crew long after I had become a prisoner of war. In September 1940, Bill Bissett, who by that time had been awarded a DFM, very sadly met his end. While dropping an anti-shipping mine near Calais harbour, they were exposed by searchlights and Webster tried the same evasive action as he had attempted over Rheims. Again he lost control and again he ordered the crew to bale out. This time, however, Bissett managed to do so and was never seen again. It was presumed that the poor fellow drowned in the sea.

When we landed back at Hemswell, our Hampden was soon surrounded by a curious crowd intrigued by the unusual strange smell of the aircraft

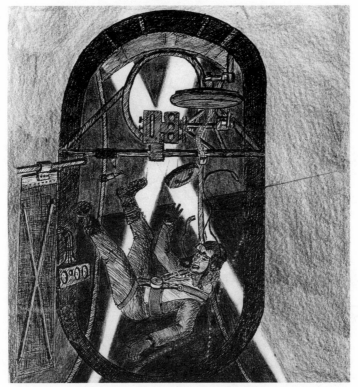

The Rheims raid: "I sailed off the floor and seemed to
float like an astronaut..." (see p. 88)

which seemed to be leaking. When it became known the toilet had caused
all this dilapidation, the indelicate remarks were classics. Unable to
negotiate the ladder because of my ankle, I was lowered out of the nose
of the aircraft and driven to sick quarters where my sprained and very
swollen ankle was strapped up. Our Elsan episode was the big joke of the
station and no one was enjoying it more than I, but these experiences are
liable to backlash and this one certainly did.

After breakfast with the others in the dining room of the officers' mess,
I went to bed and was soon asleep. Then I was in that darkened glass nose
again as it pointed up to the sky. I was floating helplessly to disaster and

struggling against invisible bonds like a fly in a web while I fell down, down, down. I woke up kicking and yelling in a state of utter, sweaty panic. Now I was really frightened and I stayed frightened for a while afterwards, the palms of my hands becoming moist every time I spoke, even laughingly, about that incident over Rheims. Nor was that the last time I was to have that particular nightmare.

At least I was able to get away from the war for a while. My damaged ankle coincided nicely with the six days' leave I was due, so while recuperating I travelled to the north Welsh seaside resort of Llandudno where Ann and her mother were now living. It was another delirious, tantalising flash of promise in what seemed like an eternity of frustration. If we couldn't be married, at least it was agreed that we could soon announce our engagement—a step in the right direction.

Back at Hemswell, I discovered that Alec Webster had acquired a new navigator in my absence and, with my ankle almost back to normal, I crewed up with an Australian, Alex Gould. During the last week of June our new crew carried out four sorties. Two were trips planting magnetic mines into German sea routes in or near German naval harbours, an operation code-named "Gardening". These 2,000 lb devices had to be dropped, trailing a drogue to ensure they hit the water nose first, from 150 feet or so above the sea. On some occasions such trips could be fairly quiet, on others quite hairy. During one of them we came close enough to harbour defences, or a flak ship, to have a lively exchange with anti-aircraft artillery and searchlights, one of which our gunners claimed to have shot out with their .303 machine guns.

Our other two operations that week targeted the Dortmund-Ems Aqueduct which carried a very busy important canal over the river Rhine. The canal was a vital part of the German transport system and in June was carrying barges loaded with war supplies to harbours on the north German coast. This was part of the build-up for "Operation Sealion"—the projected German invasion of England. A plan was conceived to drop these mines from 100 feet or so into the concrete aqueduct and, by repeated blasting, eventually to crack the structure causing it to leak and drain dry—almost a preliminary to the Dambusters' raid nearly three years later. The achievement of this objective required several raids by a few experienced, specially selected, trained and rehearsed Hampden crews, all of whom met frightful opposition from the enemy. The Germans, having realised from previous attacks what was afoot, had lined the sides of the Aqueduct with searchlights and flak coned at the height from which they knew the bombers had to drop the mines. When they heard an aircraft approaching, they had only to switch everything on and press all the buttons so that the mine-layers had to run the gauntlet of blinding dazzle and a hail of flak while lesser mortals like us attacked from a little higher to draw off some of the defences and do what damage we could with high-explosive bombs.

Our losses on these sorties were tragic and the bravery of those low-flying crews was incredible. One such was our old mate, Babe Learoyd of 49 Squadron. On the night of 12/13 August, the two Hampdens preceding him were shot down from a height of 100 feet (from which there was no possible escape by parachute). On that occasion Babe returned to base in a flying wreck which he considered was unfit for a night landing, so he circled the field until dawn when he landed the heap without further drama. He was awarded the Victoria Cross.

The collective reward for these hammerings was a series of photographs taken by Photographic Reconnaissance Unit aircraft showing invasion barges stranded in the dry canal. Although we succeeded in closing the waterway for only ten days, at that time every single day was precious. We were desperately trying to hold on until bad weather in the late autumn would make a seaborne invasion impossible. Although we gained those ten days at a high price, hopefully it made a greater difference than one might think.

My time as a navigator was coming to an end. At the beginning of July I was suddenly given my own command. My crew—sergeants Murdock, Brock and Joyce—were all inexperienced and insufficiently trained, but the least ready for night operations in foul weather was myself as captain. Now that I had full responsibility for the lives of three other men, I felt my lack of preparation more acutely than ever. I worried more about my inexperience than I did about the enemy. But it was always the old story; we couldn't be spared for training because we were so badly needed. How many others, I wonder, were caught in this supply and demand trap and, totally unprepared, thrown into the deep end of the air war when "bomb 'em regardless of weather" became the demand from on high? It is little wonder that, at the time, a third of Hampden losses were due to causes other than enemy action. Aircraft were piled up, iced up, ditched in the sea out of fuel, just spun in from turbulent cloud, or crash-landed. One crew in Ireland thought they were in England, another found themselves in a forest clearing in Scotland which turned out to be the Black Forest of Germany. And that was just the Hampdens! Perhaps the classic of all time was the Whitley heavy bomber which took off in May 1940 from RAF Dishforth in Yorkshire to bomb Germany at night. The crew became well and truly lost in very bad weather. Eventually they spotted and bombed a German airfield which, they later learned, was RAF Bassingbourne in Cambridgeshire. Next day some Bassingbourne aircrew flew over to Dishforth and dropped from their aircraft a huge German Iron Cross, just to rub it in a bit. It so happened that this particular debacle caused no harm to anyone and much laughter, but most of the other incidents were tragic.

All too soon our lack of preparation would make itself painfully evident. Our first operational sortie as a complete crew in late July had to be abandoned soon after take-off when our radio transmitter gave up the ghost. That was depressing enough, but it paled into insignificance beside what happened a couple of nights later. On this occasion, we were sent off in particularly doubtful weather conditions with a liberal scattering of thunderstorms. To all pilots, thunderclouds are bad news, coming as they do in only three varieties: nasty, extremely nasty, or killers. The danger is not so much from lightning strikes, which curiously enough are not particularly serious in the air, but from extreme turbulence, which can snap an aircraft in two like a biscuit. Even modern commercial aircraft give thunderclouds a wide berth, usually by climbing to the clear air above. In those days our bombers could never get remotely high enough, so we had no choice other than simply to plough through.

On this dirty night, as the guiding line of paraffin flares flashed beneath us, we were suddenly entirely dependent upon our dimly luminous instruments. It was not a long flight to the coast, and we climbed up through solid murk towards an operational cruising height of about 1,500 feet. Heavily laden with bombs and fuel, we were at about 8,000 feet when we hit a vicious invisible thunderstorm waiting for us in the dark confusion

94

of other harmless clouds. The first indication of trouble was the sudden onset of loud rain or hail clatter. This almost drowned out the engine noise and was accompanied by the harsh crackle of electrical discharges on the radio in our earphones. Lightning! Next came increasing turbulence, tossing the aircraft about so much that holding any semblance of order on the instrument panel demanded intense concentration and—questionable technique that it was—a struggle with the bucking control column. Then, suddenly, we were pressed in our seats as the vertical speed indicator swung crazily to climb. We were being hurled upwards by the mighty forces of nature like a leaf in an autumn tempest. More deafening clatter and bucking; direction indicator spinning; artificial horizon lurching all over the place, and an extremely worried pilot attempting to control his panic. Then a flash so bright the whole cockpit was momentarily as black afterwards as for a blind man. Slowly seeing again, drunken instruments told me we were almost out of control.

At last came a fearsome fiery glow such as I had never seen before, nor been told or warned about. It started as a thin blue electrical circle of light at the tips of the propellers which expanded to become a wide band of blue-white glare close on each side of my cockpit. The ring-and-bead metal gunsight in front of my face, outside the windscreen on the nose, became an eerie ball of glowing light. Then leaping, crackling sparks ran up the nose of the aircraft towards me and over my windscreen. This spectral, blue-white glow intensified until it seemed the whole aircraft was being enclosed in it. There was strangely no heat or discomfort apart from the bucking from the turbulence and the spasmodic clatter of hail thundering against the metal skin of the Hampden. The whole crew was terrified, but I knew we were over the sea and baling out was not an option.

Then the vertical speed was off the clock downwards. Pull on the control column, airspeed falling away, near to the stall, controls mushy, must let her go down now or spin, still plenty of height. The next second the clattering ceased as suddenly as it had begun and the eerie fire subsided and was suddenly gone. We were in control again, but physically and mentally exhausted. It was then that Sergeant Brock reported the inside of the fuselage, aft of his position at the radio, seemed wet with some sort of oil and the deck was a mess. Sergeants Brock and Joyce both said they thought it was hydraulic fluid leaking from a ruptured pipe amidships that served the flaps, bomb doors and/or the undercarriage. If so, this could soon affect their operation. Pinned in my tiny cockpit, there was no way I could go aft and look at it myself because in a Hampden the pilot was confined to his seat for the duration of the flight and it seemed essential that we should get the aircraft back on the ground while things were still operating properly. I turned back, secretly ashamed to be grateful for the legitimate excuse to do so—less than a hero and hardly believing we had survived such a strange onslaught by the elements. I landed at the first available RAF airfield. There it was that our hydraulic leak turned out to be Elsanol AGAIN! The violent bucking up and down in that ferocious storm had catapulted the brown fluid out past the fastened lid and sprayed the rear of our aircraft.

The fireworks, we learned later, had been a relatively harmless phenomenon of static discharge once known as "St Elmo's Fire". This had terrified and excited superstitious seamen over the centuries, when electrical night storms had planted a ball of fire at the masthead. But we had never seen nor heard of it before, not even in training lectures. Nor have I ever heard of it being anything like so terrifyingly spectacular as it was that night on Ops.

I began to despair of *ever* becoming an intrepid RAF pilot on these damned night bombers. Affecting my morale more than anything else was concern about my own inadequacy and a dread that I might lose my aircraft and crew through some personal failure. I had felt such pride in the RAF since I was a kid and would have given anything to transfer to fighters away from the black misery of those hopeless night operations. I was not afraid of flying, or combat, or dying, or the weather, but more of myself. I felt uneasy about the relief with which I had quite reasonably aborted a sortie with that apparent hydraulic leak. I became obsessed with a resolve that I would never turn back again—an obsession which could and perhaps did affect decisions, sometimes unwisely, throughout the rest of my flying days. Quite often, discretion really is the better part of valour.

Between 10 and 26 August, my crew flew six more operations, some of which I cannot remember individually, although the highlights stand out. They were all either bombing attacks against industrial targets, or anti-shipping mine-dropping sorties, in and around Heligoland or French ports. These were part of an attempt to hobble the German navy and to hamper preparations for Operation Sealion—the invasion of Britain. I was not aware of any more failures.

One, though, was memorable for all the wrong reasons. We had set off to bomb a German oil refinery at Benrath near Düsseldorf. On the way back, our dead reckoning navigation led us to believe we should hit England somewhere between Aldeburgh and Great Yarmouth on the east coast. When our ETA was up it was still dark and murky so that little could be seen, but to our great relief, the radio transmitter was behaving perfectly for a change. Sergeant Brock was getting regular updates from Hemswell, which was homing in on our transmissions and telling us the course to steer to reach home. There was only one snag. Murdock the navigator and I both reckoned that from where we had calculated we ought to be, we should be heading in a northwesterly direction. Instead Hemswell's messages were directing us to steer southwest. At first, Murdock and I would not believe them. If Hemswell was right, we were up around Grimsby and we couldn't believe we could be so far off track to the north. However, it was still pitch dark, we could not see anything, and the headings continued to come in to Brock, all within a few degrees of one another. There comes a time when you just have to accept they are right and your own calculations are wrong. So we headed southwest.

At about our calculated ETA for base, I saw a dark shape slide past us on the starboard side just visible against the grey light of dawn. "Phew! That was a close one," I told the crew. "One of the other kites joining the circuit. We must be home!"

Well, when you spot one of something, your eye gets in and you spot the rest, like buck in the bush if you are out hunting. And I *did* spot the rest. Balloons. Barrage balloons. Lots of them to left and right, above and below, and each attached to an invisible steel cable lethal to aircraft. We were heading into the London Anti-Aircraft Balloon Barrage! Panic stations— parachutes on—everyone's eyes popping out like dogs' balls, trying to spot those shadowy monsters and trying to guess where the invisible lethal cables lay towards the wind. The instructions issuing from the glass nose were quite unlike the passionless drone of a bomb aimer with his "left-

left-steady-steady-right-steady". This was: "Left, for Christ's sake. Left! More! Oh Jesus, there's another one! Right, sir, hard right! Oh shit! Left, left, quick!" And meanwhile, I was climbing that Hampden for all it was worth. How we cleared the balloons I'll never know, but as soon as we did so we spotted an airfield. Being short of fuel after a long night's work (and mentally of everything else), we landed at RAF Kenley, a fighter station just south of London, in the early light of morning.

It is interesting here to note that, according to Bomber Command postwar statistics, while it is believed that only one Hampden bomber was known to have been lost to a German barrage balloon, no fewer than five Hampdens fell victim to our own.

Later on, having telephoned our base from Kenley to report what was going on and having re-fuelled and drawn breath, we took off, carefully avoided the balloon barrage, and flew back to Hemswell. I was immediately invited to stand on the squadron commander's mat, now belonging to the famous Wally Sheen himself. It is my firm belief that if one is in the soup, it is never advantageous to be judged by another who has just got out of it like poor old Wally. He had recently returned from leading an abortive chase of the battleship *Deutschland* with some of his formation running out of fuel and others being shot down by RAF Spitfires. Such chaps seem to be only too keen to prove that they are not the only "ninnies" and I have concluded it seems to help them to magnify the shortcomings of others. Wally harangued me as if I had spent an illicit night cavorting around beautiful bordello beauties instead of bloody barrage balloons. He would listen to no explanations, nor any mitigating circumstances. I was a four-letter part of the female anatomy. I decided Wally Sheen and I did not like each other very much.

After Wally had finished making himself feel better, I found the station signals officer and asked him to try to sort out the mystery, which he did very quickly. We had indeed crossed the coast more or less where we expected to be, and Hemswell had been sending us instructions to fly northwesterly: 330 degrees magnetic. But it appeared that poor Sergeant Brock might have developed a strange quirk in his reading of Morse. It appeared that he had heard a "three" as a "two" with the result that all our bearings were exactly 100 degrees out, heading us for London instead of

Hemswell. It never occurred to me at the time that the error could equally have been caused by bad sending of Morse, and not just the receiving by my wireless operator. But no matter who was really to blame, poor old Brock got it. Wally never relented, even when the explanation was known. I felt a bit aggrieved about that. After all, he knew as well as I did that it was dinned into us that we *must* believe our instruments rather than our own judgement. Brock spent several hours having more Morse pounded into his ears by a signals instructor and we all hoped for better things next time.

And, for once, we got them. We were detailed to bomb the oil refinery at Salzbergen, just across the border with the Netherlands. Once again it was a cloudy night, and after three hours droning along in the darkness without a sight of the ground we were what in piloting parlance is referred to as "temporarily unsure of our position", or, in plain English, "good and bloody lost". By this time, the original rule which said we must drop our bombs only on the briefed target or either bring them back or drop them in the North Sea, had been superseded. We were now permitted to select secondary targets of our own choice provided they were "self-illuminating", of strategic importance or part of the communications network. These were quite restrictive categories and we were by no means encouraged to take a whack at any old thing that showed up.

It didn't look to me as though we were going to see anything in any of these categories, so I gave orders for the gyroscopic bombsight to be shut down, in accordance with procedure, and we pointed the nose westward for the long haul home. The trip had been relatively uneventful so far, with the odd searchlight probing for us through low cloud and an occasional thumping from heavy flak as we flew over unseen defended areas. Although we continued to peer about in the thinner murk, which was now clearing somewhat, I suspect we may have been to some extent emulating the bombsight and were a bit switched off.

Sergeant Murdock's terse report, "Aircraft to port, captain, down there at about nine o'clock," snapped us all into a state of excited alertness. Night bomber crews did not much like to see any other aircraft at all. If they were friendly they were too close from a collision standpoint and if they were unfriendly they were almost certain to be enemy fighters with whom contact was likely to be extremely unhealthy. This fellow was not conforming to any normal expectations and had suddenly switched on his navigation lights—an extraordinary thing to do in wartime with lots of other chaps prowling around the skies with evil intent. It was certainly not one of ours. We never advertised our position in enemy skies by switching on navigation lights. So he must be a German, and I could see that he was not far ahead, turning left, a little below us and travelling at about the same speed. This persuaded me that this enemy aircraft was not very likely to be a fighter unless, of course, he was throttled back for some reason or about to land.

The Hampden pilot had only a single Browning machine gun fixed to fire straight ahead and a primitive ring-and-bead gunsight, but it was better than nothing and good enough to blast at a sitting duck like this fellow. In any case, I was desperate to do something valiant. I pushed my throttles wide open and curved down after him, flipping the gun button on the control column from "Safe" to "Fire". With a fire power of only 1,200 rounds per minute, as opposed to a Hurricane's or Spitfire's 9,600, it was obviously essential to creep right up close and let fly from only a few yards behind him. This I intended to do to this unsuspecting German, who was displaying such confidence (or temerity) by lighting himself up like a Christmas tree. As we closed him I briefed my rear-gunners that I would open fire from dead astern then break off to port and fly close past him to give them a beam shot to starboard with their two machine guns each, if they could bring them to bear. As we came closer to the enemy we were just beginning to discern his shadowy silhouette, slightly blacker than the dark sky, and were all expectantly silent. The same thought was in everybody's mind. If this *was* a fighter and we did not get him first go it was almost certain he would get us instead. Then we saw his white downward identification light begin to flash close and brilliantly. My thumb was on the firing button and I was about to give him a burst when the black velvet of the ground below was suddenly pierced by a pattern of sharp lights. In that moment I realised that he had requested an aerodrome to put on its lights, and that was what we were looking at—a bigger and better target than a solitary aircraft.

Instantly abandoning our stalk, I rapped out the familiar orders: "Bomb sight on, master switch on, bomb doors open," and told Murdock to select all our bomb load for dropping at one-second intervals. Within our Hampden the spell of tense waiting inactivity was broken. Now there was a flurry of action to get those bombs away before the lights went out. The other aircraft had peeled off to port and was dropping away obviously to make an approach on to the electric flarepath. We watched him turning on to finals as we, too, made a fast turn to try to line up with the hangars. They were easily identifiable with their red obstruction lights exactly similar to our own hangars back at base. We were lined up at last and the German was touching down.

"Bomb sight operational?" I asked Sergeant Murdock.

"Not quite, sir, give it another few seconds. Can you dog-leg?"

"Yes, but only a little bit. We haven't got much time."

"Coming on now, sir. Turn left, left—left, left, steady, right steady—steady..."

And out went all the lights below. Nothing but darkness, blacker than ever, in contrast to the recent bright display. A chorus of four letter words from the crew expressed our disappointment. There was only one thing to do.

I gave the order, "Stand by to drop a low level stick—never mind the bombsight—keep the setting at one second intervals."

"Right, sir, one second it is. What are we going to do?"

"We are going to ask them to light up."

Somebody said "Christ!" and I knew what he was thinking. Our Bristol Pegasus engines sounded nothing like most German engines—the difference should be obvious to the initiated. Maybe they had twigged our presence already, maybe even now they were radioing other aircraft to deal with us. If we now lit ourselves up it would be our Hampden that had become the sitting duck. I switched on our navigation lights and looking at that red glow on the port wing tip and the green glow to starboard I felt naked. One of my crew said, "And the best of British luck to all of us." It was a sober enough prayer, but I wasn't sure whether or not there was an element of reproach in it.

Murdock steered me on to where he thought the aerodrome was and, selecting "down" on the identification light switch, I then flashed the same Morse letters as we had seen the German send. I assumed that the Germans would be calling us on their local frequency and perhaps getting suspicious because we did not answer. Would they, with luck, assume our radio had gone on the blink? Or perhaps they worked on lights alone? Or were they already wise to us and planning a warm reception? As their lights came back on below there was a quiet cheer from my lads and we banked into a downwind leg and then a wide descending turn with power to line ourselves up with their flarepath and began a normal final approach as if for a landing, with the row of hangars nicely lit up just off to the right.

"All ready, bomb aimer? Check again master switch, bomb doors, selectors on for the whole lot, one second."

"All ready, sir. One second it is, standing by for a visual low level."

"Right! Don't press the tit until I shout NOW."

"Okay, sir. All ready. Standing by."

I could have controlled the bomb dropping myself in the pilot's cockpit but decided it would be better for several reasons if we shared the operation. My mind went back to those fun low-level bombing practices I had so enjoyed on the dummy submarine marked out near Scampton. I had been pretty good at it. Now for the pay-off. We made a perfectly normal approach to that flarepath, lower, lower, slower, and only at the last moment poured on some power and banked right to line up with the hangars a few feet below. I expected the Germans to open up on us at once, but they didn't. As we approached very close to the hangars I shouted "NOW" to Sergeant Murdock. The Hampden bucked slightly and Murdock's voice came back, "Bombs gone." Off went our lights and only then did some very light tracer begin to fly up at us as we weaved away climbing into the darkness, which had just been punctuated by our bomb flashes.

"We got 'em, we got 'em. Wacko, sir, we got 'em!"

Brock and Joyce in the rear positions began an excited gabble like kids at a firework display. I had to suggest they calm down and give a coherent running commentary while I concentrated in getting to hell out of it, which we were always good at and eager to boot. After the first flashes we thought for a moment we were going to be disappointed and then the fun really started. One of the chaps in the back end said, "Boof!" and the other said, "Wow!" and I said, "What the hell does that mean?"

"A bloody great explosion of fire, sir, and Boof—there goes another one."

The two sergeants were away to an excited commentary as they described the growing fire, billowing smoke and red explosive blossoms. For the next few minutes there were a few more "boofs" and "wows" and "there goes another one", a gloriously satisfying end to an unpromising night's work. Whether every "boof" was an aircraft blowing up or other things as well like petrol bowsers and such we could not tell—but it was quite "warming" and very satisfying.

At our de-briefing by the intelligence officers back at base we were able to give only our approximate position at the time of bombing and I do not know what steps, if any, were or ever could be taken to attempt positive identification of the aerodrome we had attacked. The anonymous compilers of our Squadron's Operations Records Book wrote the next day that we had bombed Lastrup, about forty miles northeast of our original target. I've no idea what led them to believe so; they certainly never heard it from me. No doubt it looked better to the powers that be than "unknown aerodrome" and, besides, the Germans were hardly likely to contradict them.

At the time that operation gave us great personal satisfaction. We knew on that night alone, we had justified our existence. Our war effort must have had a credit balance in enemy aircraft destroyed. Wally Sheen, for his part, didn't give us so much as a pat on the back. All the same, satisfying though our last operation had been, one could not help being aware of the disappointing inadequacy of such haphazard successes in the general conduct of a bomber offensive. This was especially so considering Bomber Command was, for some time, the only arm of the Allied fighting services still in a position to hit the enemy where it really hurt, apart from a few very gallant nuisance raids by the Royal Navy and brave commandos.

Then, on the night of 24 August, the Germans initiated a further escalation of the air war by dropping the first bombs on central London at night. For a man like Winston Churchill, there could be only one answer to that. Bombs on Berlin—irrespective of weather, feasibility or chances of material strategic advantage. A gesture was needed for political purposes and the morale of the British people. The cold statistics of our first Berlin bombing raid on the night of 25 August are depressing. Scraping together the Wellingtons of 3 Group, the lumbering Whitleys of 4 Group and the Hampdens of 5 Group, eighty-one twin-engined aircraft were dispatched on that raid. Of these, only twenty-nine claimed to have bombed Berlin.

Even this figure of twenty-nine must be treated with caution. In June and July 1941, by which time cameras that automatically took a photograph at the moment the bombs were dropped had been fitted to some aircraft, it was revealed that of those crews that reported having attacked their target in Germany, only one in four had got within five miles of it. When the target was in the Ruhr, full of smog and searchlights, it was only one in ten. Twenty-seven other aircraft of that force of eighty-one thought they were in the vicinity of Berlin but could not locate the target. They brought their bombs back to base or jettisoned them in the sea. Eighteen more found alternative targets and bombed them. Seven crews aborted for various reasons and it is known that at least five aircraft ditched in the sea out of fuel. Some of the luckier ones were picked up later. The others perished.

The raid Bomber Command was ordered to carry out the next night, 26 August, was no less demanding. For my crew and I, it ended on a beach on a Dutch island, standing beside our aircraft with hard-faced men pointing guns at us.

Chapter Six

"Kommen sie mit!"

We had landed on the Vliehors, a vast stretch of firm sand on the west side of Vlieland, the island which is one up from Texel, the most southerly of the chain of Dutch Frisian islands. The aircraft was intact, and from all appearances completely undamaged. Brock and Murdock's efforts to set it alight had failed, as there was not enough fuel left in it to fill a cigarette lighter. Our captors told me that one of our bombs had hung up, as bombs occasionally did, and was still on the bomb rack. The Germans said that if it were a booby trap, I would be shot.

We were marched along, the entire crew, in conformity with my instructions, still looking unreasonably cheerful. Perhaps our pantomime gave a morale boost to the few Dutch onlookers we passed, one of whom was taking photographs. It was not easy to keep this up, what with exhaustion, backache and the gloomy outlook of imprisonment. Walking was, at first, literally a pain in the bum for me after sitting on a parachute pack, unable to move, for ten hours.

We were taken to the mainland via Texel in an open launch guarded by a German officer, one NCO and a rifleman with a Schmeisser sub-machine gun. On the voyage, I winked at the old Dutchman who stood at the wheel. The Germans were in the bows looking ahead. I broached the idea of dropping them overboard and heading west for England, at which the old Hollander nearly had a fit. He whispered breathlessly, "Dese blotty Chermans. Vee hef to do everysing dey say. Dey vood shoot my femmily. Anyvay, dere is not fuel enough." That was the end of that brilliant idea.

Our initial interrogation on the mainland was superficial and I remember a nicely fatuous answer given by Brock, when asked what our target had been.

"Oh, that's Top Secret," he said. "They NEVER tell us that."

That sort of badinage is all very well to keep one's morale up, but really the only safe way to get through interrogation is to stick to name, rank and number. Any further loosening-up of the tongue can always lead to slips and only serves to prolong the ordeal.

Earlier in the summer, we at Hemswell had had a visit from a renowned escape expert, Squadron Leader A.J. Evans. During the First World War he had succeeded in getting away from both the Germans and the Turks. The book he wrote about his adventures, *The Escaping Club*, must have been read by every British schoolboy between the wars, including me. The opening remark of his presentation certainly carried an impact. "Let's face it," he said, "most of you chaps are either going to be killed or become prisoners of war." There were, he told us, three things we needed to do if we found ourselves behind enemy lines. The first was to try to escape and rejoin the fray. The second was to devise in advance a secret code and teach it to the person we would naturally write to most frequently, if we became prisoners. Taking this advice to heart, I hashed out a code after the lecture and showed Ann how to use it. But the third thing really stuck with me. It was, he said, the duty of a prisoner of war "to be as big a bloody nuisance as possible to the enemy". Those were his actual words. It seemed a pretty unequivocal instruction and I never forgot it.

Some lessons, though, are only learned by experience. The place they kept us that first night was a kind of two-storey guesthouse. After I was locked in my first floor room, I saw through the keyhole that a German guard was standing in the corridor outside my door. Another stood under my window and I accepted that escape was impossible. What a piece of cake it would have seemed to me as an experienced escaper a year or two later! I would have tried to go up through that ceiling, along the roof space and out the other end of the building well before the light of dawn.

By the time I flopped onto a bed, I was utterly exhausted, mentally and physically, having had no rest for about thirty-six hours. The future of all of us now seemed as uncertain as it had been on Ops and my last thought was about those "missing" telegrams going out to our families—to my father and to Edie. I knew she would be terribly upset and I wondered how Ann would be taking it. When would I see her again, if ever? Then I fell asleep.

"Kommen sie mit!"

It seemed I was immediately awake again. I could not at first realise where I was and thought I was waking from a bad dream. But the nightmare was real and the awful truth dawned, as it would every morning for nearly five more years. My youthful RAF ambitions had been dashed with an inglorious end and my aircraft, if it had not been taken, as I hoped it would, by the incoming tide, might possibly be intact in enemy hands. The misery of it all was overwhelming. Then there were clomping boots in the passage and a German shouted that I must get up and be ready to move. It was 5.30 in the morning.

Another golden opportunity slipped by on our way to Germany in two open cars, each with one German officer and a guard. Here and there, we stopped to "splash our boots" and I can remember at least one occasion when the slightest diversion would have enabled me to throw myself into the underbrush and run for it. We were not on the ball, and neither, at that stage, were they.

It was with pride our escort announced, "Vee are now in Chermany," and with a sorry lack of appreciation, I hardly reacted at all. For as we crossed that frontier, every man's hand was turned against us. Until then, we had been among those whose inclination was to help, even if they were too scared to do so. We should never have crossed that frontier! Inexperienced and in a state of demoralised unreality, we thought we were heavily guarded. Escaping was, I supposed, something you did from a prison camp with a disguise and maps, compass, rations, money and a plan. Little did I realise that in reality I would be surrounded by more numerous, more watchful guards with Schmeissers and Alsatian dogs, whose only job was to prevent us from breaking out and who were, by and large, extremely good at it. Like so many others, I had let the best chances pass. I had not learned that the best time to escape is usually as soon as possible.

In due course, we arrived at the Luftwaffe's reception and transit camp for newly captured airmen, Dulag Luft, at Oberursul near Frankfurt am Main, where I was separated from the others. I saw nothing more of my crew until after the war.

For the first week at Dulag Luft, prisoners were kept in solitary confinement as part of the softening-up process during their real interrogation when a number of ploys were tried to get them to divulge information. The cells were no doubt bugged and at some stage, another "newly captured officer" might be popped into his cell. The Germans already had a wealth of knowledge about squadron personnel and activities in England, and the newcomer would easily sound quite genuine, and simply encourage some revealing chat.

The formal questioning was carried out by several intelligence officers in turn, each with his own technique so that wheedling would be followed by blustering and bonhomie would be followed with threats. But careful adherence to the "name, rank and number" routine saw them all off.

At last I was informed that I should be joining the other prisoners in the main camp after the completion of a few routine formalities, one of which was an interview with a visiting Swiss gentleman from the International Red Cross whose business it would be to see that news of my safety was conveyed to the folks at home through Red Cross channels via Geneva. He was a nice avuncular old gentleman with white hair and a kindly sympathetic nature. He realised how terribly worried my family must be as up to now I would still be posted as "missing". Now, if I would please complete this International Red Cross form for him, he would get it straight off to his headquarters in Geneva and my concern about my family's anxiety would be over.

"Uncle" handed me the form and smiled benignly as he offered me his pen. The form was emblazoned with the Red Cross and had indeed originated in Geneva—it said so on top. It required me to fill in my full name, rank and number, date and place of birth, which all seemed innocuous enough. Then it wanted to know my squadron, flight, station and more little tidbits of information which I felt sure could not be of the slightest interest to the good Red Cross souls in Geneva. I told him I was sorry but I could not divulge that information. He was terribly hurt. Did I doubt for one moment that he would treat it with the utmost confidence? I did want my family to know that I was safe, didn't I? Surely I was prepared to cooperate with such a wonderful humanitarian organisation as the International Red Cross, wasn't I? I told him I certainly was—but not with some imposter who wanted to know a whole lot more about my unit which was none of his bloody business. That did it! The dear old gentleman flew into a Teutonic rage, told me I could rot for all he cared, and that my family

Portrait of PDT by his friend and fellow-prisoner, the
master forger John Mansel.

could just go on wondering about my fate. He stormed out and slammed
the cell door.

I did not know until after the war that the names of newly captured
aircrew were being immediately broadcast to Britain, along with German
radio propaganda, in order to encourage people to listen.

Later that day, I joined the rest of the prisoners in the main camp. There
were a few familiar faces and the majority of the inmates were prisoners
of quite long standing who, it seemed, formed a sort of "permanent staff".
New arrivals stayed only a short while until there was a big enough batch
to move them on to a more permanent prison camp—an operation which
became known as a "purge".

Conditions at Dulag Luft were surprisingly comfortable. The food was not marvellous, but plentiful and not bad either. There was a good supply of Red Cross food parcels, one of which each prisoner in Germany was, in theory, supposed to receive weekly. These were little bigger than a shoe box and packed with concentrated goodies.

Each room housed no more than four prisoners and the senior officers had even more privacy. Everyone was issued with Red Cross clothing from a central store. The Germans were friendly, even sympathetic. They organised delightful walks for us in the truly beautiful countryside during which we were permitted to rest at the occasional picturesque guesthouse and buy a beer with our *Lagergeld*—camp "Monopoly money"—issued against a stoppage from our pay in England. We were also allowed to write home on a prison camp letter form and, naturally, wrote very favourably about our treatment.

Dulag Luft had the atmosphere of a gentle spa resort with the British permanent staff rather smugly aloof and laying down the law for the transients. Rule number one seemed to be—NO ESCAPING. Having cased the joint, I was particularly resentful of this because, despite the barbed wire fences, it looked fairly easy, especially because the guards were so amiable and sloppy.

When I and a few others tended to chafe against the "no escaping" dictum, we were gently but firmly reminded that we were still under the orders of the senior officer present, Wing Commander H.E. "Prickie" Day, and that Dulag Luft did not appreciate "troublemakers" who during their brief stay would only mess things up for the permanent staff. Many of us considered this a despicable attitude and had little respect for Prickie Day and his boys. It seemed strange that a man with such a high reputation in the RAF could suddenly have become so malleable in the hands of his enemies.

Little did we know, nor were we supposed to know, the truth of the situation. Hare-brained transients would, indeed, have messed things up for the "permanents" and particularly their escape plans which had been carefully laid and cunningly disguised by Prickie Day himself. In our ignorance we didn't realise that the man we despised as a wimp would soon become legendary as perhaps the most dedicated, devious and brilliant escaper of them all. "Wings" Day, as he would later be called, became one of only two officers that I know of who were awarded the DSO for their conduct as prisoners of war.

In order to go on the walks from Dulag Luft, it was necessary to give our word not to escape, and everybody did this as a matter of course. Nonetheless, we were accompanied by many guards with rifles and a few guard dogs. As one of our German camp officers explained to us, he and his comrades would have no compunction in breaking a promise given to an enemy, and it was assumed that we would do likewise. I never gave my word again for anything in Germany. And indeed, I felt the sooner I got away from Dulag Luft the better. With the obviously "bolshie" attitude of several of us, our departure was not long delayed.

I was on the first purge to the Luftwaffe's new permanent camp, Stalag Luft I at Barth on the Baltic coast. We were sent by train, packed into third-class carriages with wooden seats, and with many stops and shunts into sidings. The journey lasted about forty-eight hours. Carefully guarded by Luftwaffe troops, we were seldom allowed to stand up or move about, with the result that I soon suffered from "Hampden Bum" again. Some of the prisoners who took off their shoes for relief found that their feet swelled up so much that they had difficulty getting them back on again. I have often heard people aghast at the inhumanity of moving prisoners in cattle trucks, but I am not sure that they are not preferable. Provided the weather is reasonable and with a good thick litter of straw, at least one could sit, stand or lie down at will—or even move about a little.

Of course, such journeys encourage a special breed of escaper—the train jumper—and it is odd how some people, like a keen escaping pal of mine, "Pissy" Edwards, tended to specialise in this hairy activity. Railroad tracks are abominably hard flinty things with poles and signal wires and little concrete markers liberally scattered along the way. Even so, these artists would hurl themselves out of windows into the dark or drop through holes cut in the floor with gay abandon anytime the "clickety-clack" sounded like something less than ten miles an hour. God bless 'em! I'll find another way!

Train jumpers developed techniques, of course, with jumping onto a down-sloping embankment a favourite. Also the classic rules for train jumpers advised that they should try it from as near the rear of the train as possible and also from the right-hand side facing forward. That way fewer guards could take pot shots, and when they did it was from the wrong shoulder.

As train-jumping became an art, so the precautions against it became more stringent. I have travelled in trains with an armed guard in each compartment, with more in the corridor and the windows laced up with barbed wire. Even then the odd Houdini had a go. On this particular journey, three officers went adrift and I seem to remember they were Pissy Edwards, "Errol" Flinn and Maurice Butt. They were all rounded up in due course and rejoined us.

Our arrival at the new camp was a dramatically staged affair in the dark—obviously with the intention of conveying the message that the Dulag Luft tea party was over and this was to be the real thing. We were marched from the railway station to the camp, carrying hardly any belongings since we had none, thickly surrounded by guards with rifles or automatic weapons and snarling Alsatians, all to an accompaniment of Teutonic screaming.

As we approached the desolate, hutted camp—floodlit and surrounded by high barbed wire fences with barbed wire entanglements between—the searchlights from the elevated guard boxes swung onto us and, for no good reason, somebody in one of the guard towers let fly a dramatic short burst of machine-gun fire over our heads. The remainder of our first night was spent in a large wooden reception block in the German compound of Stalag Luft which stood, like all the other prisoners' barrack blocks, well off the sandy ground on short stilts—a useful precaution against tunnelling. The next day we were stripped and searched, individually and very intimately.

The RAF was already creating a reputation as the most escape-minded of our three services and the Luftwaffe, who insisted upon guarding their own, were therefore becoming ultra security conscious. An influx of new prisoners could always mean an influx of smuggled escape material, such as maps, compasses and real Reichsmarks as opposed to *Lagergeld*. The Germans already knew about our silk maps sewn inside tunic linings and the occasional brass button which unscrewed and contained a little compass. We were checked for all these things and more.

After the search and only our second hot meal of slop since leaving Dulag Luft, we were harangued by the camp's security officer, Major von

Stachelski, a pint-sized martinet who seemed to jump up and down as he stressed each point of the impossibility of escaping from Barth and the dire penalties for those attempting to do so.

Next morning, we were herded towards the main gate of the inner prisoners' compound to join the regular inmates who were crowded round as a sort of curious news-hungry reception committee, eager to see who was in the latest catch. My first sight of these people gave me a strange impression. They were not the poor human wrecks and living skeletons of the concentration camps, but were, to our unaccustomed eyes, a motley conglomeration of weirdly dressed, somewhat tatty scarecrows, and all seemed to be wearing an indefinable, slightly vacant or dazed look.

I remember distinctly how this odd appearance struck me at the time, then how it was no longer noticeable as it became commonplace, remaining so until I was free again. Then, for a little while after the war, I discovered that I had an extraordinary facility. Going up to a complete stranger in a train, pub or officers' mess I would say, "Hello, you're an ex-POW, aren't you?" To which each time the reply, without fail, was, "Yes, how the hell did you know that?" I did not know how myself, but I am sure it was in the eyes—a sort of distant longing, a sadness, a resignation, a *je ne sais quoi*.

As we stood at that huge double gate—us on one side, them on the other—waiting for the guards to open it, there were shouts of recognition and surprise. The first officer to claim my own attention was a chap called Barratt whose kit I had packed up one day in Hemswell when he was posted missing. Then I saw one officer after another from Hemswell, and others well known from Scampton and yet more from other 5 Group stations, whose faces were vaguely familiar from the "Snake Pit". It looked as if there were enough from 5 Group to re-form a squadron or two; these were the lucky one in five survivors of those posted as missing.

When we mixed together, greetings were quickly followed by avid demands for news of the war and particular friends on the squadron. With access only to German news media and propaganda, new prisoners with the other side of the story to tell were always the greatest morale boosters until the advent of smuggled radios.

During the following weeks, as the Battle of Britain soared into its full fury, we were inundated with German newspaper and magazine photographs of the smoking ruins in London and the smiling carefree faces of gallant German bomber crews. Their destructive capability was reported as formidable and their losses negligible, so that the demand from newcomers at the prison gate became simplified and formalised as though we were following an international cricket match. "What's the latest score?" and the cocky replies like, "Last Tuesday was 37 for 9. We've got 'em on the run!"

The new camp was the stereotype model with lines of creosoted wooden huts standing two feet or so off the soft sandy ground. Roofing felt covered the low-pitched roofs and the ceilings were of soft thick cardboard-like material. Each barrack block had a passage down the middle with a door at each end. Off the passage on both sides were the doors to rooms, each with two double-tiered wooden bunks with cross-wise bed boards supporting straw-filled sacking palliasses.

Every room had a window with hefty wooden shutters which, before dark, were bolted shut on the outside. Each was furnished with a bare wooden table with four stools and a wooden locker. On a concrete slab was a small iron stove, with a pipe going up through the ceiling. By normal prison camp standards, with sixteen or so men to a room, this was cosy and life could have been tolerable but for acute deprivations like hunger, claustrophobia and boredom and, of course, indeterminate separation from loved ones.

In the middle of each barrack block was a small kitchen with a sink, a cold tap and two small cooking stoves. At both ends of the central passage stood a wooden box with a hinged lid in which reposed a latrine bucket. This contraption we called a "thunder box" and, unscreened from the public gaze, was for use from dusk until morning *Appell*—roll call—during which period we were locked in the huts with the windows shuttered, barred and bolted.

During these hours, from 4.30 pm until 7.00 am, a horrible fug developed in these huts which was a mixture of hairy under-washed bodies, unappetising cooking smells (if there was anything to cook) and an odorous contribution from the thunder boxes, especially when mild tummy troubles or serious dysentery was prevalent.

Worst of all, to my sensitivities, was the ceaseless hubbub of voices, clomping footsteps, dragged furniture, clattering pots, peals of laughter and the arguments for hours on end with no escape to quiet or privacy. This was the feature of hut life which, more than anything else, drove me up the wall.

Another hut housed a dining room with long bare wooden tables and benches and, luxurious gadget, a hand-operated bread-slicing machine. Here prisoners congregated during the day to sit and read or play cards or chess. One hot meal per day was sent into the dining room from the cook house which was outside our compound. It arrived at our main gate in a number of metal containers similar to five-gallon milk cans with lids.

These large cans invariably contained some kind of slop with, on rare happy occasions, little bits of meat floating about in it. Often, it was unrelieved cabbage slop or turnip slop or carrot slop, sometimes with an unexpected bonus of protein in the form of a boiled earthworm spiced with a sprinkling of grit. From time to time we had a soup made from klipfish, an unlovely Norwegian form of salted cod which, before cooking, looked like dried bark. It also smelled pretty bad, though not quite as high as the abominable weekly issue of cheese, shaped like a slimy yellow sausage and aptly named "dead man's finger".

The daily bread ration was one-fifth of a sour-tasting loaf for each man (about five slices if he took care), plus half a matchbox-sized piece of margarine; a dessertspoonful of sugar; and every so often a dollop of "jam" which was bright red, stained plates and lips and tasted bitter. It was doled out from large tins inscribed *"Nur für Kriegsgefangene"*—For Prisoners of War Only. There was also a weekly issue of a bit of wurst which was not too bad and the occasional Wehrmacht *Suppe* which was better than most. This uninteresting diet was washed down with ersatz coffee, reputed to be made from burnt acorns. I doubt it was, because I do not believe acorns could taste so vile.

The whole complex was set in a wide, treeless, sandy waste. Surrounding the prisoners' compound, about ten feet in from the main fence, was what was known as the "warning wire" or "death wire". This single strand of barbed wire on wooden posts stood a little above knee height. Anyone touching, stepping over or crawling under that wire could be shot without warning. The main fence consisted of two parallel barbed-wire fences about eight feet high and six feet apart. These were of closely meshed squares of barbed wire with coiled wire on top. The six feet between these two fences was covered with a thick, coiled barbed wire entanglement. The whole fence system was brightly floodlit at night and immediately outside it, all day and all night, German guards with rifles patrolled beats and a dog handler or two had roving commissions.

At intervals along this formidable main fence, and at each corner, heavy poles supported watchtowers, each one equipped with a machine gun and a searchlight which constantly swept the deserted compound after dusk. Any prisoner seen moving about after dark could be shot.

The main and only access to this prisoners' compound consisted of two well-guarded gates—one in the inner and the other in the outer fence. They operated rather like the entrance to an aviary so that at no time were both gates open at once. A guard was permanently on the gate ensuring that nobody could go out who had not officially checked in via the guard room.

Outside the prisoners' compound was the German compound with a single six-foot barbed wire fence around it. This appeared very similar to our own and contained the guards' barrack blocks, dining room, recreation room, ablutions, and latrines. It also contained the prisoners' punishment cells and reception block as well as the *Kommandantur* (Administration Offices) stores, armoury and so on. The German troops had to book in and out of their compound through their own main gate at the guard room. There was one other gate in their fence and this led into an enclosure, again surrounded by barbed wire, which was big enough to kick a football around in. In compliance with the Geneva Convention, prisoners were marched under heavy guard into this enclosure for an hour or two's exercise a day. Even though prisoners were required to sign an agreement not to attempt to escape, the enclosure was surrounded by armed guards and dogs. Having already decided never to give my parole, my immediate reaction to the sports field was that my hosts could stuff it!

The other main form of exercise was walking repeatedly round and round our compound just inside the warning wire on the soft sandy soil. This tended to churn up, except when frozen, and was an uncomfortable and extremely boring pastime, relieved only by occasionally varying the direction of the circuit from left to right. Trudging around became a problem for me because of my Rheims ankle injury which soon tended to ache. Some prisoners walked in bare feet and the odd chap had scrounged— from goodness knows where—a pair of clogs or wooden-soled jackboots before arrival at the camp, but these were very scarce. There were no facilities for shoe repairs.

The first addition to my wardrobe was a shirt given to me by another, older prisoner who had received a parcel from his family after I had been "in the bag" for seven or eight weeks. Up until then, when I washed my shirt I wore no shirt and ditto vest, pants and socks. We were issued with no clothing whatsoever, although it was winter and bitterly cold up there near the Baltic coast.

Under these circumstances, we were somewhat bitter when mail began to arrive for the older prisoners. Anxious relatives wrote of their relief on hearing BBC Radio News announcements that Red Cross clothing was now available to British prisoners of war, and their letters usually concluded with something like: "We were so relieved, dear, that daddy has sent a generous cheque to the Red Cross in appreciation." No such clothing had reached Barth although there had been some at Dulag Luft. Our bitterness would have turned to intense anger had we known that, after the war, the British Treasury would insist that officers be charged for every item of Red Cross clothing they eventually received as a prisoner, claiming that the clothing was from service stores and the Red Cross was merely the agent for getting it to them.

The worst hardship of all, before Red Cross food parcels arrived, was undoubtedly hunger. This was a frightening, constant, gnawing misery, gradually putting you into a desperate state of mind so that you would find yourself wandering around, scrutinising every substance and object in the belief that somewhere—if only you can find it—there MUST be something edible. Because of hunger many prisoners gave up taking exercise and took to lying on their beds all day which is, of course, the beginning of the end. By midday, I think nearly everyone was sitting at their windows just watching for that main gate to open and the cans of slop to come in. I think of this now when I see the big cats in a zoo walking endlessly back and forth in their cages just before feeding time, and I feel for them.

I had roomed up with two other officers, John Haskins, a red-headed mate from my old 49 Squadron, and "Bunt" Howard, a dumpy rosy-faced Fleet Air Arm pilot. We pooled our meagre rations and it is interesting how, in extreme conditions, men naturally adopt and take quite seriously procedures which in normal life would seem ludicrous. I remember when the first small batch of Red Cross food parcels arrived and were issued at the rate of one parcel per three men, our mess of three shared a tin of baked beans, and each bean was counted out one by one, with lots drawn for the odd two over. There was no sense of the ridiculous about this. For smokers, hunger seemed even worse without cigarettes. When a few French Gauloises appeared from somewhere and I had my first drag, so powerful was the sensation that it was still vividly revived in me years later each time I smelled that distinctive aroma—even though I had long given up smoking.

As food and cigarette parcels began to dribble into the camp, everything quickly acquired an exact market value for trading and swapping, such as four cigarettes for a slice of bread. Dog ends were carefully stored for re-rolling and even a cigarette tin full of "dog ends" tobacco had its market value. These were known as "ends". When they were re-rolled into cigarettes and smoked, the ends were again saved and known as "ends of ends", which had a lower market value than "ends". All this was taken quite seriously.

One day I hit upon a crafty scheme. I noticed there was a crack in the base of the bread cutting machine, and that this filled with crumbs. I spent a few days reading at the table by the machine and after anyone sliced some bread, I furtively ran a sliver of wood along the crack and harvested a few crumbs into a paper bag. At the end of each day, I had quite a little pile in the bag. At the end of the week, the bag was half full and I remember the battle I had with my conscience before I told Bunt and John what I had been up to. We made and shared a tiny bread pudding with a blob of ersatz jam in it.

The Pomeranian countryside surrounding the camp was flat and bleak, relieved only by a dark wood of fir trees which reached a long narrow finger out towards the prison camp, ending about fifty yards from the perimeter fence of the German compound. Out of sight, some miles behind the trees, there was a Luftwaffe Operational Training Unit converting newly trained

PDT and friends at Stalag Luft I, Barth, 1940.

aircrew onto Junkers Ju-88 twin-engined bombers, such as were at that time knocking hell out of London. These aircraft often flew over the camp and as they did so, it became almost a ritual for chaps in the compound to look up at them and spit out some uncomplimentary epithet, more often than not, "Spin in, you bastard!"

I decided that if I were able to escape, I would make for that Luftwaffe airfield and try to steal an aircraft of some sort and fly to neutral Sweden, which was not very far away. I was especially keen on this idea as a way of evening the score: they had got my aircraft so I must try nicking one of theirs. The immediate problem was how to escape.

The Senior British Officer (SBO) at Barth was a wild man with a mane of hair and a beard, a glint of devilry in the eye and a piratical laugh. He was Squadron Leader Brian "Auntie" Paddon. Why Auntie I have not the faintest idea, because there was nothing of the old woman about that one. After several escape attempts, he ended up in Colditz Castle, the last stop for the baddest of bad boys. He was renowned for his furtive conspiratorial glances whenever engaged in matters escaping, and everyone was certain he would never avoid detection outside. His manner almost broadcast to the Germans, "Look out, chaps, I'm up to something!"

Apart from the gallant but abortive efforts of the train jumpers and one or two failures to get through the gates and away from the cell block, there had been no serious or successful escape attempts from Stalag Luft I. It was an extremely difficult type of prison camp to escape from, especially for relatively green prisoners with no precedents or experience. Also an empty belly does little to encourage enterprise. I spent many sleepless nights on my top bunk fretting about my family's anxieties and especially my darling Ann.

Most of all, I was plagued by misgivings about our crew's inglorious end and was sick with remorse about "if only this, and if only that". Why had we made a complete balls of things, with our eventual desperate decision to turn back eastwards towards what must have been an illusion on the early morning horizon? So many times I tried to reconstruct that last flight and fathom the errors that had led to our captivity and the loss of our Hampden, and so many times I awoke from fitful sleep with the recurring Rheims nightmare. I was not alone in this and there were occasional desperate shouts in the middle of the night as some poor fellow dreamt of his final undoing with engines on fire or wings dropping off, some of them performing a spectacular bale-out from a top bunk and landing in a heap on the floor. It was all a part of life and treated as a huge joke by everybody else, if they did not curse the silly sod for disturbing their own rest.

My own remorse resolved itself into an absolute determination to escape and, if possible, to even the score by making it with a German aircraft. It seemed farfetched, but gradually the idea became almost an obsession and I found myself thinking of little else but the ways and means to get home and continue my RAF career from where I had left off. Single-mindedness is often the key to success in most things and, if what I am told is true—that I was to chalk up the all-comers British record number of escape attempts during the next twelve months—I attribute this entirely to that state of mind. I schemed and thought about little else, except Ann who was almost constantly in my thoughts.

Escape from a camp of this sort could, it seemed, be narrowed down to a few limited avenues. There was the wire and there was the gate. The wire presented three possibilities: over it, through it or under it. None of these seemed feasible, or rather, nobody at this stage had dreamed up the quite fantastic wire schemes that eventually began to evolve as the years went by. Tunnelling in soft sand from huts on stilts that were far from the wire seemed an impossibility, although such schemes were being contemplated.

That left the gate. There are two ways through a gate. Openly by some ruse, or hidden in a vehicle. Traffic through our gate, both on foot and wheels, was very light and highly regulated. There seemed no flaw in the German check systems. Long-winded schemes like feigning sickness or insanity, such as some people worked in later days to have themselves removed to easier departure points, did not occur to me. I had to get out of this camp NOW! Who and what went through that gate? Why, how and when?

The only regular arrivals and exits through the gate were of food, snooping Germans and the daily party to the playing field. The last was out because they were all on parole and, in any case, carefully guarded on the march and on the little playing field. Curse the bloody parole system! Why did prisoners have anything to do with it? Was it absolutely necessary to give parole to get into a football party? Was there perhaps a flaw there? I excitedly put all my attention to examining the parole system.

At about 10.00 am, a German guard came in with the parole book and those wishing to go out that afternoon signed their names. Unobtrusively following the guard around and counting how many people had signed, I noticed that by the time the party went out, at about 2.30 pm, there were frequently one or two people who had changed their minds, meaning fewer left than had originally signed. Each man should have been made to sign as he went out through the gate, but so long as the Germans had as many or more signatures in the book than they had in the outgoing party, they were satisfied. Fools! I joined an under-strength party and went to the playing field without signing parole. It was easy. I went, as some others did, as a spectator, not a player, with the familiar bed blanket round my shoulders. My sole purpose was to find a way out of that playing field, but even after several visits I realised there was no obvious way out. My frustration was uncontrollable.

Then, one day as we were marched back through the German compound three abreast, a Luftwaffe *Unteroffizier* in full uniform passed us close by going in the opposite direction. There he was, within spitting distance of me, a free man and here I was a prisoner. I almost envied him. Tonight he could enjoy himself at the local pub—maybe see his girlfriend. If only I could be him, just for one evening. If only I could be him.

In a flash I had my scheme and was bursting with excitement and impatience to put it into effect. At our main gate, the Germans made a foolish error. They did not first count the party outside the gate and then let it in; they let it in and then counted. Then, satisfied that the same number had returned as went out, they took no further interest.

I realised there were difficulties, of course: how to change identity in a split second from prisoner to German NCO; how to avoid detection by the escorting guards; how to do all this under the noses of the guards in the machine-gun towers that watched the party's progress step by step; how to fiddle the numbers at the gate. But these, I felt, were mere details. Once one has the bones of a good scheme, I have always found the difficulties are technical problems to be overcome and that the ways to overcome them can nearly always be found with enough determination. They have to be.

I went to Auntie Paddon, bursting with enthusiasm, and his reaction was predictable. He chuckled at the audacity of the scheme. One moment a prisoner going one way and the next moment a guard going the other way—a classic! He loved the idea and his gleeful enthusiasm matched my own.

"Plan to beat the snags and have a go. I will give you all the help I can," he said.

His blessing was all I needed, but then the "doubting Thomases" started, especially two of the other senior officers.

"It could never work!"

"There are too many German eyes on us all the time."

"What about the German machine-gunners in the boxes on stilts?"

"The other chaps being on parole could not cooperate and assist an escape."

"Even if that part of it worked, how could you get out of the German compound? The German gate at the guard room was impossible."

"If they did not get you leaving the column, they would get you going over the German wire. If they didn't shoot you then, they would shoot you later for wearing German uniform."

"It was madness and Auntie Paddon was an irresponsible ass to condone it."

But for every one of them, there were others who chuckled, said it was worth a bash and encouraged me to press on.

My original plan was to make for the Luftwaffe Operational Training Unit and try to swipe a Ju-88 for a quick flight to Sweden. I did not underestimate the difficulty of this, but I would be in Luftwaffe working uniform and that would help. The biggest hurdle would be starting the engines. Starting up an aircraft, especially a sophisticated one, cannot be compared with starting a car. There is usually a complicated rigmarole to go through and, if it is like a Hampden, somebody has to prime the engine with fuel from underneath while the pilot goes through his routine in the cockpit. We had no pilot's notes for any German aircraft at that stage of the war and had only a smattering of what various cockpit instructions could mean. At least I knew "*Benzin auf*" and "*Benzin zu*" meant "fuel on" and "fuel off", but that was about it.

Then a bright new prisoner turned up who had managed to remove a railway map from a carriage compartment on the way up from Dulag Luft and to conceal it during his search. It showed a dotted line marked "Train Ferry" from Sassnitz on the island of Rügen to the port of Trelleburg in Sweden. Rügen was joined to the German mainland by a railway bridge from Stralsund, and Stralsund was no more than about six hours walking distance to the east of our camp. If the train ferry was still operating in war time, this was it. We also learned that the passenger ferry used to carry German coal to Sweden and return with Swedish iron ore, but no matter how we tried, we could not establish whether it was still running in wartime without arousing suspicion.

Then a doctor from Sweden, acting for our protecting power under the Geneva Convention, visited. He was allowed to chat with us but was, of course, honour bound not to assist us in escaping. By subtle roundabout conversation, I managed to elicit from him that he had crossed by ferry. My hopes soared as I realised I could make a viable plan.

Preparations for my escape consisted mainly of manufacturing a Luftwaffe working uniform of air force blue trousers (our own were near enough); a black lightweight loose-fitting fatigue jacket under which no German uniform shirt was necessary; and a jaunty field service cap always referred to in the RAF by a very rude name. (Oh, all right, we called it a "c*** cap." You just had to know, didn't you!)

The German cap was similar to our own and I still had mine, which had been stuffed in my uniform pocket while I was flying. A little tailoring and embroidering the Luftwaffe eagle on the front would fix that. German jackboots worn outside the trousers threatened to be the biggest problem. The silverish braid for an *Unteroffizier*'s stripes and collar band could no doubt be made from suitably doctored silver paper from Red Cross chocolate, if any came to hand. A Flying Officer Jones of 61 Squadron had been shot down wearing a snazzy black, lightweight flying overall and I managed to talk him out of this with the help of a tin of cigarettes. Cut in half just below the waist and modified, it made the German fatigue jacket.

Then I spotted a pair of jackboots tramping round the compound. They were Polish and had wooden soles, but with any luck this would not be noticed. Some swift bargaining and they were mine. I decided to make the German uniform convertible into something that would do for a Swedish seaman, and manufactured a convincing seaman's cap from a black beret and the shiny black cover of an exercise book for a peak.

I checked the wording of the parole for footballers. They promised not to escape but it said nothing about assisting escape. My plans for upsetting the count when the footballers returned and for distracting the machine gun towers were also complete. I saved scraps from my daily food issue and bartered them for a small store of escape rations—raisins, chocolate and, best of all, a tin of Nestlé's Condensed Milk.

At that stage in the escaping game we had no forged papers, nor any German money, which was a terrible handicap. A few German Marks would, in the event, have made a world of difference for me.

Meanwhile, life in the camp went on as usual with only a rare incident to punctuate the dreary passage of time. One such occurred just after Squadron Leader Geoffrey "Little Steve" Stephenson, an ex-Central Flying School pundit, had finished giving us a lecture on the theory of flight. He had been talking about the incipient spin developing from a slow flat turn. As we walked out of the lecture, a Ju-88 droned overhead in the cloudless winter sky. He was making a slow flat turn to starboard. The usual chorus went up. "Spin in, you bastard." And he did! As we heard the thump and saw the black ball of smoke rise from the point of impact, I swear that a spontaneous cheer went up from every man jack who saw that German bomber go in. After all, it was one less to knock the hell out of London and the coincidence after Little Steve's lecture was downright uncanny.

One of the national traits for which I give the natives of Perfidious Albion full marks is hypocrisy, and this unlovable streak in my countrymen came out clearly after the crash of the Ju-88. There were those who, on second thoughts about the jubilant cheer, saw fit to mutter about the "damn poor show", "disrespect for the dead" and "comradeship of the air". The English are rather good at these sudden shifts of conscience, which is why a strategic bomber force cheered to the echo for its gallantry in wartime has, to some, become a shameful memory.

One of my main concerns about escape preparations was security. There was not a single officer in the whole camp who was not well known to several others, so there was hardly any question of a stool pigeon among us. Nonetheless, we had the impression that the Germans were too well acquainted with what went on in the privacy of our barrack blocks. Auntie Paddon and "Big Steve"—Lieutenant Commander Stevinson of the Fleet Air Arm who stood head and shoulders above our "Little Steve"—suspected the quarters were bugged. They made a search for microphones and found them. They were above the ceilings at the holes cut for the stove pipes.

Auntie was not the man to pass up such a discovery without a hearty demonstration of one-upmanship. A crafty leader might have kept quiet and usefully fed the Germans false information, but Auntie had a simple boyish heart. His direct retaliation was a super morale booster, so essential to prison camp survival. He somehow connected the microphone leads up to the camp's main electricity supply in such a way that the eavesdroppers in the *Kommandantur* suddenly had their equipment go up with a puff of smoke.

Within the hour, a riot squad charged into our compound—helmets, rifles, bayonets, big boots and all—their entry through the gate enthusiastically greeted by a cheer party. With orderly precision, they split up and pounded into our barrack blocks where ladders were pushed up into ceiling trapdoors and suitably briefed heroes disappeared into the roof space. This was exactly what Auntie had anticipated and, it is said, that was why he had ordered a few strategically placed rafters to be almost completely sawn through. The sudden rending of timber, bursting ceilings and the shrill descent of German troops onto the floor of one of our rooms, were greeted with further cheers and chaps rolling around in paroxysms of laughter. It is no wonder that some of them suffered a good clump round the ear'ole and a miracle nobody was bayoneted.

Soon after the dust had settled, my first escape attempt was ready and with a bonus. The capers in the roof had given me an idea for covering up my absence at the first evening *Appell* after my escape. Morning *Appell* was held outside in the compound with a German NCO going through each block to count the sick who were confined to their beds. The evening *Appell* was held in the barrack blocks after the window shutters had been closed and bolted. For this count, we stood by our beds and again the sick were allowed to be tucked up. As long as a human head was visible, the count was deemed satisfactory.

I had a top bunk and we loosened a ceiling panel just above it, and then loosened another panel just above the bunk at the other end of the block belonging to a fair-haired chap similar to me. Starting, as usual, at our end, the guards would count the other chap lying "sick" in my bunk with only the back of his head visible in bed. As soon as they left the room, he would climb up into the roof and as silently as possible would scuttle along the low roof space and drop into his own room, ready to be counted again as himself, assisted by an exceptionally noisy and uncooperative roll-call organised by the rest of our lads. Variations of this *Appell* fix continued to be used in prison camps throughout the war.

Provided this trick worked, I should have a clear start of about sixteen hours before my absence was revealed on the outside morning *Appell*. That, too, could have been fixed with the tricks that gradually developed through the war, but at this stage we were only learners.

Distractions and diversions had been planned and practised insofar as they would not arouse suspicion. The attention of the machine-gunners in the towers was to be diverted by a free fight developing from a ball game— very "un-British" in those days, but it would be made convincing enough. The count of the incoming football party was to be confused by a collision with irresponsible idiot runners round the compound who, in the ensuing melee and screaming of outraged guards, would leave one of their number with the footballers to make up for my absence.

The trickiest part of all was my actual departure from the column of prisoners and my about turn into a completely changed identity from prisoner to German soldier in half a second. The change of guise was no great problem. We hoped nobody would notice the wooden soled boots or the subtly different blue of my own air force blue trousers. The black working jacket with *Unteroffizier*'s rank badges would initially be hidden under the familiar bed blanket over my shoulders which had only to be thrown off to a chum, and the Luftwaffe field service cap had then to be clapped onto my head. A small sack, which a German on fatigue duties might possibly be carrying with tools or something in it, would also be under my blanket. This would contain my rations, seaman's cap, Ann's knitted sweater for a bit of extra warmth, and my own shoes to replace the jackboots which, with their wooden soles, would be hopeless for the long walk to Sassnitz via Stralsund.

Success or failure depended upon that break from the column of prisoners—perhaps even life or death, depending on the German reaction to the uniform issue. I had arranged to signal the start of the attempt to all concerned by starting up the old First World War song "Pack Up Your Troubles in Your Old Kitbag". We are not a singing race like the Welsh or, indeed, the Germans, whose practised and stirring marching songs we heard every day with irritation and a sneaking admiration. But during the weeks before my escape, the football party became great singers on the march too. The noise must have been excruciating for the German perfectionists. I was the song leader, and the plan was that if "Pack Up Your Troubles" started, I was about to have a go and everyone must swing into his briefed routine.

I would be positioned on the left of the column which was following a right hand circuit round the outside of the main fence of our compound, close under the machine gun towers. I would take a position immediately behind one of the flanking guards who, unwisely, marched much too close to our column. The prisoners in the files behind me would bulge outwards to the left slightly to obstruct the view of the next guard down the column. Some of my mates would point excitedly up at the sky to the right so that, hopefully, the guards would look up that way as well to see what was so interesting. I would throw off my blanket to the chap on my right, clap on my Luftwaffe hat, sling my sack over my shoulder, step out of line, turn about, and walk back past all the oncoming guards as one of their comrades. That, anyway, was the hopeful plan.

Nights in prison camp always tended to be restless, but during the work-up for an escape, they were much more so. Many hours I spent awake, thinking of home, the war, and most of all, my lovely Ann. But for the past weeks, in addition to imagining our reunion, I now saw each move of the escape, each development on the way, crossing the guarded railway bridge to Rügen, the marshalling yard at the dock at Sassnitz, burrowing my way into the coal of a loaded truck. I saw all the details and planned for them carefully.

I learned, with bitter experience, that this is not a reliable process, for one tends to imagine what one wants to imagine. You see yourself climbing over the five-foot fence made of old railway sleepers, like the one near my home town, Grays, and dropping into the blacked-out darkness of the marshalling yard. Inside, you quickly identify the railway track that runs to the ferry, and on it, waiting to be shunted onto the ship, is a line of

A FIGHT!

A GERMAN IN FATIGUE
UNIFORM WALKING BACK
THE OTHER WAY

LOTS OF
CHATTING
& POINTING

Sketch by PDT of the diversion for his escape from Barth.

trucks full of fine coal, each with a destination card in a wire holder which boldly states "Trelleborg". But things never turn out like that. Instead, you find a nine-foot brick wall with spikes on top; the whole marshalling yard floodlit except during air raid warnings; a confusion of tracks with trucks all over the place bearing chalked hieroglyphics on them which you cannot decipher; the coal is in huge lumps into which you cannot burrow and there are guards with police dogs on patrol. As the trucks move slowly onto the ferry, each one is searched.

As an escaper, one must learn to imagine the plan for the worst eventuality. Germany was a police state. The Jews were being persecuted to death. Many were on the run. So were slave workers from the occupied countries and a few deserters from the Nazi forces. As the war progressed, there were thousands on the move illegally for one reason or another and the network for catching them became progressively finer. This was the escaper's most serious obstacle.

In the still moments of the night, my morale often soared but plummeted when I allowed myself to dwell on the warnings against wearing German uniform. And, if it came to it, how would I stand up to a firing squad? Could I maintain the traditional proud defiant attitude or would my courage fail? I had to tear my mind away from such morbid thoughts.

The great day arrived and off we went to the football field. It was bitterly cold, standing there as a spectator. My blanket did not prevent the shivers with nothing especially warm under the flimsy black jacket. Then the guards ordered us to form up for the march back to our compound and we were on our way. Everybody put on a good casual jocular act. Inside the compound, the ball game was in full swing and some prisoners were running around the inside perimeter. I manoeuvred myself to be immediately behind a guard on the left of the column. As we passed under one of the machine gun towers, everything looked right and I started a lusty "Pack Up Your Troubles". The other chaps took it up. I glimpsed the beginning of a hullabaloo inside the wire—the fight was on! I assumed the column behind me had bulged out, whipped off the blanket, which was grabbed by the chap next to me on my right, stuck the German hat on my head, turned about and tried to look unconcerned. My friends tramped on singing their raucous song and, as briefed, none of them paid any attention to me but some were pointing up into the sky over to the right. The guards did not so much as glance my way.

Stage one was a complete success and a new escape method was established which was used often with variations throughout the rest of the war. (It was at first referred to as "doing a Tunstall" but later acquired a more appropriate name, "a chameleon".) The fight inside the wire was planned to continue for three minutes which would give me time to walk between two German barrack blocks to their high perimeter fence which I intended to climb up and over, trusting to luck that the machine-gunners' attentions would still be on the fight.

"Kommen sie mit!"

I rounded the end of the German huts and walked slap into a small bunch of off-duty guards, sitting on chairs outside their hut wrapped in their greatcoats and enjoying a lively conversation. As this completely strange *Unteroffizier* approached, they turned their faces towards me and the conversation stopped dead. No wonder. It was not such an enormous guard company and no doubt nearly everybody knew each other, and in any case, why was this strange *Unteroffizier* walking between the huts towards nowhere but the wire? They stared silently and I was sure the game was up.

I could not turn and run; there was nowhere to run to. I smiled at them and then began whistling a German tune nonchalantly and swinging my little sack as though I hadn't a care in the world, but they still stared, damn them. At that moment, fortune smiled upon me. By the wire, I saw some rabbit hutches, obviously the property of some enterprising guards who fancied an extra meat ration. I walked to the hutches and with my back to the curious guards, delved into the sack and pretended to be pushing some vegetable scraps through the wire and stroking the rabbits' noses. Gradually I heard the conversation start up again behind me and I worked slowly along the line of hutches until I reached a position where I was round the end of the hut and out of their line of sight.

Unfortunately, I was still in the sight of the gun tower and after the time-consuming pantomime at the hutches, the free fight diversion had finished and the machine-gunner again had his attention on his job. There was nothing for it but to toss my sack over the wire and climb after it trusting to luck that nobody looked my way. The skin of my back crawled against the anticipated burst of fire. I jumped down from the top strand of wire, landed on hands and knees with a sharp twinge of pain from that bloody ankle I had injured over Rheims. I grabbed my sack and ran, limping a bit, fifty yards for the cover of the finger of pine wood which pointed towards the wire. Arriving there, I threw myself beneath the trees and for a while lay panting with effort and fright. Then I cautiously made my way up the length of the narrow strip of wood, so narrow that I could see both edges, but was concealed from the prison camp so long as I kept in the centre.

It seemed wise to make some distance from the prison camp before stopping to change disguise and soon caution had to be abandoned for faster progress. Speed was the essence of success. Ideally, I should be hidden in a coal truck before my absence was discovered, for the Germans were certain to increase their vigilance at the docks with an RAF officer on the run. It was obviously desirable to be across the guarded bridge and on the island of Rügen before any warnings were broadcast about an escaped prisoner.

I straightened up and was about to crash through the woods when a German spoke out and shocked me to a full stop. I could not see him and assumed he was hiding just ahead of me. Then his voice continued softly and without challenge and I realised he was not speaking to me. I sank slowly down again onto my hands and knees. The voice was directly in my line of advance and to detour much to left or right would again expose me to view from the camp. I listened carefully as the voice continued softly in playful affection and I concluded I had stumbled upon an off-duty soldier necking a Fräulein in the woods. The irony of it struck me with bitterness. Whatever the sum total of my motives for escape—duty, boredom, hunger—a powerful desire was to hold Ann in my arms again. Now it seemed my consuming love and longing was to be frustrated by the casual amour of a German soldier. *"Deine schönen traurigen Augen staunen in mein Angesicht. Machst du mich, liebst du mich?"* He was slobbering on about her beautiful eyes gazing into his and asking her if she really loved him!

It was love talk all right! To skirt round them, I must first locate them exactly, so I began to crawl forward like a cat stalking a sparrow. Then, a few yards away, I spotted the German sitting in a small sunlit clearing with his back to me. On his shoulders he wore the silver braid of an *Unteroffizier* and on his heavy leather belt snuggled the holster of a Luger pistol. He was a prison camp "dog handler" and between his palms he lovingly held the muzzle of his Alsatian guard dog, almost facing my way but gazing into her master's eyes.

I froze with sudden shock, then slowly sank down until my nose was in the pine needles. My memory flashed back again to that day at the lake when I was with my father, and Compton, the Head Gamekeeper, almost came upon us with his dog. I thought of my father's steadiness and his teaching and of my Boy Scout games at Orsett. Inch by gradual inch, I worked my way backwards from danger with my nose still on the ground and my mind as blank as I could keep it. Well clear of the German, I chose the downwind edge of the woods to keep my scent away from the dog and painfully slowly, wriggled past them on my belly. At last I was clear enough to get up and run.

The finger of trees led into a larger wood where I changed my garb to Swedish seaman, with the peaked cap, the black jacket with the military rank badges removed, and my own shoes. The jackboots and Luftwaffe cap I buried in pine needles. Already the sun was low above the horizon and the intense cold of the November evening was taking a grip. I was glad I had to move fast and set off for Barth to find the road for Stralsund.

By the time I reached the small town of Barth, dusk was falling. It was just as well because most young Germans of my age had been called up and I preferred not to be seen too clearly. I had no road map of the area and was working on my memory of the small-scale railway map which had found its way into the camp. I had no compass, but thanks to my scout training and the clear sky, the stars would soon be good enough. There must have been signposts, but I saw none and dared not risk asking anybody the way. I had to sort it all out as best I could. Eventually I found the road that seemed to be heading southeast. I assumed it would be the right one and eventually headed in a more easterly direction towards Stralsund.

Ever since my ankle was sprained over Rheims in mid-June, it had started to play up a little if it became overstressed. Now, after my leap down from the fence and plodding along a road, parts of which seemed to be cobbled, it began to ache and I developed a slight limp. It was worrying considering how far I still had to tramp—at least another thirty-odd miles, nearly eighty kilometres to Sassnitz. Then I would probably need some agility to board a coal truck.

With a clear brilliant starlit sky, the cold was intense and soon became a serious concern, especially as I was now slowing down with increasing pain in my ankle. I realised the situation would become progressively worse and it would soon be essential to get some sort of transport—but how, with not a pennyworth of German money? I plodded on, becoming more concerned that the growing pain would put paid to my attempt, especially as I could not hide up to rest in this freezing cold.

Then I saw the headlights of a vehicle coming towards me and flopped into a dry roadside ditch. Just before it reached me, the light truck turned to its left off the road into an open gateway. Its load had a familiar clatter which I recognised as empty milk churns. It had turned into a farm entrance on my right. There was no mistaking on the soft sides of its drive the prints of hoofed feet and I was certain I could smell cow pats. A dairy farm! The signs were so familiar to me after working on my sister's farm just before I joined the RAF. I listened intently and, sure enough, I heard the familiar sounds of a busy milking shed, the soft mooing of cows and the clatter of milking time.

I thought of the milk deliveries to Tilbury from Lucy's farm at Chadwell St Mary, which I had made regularly with a Ford car and trailer. There would have to be an early morning delivery from this farm to the nearest big town—most likely Stralsund. The truck I had seen with the familiar milk churn rattle had come from the direction of Stralsund and must obviously be for that very purpose.

I cautiously followed the truck up the drive. An outside light had come on at the sheds. The driver turned his truck round and backed up to a large door under the light. There were voices and the sound of empty churns being unloaded. Then everyone went inside and the light went out.

Great! The light would soon come on again. They would load full milk churns and the truck would go back to where it had come from. And with a bit of luck, I might be on it. I silently crept my way up to the dark buildings, half frozen and limping quite badly. There was a wide chink between the double doors of the milking shed and warm air drifted out of it. For a few moments, I stood with my back pressed against it for the blessed warmth.

There was no way I could hide in the open truck. They would see me when they loaded it. I knew I must leap onto it as it drove off, but how could I do that without having been discovered lurking in the vicinity before it set off for Stralsund? Just to the right of where the truck was parked, there was a huge heap of leaves—probably beet tops used as cattle fodder, after they had wilted a bit to reduce the acid content. I knew about these things.

I would hide myself in the heap of leaves and, with a bit of luck, be able to burst out at the crucial moment and jump onto the back of the truck. Unfortunately, the leaves were sparkling with frost. They were frozen stiff and as I crawled into the heap and covered myself, they rattled. It seemed a dreadful noise, but with all the clanging and shouting in the milking shed and dairy I was fairly sure nobody would notice. I settled down to watch and wait and then a new problem descended upon me. I was becoming frozen like the bloody beet tops and began to shiver uncontrollably. There was nothing I could do about it. The new problem was that my violent shivering made the frozen leaves rattle and I was sure somebody would hear them when they opened the door.

After what seemed like a very long time, there were raised voices, more clattering, I could see the light had come on and hear churns being loaded— all so familiar. Then there were cheerful *"Wiedersehen"* shouts, the dairy door closed, the light went off, the truck engine started. Time to move—fast!

I burst out of the beet leaves like the Demon King in a pantomime and as the truck began to move off, I leapt on the back, climbed over the tail board and hung on. I ignored the pain in my ankle. The driver was a bit of a lunatic, or running late. He tore down the drive and I braced myself for a hairy swerve to the right onto the road bound for Stralsund. Braced as I was, I was nearly thrown off the truck because he did not turn right for Stralsund. He turned left for Barth!

I could hardly believe my abominable luck. Now the man was driving back towards the prison camp at high speed over all the miles I had so painfully trudged. I could do nothing about it and felt desperate. I had to get off that damned truck as soon as possible—but how? I knew there would be a sharp right turn into Barth and braced myself for a leap off as he slowed down at the corner. I was right, he did, but being the crazy driver he was, it wasn't all that slow and I just had to jump no matter what. So I did—and made a horrible crash landing. The awful rolling tumble knocked the wind out of me and the pain in my ankle as I hit the ground was excruciating. I knew I was now in a dire predicament. I had hoped to be in Stralsund before full light of morning and somehow cross the railway bridge onto the island of Rügen at the northeast corner of which was Sassnitz and the train ferry terminal. I had hoped to hide up on the island and get to Sassnitz during the cover of darkness next night. I should never have made the attempt in such cruelly cold weather. In the escaping game, one learns slowly and painfully.

The next *Appell* at Barth would be at 8.00 am, after which I would be hunted and here I was, back almost to square one. I wanted to lie down and sleep but if I had done, I could have died of hypothermia. The situation was desperate and the time had come to abandon all caution. It was still pitch dark and I hobbled about a bit in a state of nightmare unreality. I thought of my friends at Barth, snug in bed, and almost envied them. Then I thought of how all their hopes and good wishes were with me and to give up now would be like letting them down too. I gathered my wits and tried to renew my determination.

Then I could hardly believe what I thought I could hear. Not very far away, it sounded as if there were girls' or young women's voices chatting and laughing. I could only think they were schoolgirls and at that early hour, they could only be waiting for transport. Where to? School? Where, if not in Barth? The only answer could be Stralsund. I hobbled towards the voices and came upon a bus-shelter by a narrow-gauge rail track. I had already seen the track earlier on and had decided it was a sort of overland tramway, more or less following the line of the road.

The shelter was full of senior schoolgirls with satchels and briefcases. When they saw me, their chatter died away and they stared curiously. I must have looked a bit battered. It was my cue to play the simpleton.

"*Gehen sie nach Stralsund*?" I asked them.

The question was greeted with titters. "Gehen", the equivalent of our "go", is not used as we would say "Are you going to Stralsund?" but, instead, implies "walking" and I should have said "Fahren", meaning are you "travelling" to Stralsund. Now they knew I was no German. Anyway, they conceded they were waiting for the Stralsund tram and that was what I wanted to know. I told them I was a "*schwedische Matrose*", a Swedish seaman, and that seemed to satisfy their curiosity.

The next thing was to see whether I could ride on the tram without paying a fare for which I had no money whatsoever. I think now I should have begged a few *Pfennigs* from the girls, but it is easy to be wise after the event. The single decker tram came in, well lit and warm looking, and the girls piled on at the front end. There was only a tram driver and no conductor, and nobody paid as they got on. Good. That meant they must pay as they got off. The tram looked to me as if it might be double-ended; like most old trams that go in both directions there was no particular back or front. So I sat at the opposite end from the driver, thinking that maybe I could slip off from the wrong end at Stralsund and make a dash for it, or just melt away in the half light of early morning. I would jump that hurdle when I came to it—if I could jump anything at all.

I was the last passenger to board the tram. Being a good Boy Scout, I had taken a small twist of string with me on my escape. I did not know the end of this was hanging down out of my left-hand trouser pocket. I also did not know the tram driver considered himself the local comedian who endeavoured to keep his lucky passengers in fits of laughter. As I shuffled past his driving seat, he took the end of the string in his fingers and as I moved down the tram more and more string emerged from my pocket with the driver now standing and pointing to his end of it. I had no idea why everyone was laughing at me. What I did know was that instead of being a nonentity, I was now the centre of everybody's unwelcome attention. Dammit—what else could go wrong?

The girls had filled the back of the tram and I had to sit in the middle, discovered about the string, joined in the joke, and played idiot which was not all that difficult because I felt like one anyway! Then, in the middle of nowhere, the tram stopped, the driver got out of his seat, donned a ticket punch and a money satchel, and it was "fares please".

There was no question of escape. I had to play it out. When the comedian came to me, I went through a tremendous routine of searching all my pockets, then looked at him with a sheepish grin and said I had lost my money. I think he said, "You must be careful or you will lose your head," because everybody laughed again and he seemed quite unconcerned and went on with his job. Maybe idiots weren't expected to pay!

There was now no question of my slipping off the tram before it reached the terminus, nor did there seem any necessity. As we entered the outskirts of Stralsund, day broke and as we stopped in the town square, it was almost fully light. Everyone piled off and the driver gave me a friendly sympathetic sort of smile as I hobbled off, my ankle hurting like hell. Unfortunately, there was a brown-helmeted policeman standing in the square, and Mr Big Mouth tram conductor, I am sure without malice, called out to him laughing. He pointed at me and said something like "You want to look after him. Got no money and don't know if he's coming or going." That was all I needed! I was limping, hardly able to put my sprained ankle to the ground, had a big bruise on my forehead, I was in a suspicious age group and dishevelled in appearance, which was most un-German. The armed policeman strolled over to me. "*Was ist los?*"—What's your problem?

"I am a Swedish seaman. I'm going to Sassnitz."

"What ship?"

I took a wild stab. "*Die Stockholm.*"

He looked unconvinced. "I have never heard of it. You have papers?"

"I lost my papers and my money."

"Where?"

"A woman. Last night. I was drunk. She took everything. My money. My papers."

"*Kommen sie mit!*"

How I hate that expression. It was so often the end of everything for so many people in Nazi Germany.

He took me to the police station and there I was subjected to further grilling. I do not think I was caught in a particularly sensitive security area apart from the proximity of an international port. I had, as it happens, been slinking around fairly close to Peenemünde where the V1 and V2 flying bombs and rockets were later to be developed. But at that time, I imagine there was no particular heat on. My arrest was a routine matter of little significance. I stuck to my story, but nobody had heard of *Die Stockholm* and they were not very impressed when I said I had been too drunk to remember where the woman lived in Barth. They decided to put me in the town lock-up, which was a completely separate building from the police station, and there I was taken presumably until the police could substantiate my identity.

It was not long after this that news of my escape and my description arrived at the police station. A policeman came over to the jail and I heard him tell the jailer that they knew I was a prisoner of war and that guards would soon be coming from Stalag Luft to collect me.

The town jailer was a creepy, wizened little man, full of curiosity. When he knew I was a prisoner of war, he became more friendly. He gave me my sack of belongings and I decided to eat the rations quickly before they were confiscated.

As I had been taken to my cell, I had noticed an opening in the passage which led to a small exercise yard. The wall round it was only about six feet high with a small tight roll of barbed wire on top. Set in the wall was a tap over a drain. I wondered how I could persuade the old man to let me go to the yard. I asked for a drink, but he brought me a tin mug of water.

Then he called to someone who was clattering with a broom down the passage. It turned out to be a blonde girl of about eighteen. She looked like a simple peasant girl, small-waisted, nicely rounded and quite pretty. The jailer opened the door and pointed to her.

"*Polen*," he said. "She is a Pole."

"You like?" he asked and pushed his forefinger back and forth between the thumb and forefinger of his other hand.

"You like ficken?" and he eased her gently towards the cell.

She smiled at me coyly and kept saying, "'Allo London."

The sleazy old voyeur clearly wanted to enjoy an exhibition and the poor girl was obviously game enough. An English ally would probably be a change from German soldiers.

All I wanted was to get to that outside yard. But how?

I thought of blood … If I could gash myself. The tin! I got rid of the old man and the girl and had to pluck up a lot of courage because I am not very good at this sort of thing. I held the tin firmly in my left hand, and put the rounded part of the palm of my right hand on the jagged edge. One, two, three, shove! The blood streamed dramatically over my hand between my fingers and dripped on the floor. It looked impressive. I called for the old man. As he came, I held up my gory hand and pointed towards the yard.

"*Wasser, Wasser! Schnell bitte.*"

He fell for it. He let me out to the yard and scampered off, presumably to get some rag. I wrenched off my jacket, threw it over the barbed wire, stood on the tap and was hauling myself up when there was a hullabaloo behind me. Two guards had arrived from Barth. They charged into the yard and pulled me down. It was the end of my first escape attempt and I still have the remnants of a scar on my right hand as a memento. And the ankle still plays up a bit when I overtax it.

My interrogation after the escape was conducted by the self-important little martinet, Major von Stachelski, who, unlike some German officers in the early days, treated escape more as an outrage than a legitimate military operation with a sporting flavour. I stood before his desk.

"How did you get out?" he demanded.

I would not tell him.

The interrogation lasted on and off for two days. Von Stachelski raged, shouted, stamped and threatened. Occasionally, some underling would come in and whisper some piece of information to him. Once, when the telephone rang, my interrogator picked it up with his normal arrogance and condescendingly announced, "Von Stachelski". When a voice answered, he leapt out of his chair and stood rigidly at "telephone attention". It was all "*Jawohl, Herr General*"—"*Nein, Herr General*"—"No, we still do not know how the prisoner escaped." As camp security officer, he was catching it from Area Headquarters. When the conversation finished, he replaced the handset, drew himself up to his full five foot six inches, clicked his heels and bowed to the telephone. It was too much for me, I burst into laughter at which point von Stachelski almost blew a fuse.

Next time he had me in, he wore a satisfied smirk on his face and said he knew how I had got out, and I believe he did have a fairly accurate idea after piecing things together. The fracas in the compound, the collision between the runners and footballers, the evidence of the troops about the strange *Unteroffizier* who fed the rabbits, and very likely the dogs had found the jackboots and Luftwaffe cap. When all this was thrown at me, I felt a chill foreboding.

"Ve know you use Cherman uniform!"

"Well, if you know, why ask me?"

"It is forbidden. You vill be shot."

But I wasn't, and after only ten days solitary confinement for escaping, plus five for laughing at von Stachelski, I was sent back into the camp.

It was the first of several times I was told I was to be shot. It is a disconcerting threat, especially from people who you know are quite capable of carrying it out. In the end, of course, they did shoot fifty RAF escapers out of hand, some of them chaps I knew well, and a number of our commando POWs, but for the time being, anyway, we had established that one could get away with using a German uniform. After that, it became a regular stunt and my own speciality.

Chapter Seven

From Barth to Spangenberg and Thorn

After my release from my fifteen days' solitary, I was a bit of a five-minute celebrity in the camp and was asked to tea a few times, to my gratification—a bit of somebody else's ration of bread and ersatz jam was always welcome. My hosts, in turn, were eager to learn details about the road to Stralsund, the tramway, the possibility of riding on the buffers of the tram, etc. Auntie Paddon said of my exit from the column of prisoners that it was the coolest thing he'd ever seen. I assured him that if he had observed me shivering under the frozen beet tops, he would have seen something a damn sight cooler.

The upshot of my debriefing, or post-mortem, was that it was hopeless to have attempted that journey to Sassnitz in such freezing cold weather without warm clothing and, more especially, without any money to travel on a tram. As it happened, a branch of Military Intelligence in London, known as MI9, was working on the problem of getting essential escape supplies smuggled by various devious means into POW camps. Once these resources came on stream, the number of successful escapes, or "home runs" as we called them, rose sharply. It quickly became evident that there was a formula to getting home. One needed plenty of German money, excellent forged papers identifying one as a foreign worker, and even forged letters explaining that worker's need to travel (strangely enough, usually to somewhere near the Swiss frontier); and, for preference, a fluent German-speaker as an accomplice, often a Dutch or Czech fellow captive.

Squadron Leader Paddon said the ankle problem was technically the result of a war wound and sheer bad luck that it had let me down so badly. I suggested to Auntie another ploy to get out of Stalag Luft and he agreed that I should have another go for the train ferry to Sweden as soon as the weather and my ankle improved.

One of my keenest interrogators about conditions outside was my good friend, Flight Lieutenant Hedley "Bill" Fowler, who, eighteen months later, was destined to make a "home run" from Colditz, with my assistance in covering up his absence.

It was Bill Fowler who looked out of his window one morning during that cold spell at Barth and saw the German guards outside our perimeter wire in full winter rig. They were well and truly muffled up against the Baltic frost, headgear pulled right down, ear muffs or scarf with huge upturned collars, long bulky greatcoats over warm jackboots—they looked quite shapeless creatures with gloved hands clasping the sling of the rifle on their backs.

To Bill's eye, when first he saw them like that, they resembled the shapeless sub-human creatures called "Goons" that featured in a very popular newspaper cartoon strip of the period.

"Good God!" said Bill on first seeing the guards so dressed, "We're guarded by Goons."

That unkind name immediately caught on with everybody and spread like wildfire throughout all the prison camps in Germany. The warning cry for the approach of guards was "Goons Up!" The machine gun towers around our perimeter became "Goon boxes", our home-made German uniforms for escaping were "Goon skins", and our favourite recreation of harassing the enemy was known as "Goon-baiting". The name will never die until there are no more of us ex-POWs alive.

About this time, I received my first letters from home. The arrival of mail through British and German censors brought me the most comforting boost a man could hope for. Letters from Ann uplifted my spirits more than anything else. In her first letter she wrote: "I will wait for you for as long as it takes," and later made loving references to our wedding arrangements. Those letters helped more than anything else to make the misery of imprisonment bearable.

Our correspondence was strictly rationed to three small letter forms and four postcards per month, all of which were censored by German military intelligence, the *Abwehr*. Our letters took weeks or even months to reach

Peter Tunstall (PDT) here second left and friends celebrating his
first escape attempt from Barth.

home, but they were nothing less than a lifeline. Physical deprivation such
as hunger, discomfort, and confinement were, as time went by, nothing
compared with the mental separation from every form of affection and
compassion. In other words, love. We were, outwardly, at least, a tough,
rumbustious crowd and it would have been infra dig to be emotional or
"soppy". Laughter was the order of the day and sentimentality was out.
Eventually, however, deep emotional upsets were the cause of some
prisoners going round the bend and even attempting suicide—an awful
strain on those of us who were their closest friends and tried to look after
them.

Every morning on waking and realising where I was, my spirits took a
plunge. Then I thought of the promise of my eventual reunion with Ann
and a life together, and my spirits rose; such thoughts helped to keep them
buoyant, no matter what.

Bill Fowler did us all a service as parcels officer and was permitted access
by the Goons to the parcels store, which was in the German compound. His
labours were not entirely altruistic. He had an escape scheme in mind—the
reason he had been so keen to pick my brain after my short visit to the
outside world.

Bill eventually made himself a Goon skin similar to mine, and smuggled it item by item into the parcels store. When all was ready and the weather was kinder, he made an easy departure from the store in German uniform, and climbed over the single perimeter fence much as I had done. He got to Sassnitz where a policeman demanded to see his papers and, having none, he was arrested.

From all these early failures, we gradually learned the pitfalls. The next man to go for the train ferry was Flight Lieutenant Harry Burton who, with incredibly good luck, made it all the way to Sweden and thence to England. At dead of night, he walked along the railway line from Barth via Stralsund to Sassnitz. When he came to towns he calmly walked along the length of the platforms. This was not brazen heroics, it was bloody daft! When he walked along the line over the guarded bridge to the island of Rügen in the dark early hours he bumped unexpectedly into an armed guard. So he said, in German, "Good morning", the guard said "Good morning" back, and Harry proceeded. As if that were not enough, he walked past three more guards and did the same thing. One wonders what they were there for!

Later he had to walk along a cobbled road and found it quieter to do this in bare feet, so he carried his shoes in his hand. Suddenly—disaster! A vicious Alsatian dog rushed at him snarling savagely. A door opened in a guard house revealing a man in uniform who eyed this strange apparition carrying his shoes. He demanded gruffly, "Who's that? Where are you going?" Harry gaily answered, "Sassnitz," whereupon the man grunted, called the dog in and closed the door! (I have always maintained that with his luck Harry could have replied, "I'm an escaping POW looking for a ship to Sweden," and the copper would have asked him in for a nice hot cup of coffee.)

Having reached the environs of Sassnitz, Harry realised day would soon break and he must find somewhere to hide up during daylight. In the darkness he saw a likely-looking spot with plentiful bushes, so he hopped over a fence and made his way inwards to find a cosy nook for a sleep He woke in the bright light of day to find himself in the middle of a flak battery. He skedaddled smartly.

Next day he walked into the docks past several sentries who gave him kindly nods. There were several German naval ships in the docks and the place was lousy with policemen who were all very nice. Harry decided the easiest way to get on to the ferry would be to cling underneath a railway mail van, so he did.

At the other end of his uneventful voyage he clung beneath it again and trundled off the ship. He then handed himself over to the Swedish police who passed him over to the British Legation and a few days later he was back in England for a hero's welcome and quite right too! He was awarded an immediate DSO and never looked back. Harry retired as an Air Marshal with a Knighthood. I have come to the irrevocable conclusion that fate does not distribute luck fairly.

The next important development for me at Barth after my escape— before the escapes of Bill Fowler, Harry Burton and another lucky chap called "Deaf" Shaw—was ominous. In February 1941 a list of names was read out by the Germans of all officers who had attempted to escape or been at all troublesome and we were told to pack our belongings. Auntie Paddon was on the list and when he asked where we were going, he was told it was none of his business. We got our kit together, such as it was, and were marched off to the Reception Block and meticulously searched.

There the Germans read to us a grisly report purporting to come from Canada about the harsh and brutal treatment of German POWs in Fort Henry camp near Kingston, Ontario. We were told that what was good for the goose was good for the gander, and we were to be transported to an unknown destination where we would receive similar treatment until the wicked British had learned their lesson. En route for the so-called "Reprisal Camp", we learned we were first to be held for a short time at an ancient castle at Spangenberg, near Kassel.

Schloss Spangenberg was a fascinating old fairytale-type castle. It stood on the top of an isolated, bush-covered hill in the middle of an open treeless plain, set in otherwise heavily forested country. The building was surrounded by a moat, which was now dry, with the drawbridge replaced by a permanent wooden bridge leading inwards to an impressive stone portal. This had massive wooden doors bound in iron, one of which stood open with a barbed wire gate and a permanent guard blocking the way in.

On the "land" side of the bridge was the guard room. The moat was lined with stone, sheer and rumoured to be thirty feet deep, and on the top of

The gate at Spangenberg, scene of PDT's most spectacular escape. (See p. 187)

the outside wall there was the familiar barbed wire fence, floodlit at night and permanently patrolled by guards. Spangenberg Castle has earned the reputation as the most escape-proof of all German POW centres of the Second World War.

The castle's dry moat had once been available to some earlier RAF prisoners as an exercise yard, but after one or two escape attempts this privilege had been withdrawn and the Germans had put wild boars in it. They were reputed to be dangerous savage creatures with tusks capable of inflicting terrible wounds. The prisoners decided to remove this further obstacle to escapes by tossing to the boars rotten potatoes which they had stuffed with broken razor blades. Sadly, the boars loved them and wanted more. They never turned a hair notwithstanding this iron-rich diet.

I found life in that old castle refreshingly different. We met up with another batch of RAF officers who had been held in a separate prison, known as the Spangenberg Lower Camp, in the nearby town. Some of them had become prisoners very early in the war, like Squadron Leader "Wank" Murray, a fine man who became our Senior British Officer. I hasten to add that Murray's nickname did not at that time carry the onanistic connotation it has since acquired.

Unlike the dismal hutted camps, Spangenberg was full of ancient character and charm and I was soon absorbed in exploring every nook and cranny of that old Schloss, especially the bits that were locked up or wired off or had *Verboten* (Forbidden) notices on them. It was an exciting pastime and, of course, the ultimate motive for all this was escape. I was beginning to see possibilities when we were again ordered to pack. We were bound for the mysterious, dreaded Reprisal Camp in Poland.

The laborious stop-go train journey with all its shunting and waiting was more of a nightmare than the previous ones. We were cramped, there were more guards, and the carriage windows were wired up. Even so, Pissy Edwards, "Nellie" Ellen of the RAF and a soldier, Lieutenant John Surtees, all managed to jump off the train in motion. Train jumping was crazily heroic in my opinion, and sadly, they were soon recaptured, Pissy Edwards having first lain unconscious for an hour after hitting his head on a railway line.

We eventually arrived at a town on the River Vistula called Thorn, pronounced "Torn" by the Germans and "Torrun" by the Poles. This was the location of Stalag XX-A, a new camp, or rather complex of camps scattered throughout the local area, that would eventually hold some 20,000 Allied prisoners. Our night arrival was another of those dramatically stage-managed Nazi intimidations which the Germans had become so good at. There was something truly operatic about it and the organisers seemed to wallow in the atmosphere of harsh oppression and hopelessness they had created. Millions of Jews knew more about that than we ever did. When we were ordered out of the train, we found ourselves once again in a brilliantly floodlit area surrounded by a large force of German soldiers with rifles, sub-machine guns and guard dogs.

A new type of character appeared on this scene in the form of some thick-necked thugs swinging long rubber truncheons and, behind the whole lot, a number of armoured cars were revving their engines and making big play with their armament and spotlights. It looked from their expressions as if everyone there had been carefully briefed for his part in this Super Horror Spectacular and, knowing the Nazi national mentality, I bet they had, too.

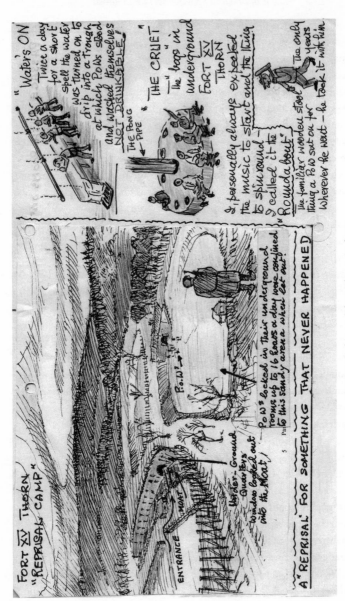

Vignettes of camp life in Thorn-Podgorz.

As I disembarked from the train, I knelt down on one knee, ostensibly to re-tie a shoelace, but really to take a peek under the train's buffers to see what was on the other side. Our gallant foes had thought of that one too and I spotted some Germans standing back in the shadows with Schmeissers at the rabbiting position. I swiftly decided that second thoughts were wiser ones. We were marched out of the town to an old underground fort named "Hermann von Salza". It, and several others like it, had been constructed by the Germans to face Russia when they occupied the area in Bismarck's time, some sixty years previously. From a distance it would appear as a slight mound in the countryside with slits for rifles and dark menacing gun-ports for cannon, mostly facing eastwards towards the River Vistula.

Surrounding the central bastion, which grew up to little above ground level, there was an enormous moat dry except for a stinking open sewer-like ditch running along its centre. The entrance was a cutting into the outside of the mound approached by an iron bridge which disappeared into a dark cave-like entrance to the central bastion. As we were herded across the iron bridge into that dark yawning mouth, I felt that if ever a destination deserved the front door inscription "Abandon Hope All Ye Who Enter Here", this one was it!

To top the lot, the place had a strange stink about it. Inside the entrance, we were herded downwards into a huge brick tunnel, with flaky whitewashed walls, dimly lit by the occasional glimmer of a small electric light bulb. The walls were hung with pipes and cables and every so often, a heavy wooden door occurred. These were opened as we went along and we were taken, sixteen at a time, into vaulted rooms which were really large cells with one heavily barred window at the end looking out into the dry moat with its smelly ditch. Each long wall of these cells was lined with the usual double-decker bunk beds. Each cell had a narrow wooden table in the middle with sixteen wooden stools. Sanitation for the cell was an open-topped "jam tin" of about two gallons capacity. We were told that we were to be locked in these rooms from teatime to breakfast time each day. With such primitive sanitation and so many people soon developing bowel problems it was not nice. To top it all off, we soon discovered the palliasses were infested with fleas and bed bugs.

We had joined several contingents of British army officers on leaving Schloss Spangenberg and had been mixed up with them so that I found myself the only RAF prisoner of war in a room of Army officers, and what a superb bunch of men they were! They had been prisoners for longer than me. Many of them were Territorial Army reservists who had dropped their civilian professions at the outbreak of war and joined up. Nearly all of them had been taken prisoner in France after gallant last stands at places like Saint-Valéry. They had been the hard-fighting rear guard for the successful evacuation of the British Expeditionary Force from Dunkirk. Some of them were middle aged and wore First World War medal ribbons. There were even one or two who had been prisoners previously, poor chaps! One army contingent had come from a similar underground fort at Posen where they had been held for a while before all the Fort Henry nonsense blew up. On arrival at Thorn as a reprisal, some of them said they were pleased with their "slightly improved conditions".

One outstanding character in that room was Captain John Mansel, who had been an architect in peacetime. John was a talented artist, caricaturist and humourist who became an outstanding forger of false identity documents, gate passes for bogus guards, travel permits and other such skullduggerous items required by escapers. John also trained others and became the leader of a thriving and essential industry.

On our first morning there, having been let out of our "bedroom" cell, we discovered further horrors of our new home. The only water available in the fort was unfit for drinking without boiling. Our washing facility was a long stone trough above which ran a rusty iron pipe with a tiny hole drilled under it every two feet or so. From this the cold water trickled meanly for an hour in the morning and an hour before we were locked in our rooms in the late afternoon. There is, though, something of artistry to be found even in the most desperate environment. At Thorn, it was the toilets which captured my imagination and charmed me, apart from their awful stink. To enter the "throne room", one climbed a flight of wooden steps as if to the scaffold and entered a perfectly round brick chamber like the inside of a medieval tower. There, at the centre, in all its magnificent proportions, was a twenty-four holer! No unimaginative straight row of gaping holes for this one, but a cunningly constructed edifice which was a masterpiece of joinery. The happy customers sat side by side in contemplation facing outwards in a circle—or rather on one side of whatever you would call a hexagon with twenty-four faces. The centre of this monster thunder box rose solidly into the ceiling, presumably serving the pit below as ventilation. Sitting there in the mornings, I sometimes eschewed the socialising which went on and let my imagination run free. I was waiting for the organ to start playing and for its steam engine to start driving the whole thing round and round, and for a gypsy lad to demand my fare of tuppence as they did on the roundabouts at the annual fair when I was a little boy in Orsett.

My own everlasting impression of Thorn was of those long dim tunnels. For years after the war they were the subject of occasional nightmares during which I was being chased along them for my life. The dreams gradually became less regular as the years went by, but very occasionally I am back there again, and the tunnels are endless.

During the day, we were permitted into the open air in the centre of the fort where there was a sandy yard below ground level surrounded by the huge grassy earthworks on which our guards stood with rifles and a few swinging truncheons. Admittedly they never used the latter to my knowledge, but they were quite impressive to begin with. It was also an unhappy and sobering discovery that this totally enclosed yard had been used by the Germans for executing Poles by firing squad. Very practical people, the Nazis!

On our first day out, the Goons sprung a search on us. While parties of them combed through our meagre belongings in our rooms, we were taken one by one from the sandy yard for a personal search. Some bright boys who had contraband on them at the time surreptitiously dug holes in the sand with their feet and buried what they could, hoping to retrieve it later. Unfortunately, this was spotted and some treasures unearthed by the Germans, which was hard luck, but gave me a splendid idea for the next search, and I prepared for it with infantile glee.

I knew another search would inevitably come before long and it did. It followed the same pattern and the Goons were especially on the lookout for illicit burials or abandonment of "hot" material. My first action in the mêlée was to drop, not too far scattered, the many pieces of a torn-up "secret message", fairly easily decipherable but not, of course, in my own handwriting. This, to my intense satisfaction, was eventually gathered up piece by piece by a meticulous Goon with a look of shining triumph on his face.

Then I buried under the sand, with one corner of it "carelessly" left peeping out of the surface, a map of the fort with intricate instructions upon it. Some other hero found that too. I hugged myself with childish pleasure as I envisaged them in the Security Office following the tortuous instructions on the map—obviously a cunningly devised escape route—which led eventually to "Black Bartholomew's Buried Treasure".

Another scene I joyfully imagined was the German Security Staff as they painstakingly pieced together the jigsaw of my torn-up copy of a message which was clearly marked "TOP SECRET" and identified as a communication from "The Espionage Section of the British Military Intelligence Contingent, Thorn" to "British Military Intelligence Headquarters, Whitehall, London". The Germans were always terribly impressed with any mention of British Intelligence, which they believed was far more effective and ubiquitous than it actually was at that time. The message, in difficult writing, described how, after gathering all available information from all sources, both civilian and military, through channels which could not be divulged for security reasons, the Central Committee of the Espionage System had come to the inescapable conclusion that Adolf Hitler was a "Megalomaniac Prize Prick".

I discovered afterwards, to my glee, that one or two other characters had been up to much the same sort of prank with delightful variations. We were later paraded and informed by the outraged *Kommandant* that it was *verboten* to ridicule the Führer or the Wehrmacht or the Reich or the German people. We all stood in sombre innocence with pained and puzzled expressions as if we had no idea what the man was ranting on about.

For some of us, Goon-baiting gradually became a facet of prison life and, as the years went by and we suffered more frustration, more provocation and more retaliatory persecution, so we became more proficient at it. There were always one or two prisoners, usually the stuffier type or more elderly army officer, who tut-tutted a bit, but usually with a very obvious twinkle in their eye. There were even a very few who were simply jealous of their petty comforts and privileges which they considered threatened by any behaviour which might upset the Germans. Those very few people were despised.

We had more understanding, but little sympathy, for those who regarded our high spirits and disrespectful conduct as something which jarred against their ingrained sense of military propriety and what was traditionally "conduct becoming an officer and a gentleman". But no amount of German military bowing and heel-clicking cut any ice with some of us, especially the more we learned of Nazi inhumanity, the barbarous concentration camps, and the murderous execution of our commandoes and of recaptured escapee POWs.

At Thorn, the Germans thought it would be a good idea to have us learn their language. It is odd how everybody thinks everybody else ought to speak their mother tongue, useful or not. In this case, it was useful—for escaping! So, as a dear old primary schoolmasterish German senior NCO began to give us lessons, we must have presented a very odd spectacle—a room full of rumbustious, tough fighting men singing, docilely and with apparent glee, under teacher's direction the nursery rhyme:

> *Hopp, hopp, hopp,*
> *Pferdchen lauf gallop,*
> *Über Stock und über Steine*
> *Aber brich dir nicht die Beine.*
> *Hopp, hopp, hopp, hopp, hopp,*
> *Pferdchen lauf gallop.*

As we sang about the dear little horsie galloping and hopping over sticks and stones, and telling it to be careful not to hurt its little self by breaking its bones, perhaps the Germans thought we were a bunch of ninnies. We certainly thought they were, to encourage us to learn German and become more efficient escapers.

Personally, I never tried to learn the German language in the recognised formal manner. That way you could never hope to pass yourself off as a native. My technique was to hear a German use an extremely useful phrase and to practise it to perfection with an absolutely natural German speaker like John Milner, who was born in Germany and had spent his school days there. This resulted in an amusing incident later on. While being interrogated by several German officers following my recapture after an escape, I demanded the service of an interpreter as my right under the Geneva Convention. One irritated German asked *Kann er nicht Deutsch sprechen?* ("Can't he speak German?") and another replied, *Ja! Perfekt, wenn er will!* ("Yes! Perfectly, when he wants to!")

From a humanitarian organisation in Switzerland, we were sent and, strangely enough in a reprisal camp, allowed to receive, a wind-up gramophone and a selection of classical records. I attended a musical concert held in a windowless vaulted room which seated about thirty prisoners who brought their wooden stools with them. I sat at the back in a dark corner. There was not a sound throughout, except for the music of Beethoven and Wagner (only Aryan composers were permitted). Sitting in that cell full of dark huddled forms, I felt attuned to the spirits of those other men. I thought too of their undoubted emotions, pondering the brutalities of war while listening to the ethereal quality of music that seemed to transcend all human divisions of race and ideology. I was deeply touched and at the same time appalled at the nature of my own species which could produce such divine music and practise such inhumanity. I began silently and very secretly to shed tears. I felt pretty desolate for a couple of days afterwards and never again listened to serious music in prison camp. I stuck to the frivolous which could not stir the depths and I never shed another tear during my entire time in captivity, not one, no matter what!

Needless to say, while all this was going on, my main attention was given to planning methods of escape. Grim as the set-up looked at first, it was really a piece of porous cake from the escaper's point of view. Getting out of the fort was going to be relatively easy. From most freshly occupied prisons, it usually is. The trick is to envisage your scheme quickly and book it before somebody else does, because as soon as they are tried, the various avenues of escape are blocked up. Any prison, therefore, becomes more escape-proof as time goes by, and successful schemes have to be progressively more brilliant or dangerous.

My departure from the fort posing no great problem, the next and vital question was, what next? One advantage was that we were now in a friendly, if oppressed, country. The Poles are a proud and very brave people with a fierce sense of national honour, and could be relied upon not to give an escaper away, even if they were unable or too frightened to help very much. They were not divided among themselves like the French, some of whom were supporters of the new Vichy Government under Pétain and to some extent willing collaborators with the Germans.

We were not too far from the Baltic and about equidistant from the port of Danzig and from Warsaw: the first meant ships to Sweden, the second provided the shelter and anonymity of a large city. What I did not like about Warsaw was that it appeared to me to be a one-way destination, and this proved to be the case for several escapers from Thorn. Mike Sinclair, Gris Davies-Scourfield and Ronnie Littledale were all sheltered there for months, but their escape attempts ended in disaster. Some officers in Warsaw had experiences at the hands of the Gestapo after recapture and saw devilish things in concentration camps before they were recaptured. Being men who knew too much, they were sent to Colditz where I met them and heard their ghastly stories. No, Warsaw never seemed like a good bet to me. I could not justify in my own mind putting gallant Polish civilians lives at risk. Apart from that, my great hankering was still to fly out of captivity and, unless there existed a compelling reason for trying another easier and more certain way, this remained my set intention.

One essential ingredient to planning a successful run after escaping is outside knowledge. There was none of this vital information available at Barth, not until people like myself and Bill Fowler had been adrift. At Thorn the situation was quite different. A few miles away there were other branch camps of the Stalag XX-A complex, including Thorn-Podgorz, for British Army NCOs and other ranks. Unlike officers, who according to the Geneva Convention were not required to work, lower ranking prisoners could be used by their captors for non-combatant labour. Troops held at Thorn-Podgorz were sent out on various work parties, one of which came into our fort daily to work as orderlies. We officers did not necessarily regard our privileged status as something to be prized. Any truly escape-minded officer would have joyfully volunteered to work anywhere at anything for the Germans if it offered good chances of escape.

The fine Scottish troops, periodically marched in to provide services to us, were invaluable sources of neighbourhood information. Having been out on other work parties, they had an excellent knowledge of the

surroundings and my immediate resolve was to find a volunteer among
them who would like to become an officer for the rest of the war, while I
clipped my hair to a short stubble and joined their happy band of workers.
Then I learned that one work party regularly went out from their camp
to pick up stones off the Luftwaffe's local grass airfield called Graudenz.
I was immediately full of resolve about this and invited two other pilots,
Don Thom and "Errol" Flinn, to join in my scheme. Lastly I found some
mischievous Jocks from the Highland Division who were delighted to
become officers on a temporary basis, and we were on our way.

We three pilots, having become Privates McLean, Menzies and Shand
(or whoever) were quite confident we should have no problem getting out
of Hermann von Salza, provided we did not bump into "Scarface" on the
way out of our fort's main gate. Scarface was a particularly bright German
Feldwebel (the equivalent of a sergeant) who was always around and
appeared to know just about everybody in the camp by sight. More on the
ball than the Nazi Security Officer, he would become the greatest danger to
escape activities despite being quite good-natured and reasonably sporting
about the whole thing.

When Scarface was not scrutinising the traffic through the gate or
poking his nose into quiet corners of the fort looking for nefarious
activities, he was an inveterate "plinker" with a small-bore rifle who stalked
the premises in search of vermin and game. He used to toss the odd crow
or cat to prisoners, all of which, I am told, were gratefully received for the
cooking pot. Above all, Scarface had a sense of humour.

As our working party formed up and started to march out with our escort
of real German guards, our hearts sank as we spotted our friend Scarface
on the bridge. I brought out a handkerchief and covered my face with it as I
blew my nose and the others did something or other, all of which probably
made us look more obviously furtive, but just at that moment, a German
officer approached from the other direction. Scarface sprang to attention
and saluted as the officer spoke to him. By the time he had finished, we
were past him and on our way.

At Thorn-Podgorz we immediately made ourselves known to the "man
of confidence", the equivalent of our SBO in an officers' camp. Sadly, I forget
his name but he was a great chap who accepted us without question and

undertook to cooperate fully. This was essential as it was he who detailed the men for the various working parties.

Two days later we were off to Graudenz aerodrome. Our hope was that we would be able to slink off from the party, quietly board a dispersed aircraft, start up and head for Sweden. In a relatively slow Junkers F.13. which we gathered were plentiful, our flying time from Thorn would be about one hour to the coast plus another hour to Sweden. Our aim was to fly at roof-top height on an erratic course to throw off interception. The F.13 was a small single-engined version of the well-known three-engined Junkers 52 transport, having a similar fixed undercarriage and a corrugated skin which, in my opinion, always made them look like a flying hen house.

We spent several consecutive days working on that airfield and once again realised that escape moves must never be planned as a result of imagining favourable circumstances. The single engined F-13s were there all right, and dispersed, but they were guarded by patrolling sentries. Our work party was so split up and carelessly guarded that it would have been quite easy to slip away from the airfield and seek help from the local Poles who we knew would be cooperative. The others were in favour of this plan, but I was dead against it for two reasons. Firstly, I was still determined to fly out of captivity, thereby evening the score; secondly, I was unwilling to expose our Polish friends to certain execution if the Germans caught them helping us. As I was the acknowledged leader of the escape, having invited the others to join in, they very decently respected that. I suggested we treat our visits to the airfield as a reconnaissance; reverse our escape back into our own prison; and there plan a more viable scheme preferably using Luftwaffe working uniforms to get into the aircraft.

Meanwhile we instructed the troops in the work party to pick up all the harmless rounded stones and to set all the sharp-edged ones into the ground at an angle best calculated to damage tyres. They set about this revised task with gusto. They were a spirited bunch of lads and we were sorry to leave their cheerful company.

Our work done, we proceeded to execute our scheme, something rather unusual in escaping annals. We marched back into our own prison camp where we immediately set about making Luftwaffe working uniforms similar to the one I had made for my escape from Barth. Wearing those, we would stand a reasonable chance of boarding one of those guarded German aircraft after having, once again, changed identity with the Jocks to escape from Thorn. They had been made thoroughly at home with their new officer colleagues and had greatly enjoyed their elevated status and seeing how the other half lived. They were perfectly willing to give it another go.

By this time, several other escapers had latched onto the change of identity lark and I became concerned lest, by the time we were ready to go again, this simple process would have been blown. For this reason, I suggested we make a German army uniform in addition to our simple Luftwaffe working rigs so that we could, if necessary, use my second escape plan—to go out as a completely bogus working party with a bogus guard an' all! The escape committee gave me excellent support and a team of experts got down to making a uniform complete with a perfect dummy Mauser rifle and a bayonet in a scabbard to be worn on the belt.

All was about ready to go using the same method as before, when I went down with meningitis. As the camp Doc later told me, I very nearly kicked the bucket, having gone from a very high fever to a full-fledged coma. Our medical facilities were rough and ready with few drugs available: one room had been set aside as a sick bay but at least we had our own British medical officer and a medical orderly, both of the Royal Army Medical Corps. It was some comfort to have one's life teetering in the hands of friends rather than enemies, not that I knew one from the other during the time I was in my feverish limbo.

As I became more *compos mentis*, I was faced with a hard decision. Our doctor said it would take quite some time before I would be fit enough to escape again and the escape committee asked me if I would agree to somebody else taking my place. It was a terribly disappointing situation after all the hard work and hope I had put into the scheme's preparation but, as I knew in my heart, the medics were right—I was as weak as a kitten. Many other people had worked hard on the thing too and their hopes were running equally high. Furthermore, it was only a matter of time before the Germans caught on to the change-of-identities caper. There was no argument about who had originated the whole thing but I had to admit to myself that it was pretty decent of them to give me the chance to opt out gracefully. I had to make the decision about who should go in my place. There were many fine chaps to choose from and I thought hard about it.

In the end I asked a Canadian chum, "Don" Donaldson, if he would like to go. Don, sometimes known as "Weasel" because of his small stature, was quite a character with a manner rather like that of Groucho Marx of the famous Marx Brothers. His remarks were very brief and to the point and he was inclined to be very rude to people he liked and meticulously polite and reserved to people he didn't. He was always extremely rude to me which, under the circumstances, I found very gratifying.

Don Donaldson was, like me, a Hampden pilot. In April 1940 he had been flying in a formation of twenty-four Hampdens sent on a daylight sortie to attack German warships thought to be in the vicinity of Kristiansand Harbour in Norway. Hampdens in daylight were no match for German fighters, and when a swarm of Messerschmidt Bf 109s showed up, the tragic results were all too predictable. Six of the tail enders of the formation were shot down almost immediately. Don's Hampden was one of them, going down in flames with a dead rear-gunner, while a Bf 109 continued to blaze away for all he was worth from astern. Don, who always had a poetic turn of phrase to describe such situations, told me, "Gee, Pete, I didn't know whether to shit or go blind!" I knew exactly how he must have felt.

Poor Don somehow managed to crash-land his burning aircraft on a small island just off the Norwegian coast. Beside the dead rear-gunner, there was his badly burned wireless operator, Corporal Henry, and an injured navigator, Flying Officer Middleton. In fact Donaldson was the only one completely unscathed out of the twenty-four men shot down. Twenty-one of them were dead already or died in their rubber dinghy after ditching in the sea. Fortunately, two fishermen rescued the survivors and took the injured men to hospital. A Norwegian doctor told Don that the Germans were approaching rapidly. He also told Don one of the Bf 109s that had attacked his formation had run out of fuel and force-landed nearby. The German pilot had been locked up.

Don immediately decided to try an escape to England in the 109 and he and the doctor refuelled it with ordinary car petrol. With help, they removed the seat from the single-seat fighter and managed to put Henry, burns and all, flat on the floor of the aircraft. Middleton sat on the empty seat frame and Donaldson sat on Middleton's lap with his head so high that they had to discard the cockpit canopy.

Our hero then made three attempts to take off with the 109, which didn't much like low-octane car fuel for a short, overweight take-off. Two attempts were aborted and on the third attempt they struck a tree and smashed a wing. Miraculously, none of our lads was further injured but that was the end of that caper. Henry was returned to the hospital while Donaldson and Middleton were taken to a hide-out a few miles up the coast and an arrangement was made for them to be picked up by a neutral Swedish boat. Unfortunately, the Germans arrived before the boat and that was that.

Don received no recognition for his heroic attempt, but I thought he at least deserved my place on the team to nick an aircraft from Graudenz *Flugplatz*. So I chose him as my replacement and he accepted with alacrity.

A few days later the Germans told us with some truculence that Don Donaldson, Don Thom and "Errol" Flinn had been caught on the airfield attempting to take an aircraft and were in big trouble. The Germans seemed reluctant to say what had happened to them and there were conflicting stories about their fate, but they were never seen again at Thorn. It was sad and very worrying.

By the time I was out of the sick bay, and strong enough to get down to serious escape activities again, the scene had changed considerably. Escapers had been getting out of the fort by various methods, mostly involving exchanges of identity with the army prisoners from Thorn-Podgorz one way or another. Two Fleet Air Arm airmen, Allan Cheetham and "Pud" Davis, had discovered an old abandoned tunnel and tried to get through it only to find themselves facing a machine gun. They were lucky to survive.

Flight Lieutenant Eric Foster had planned to go out in a visiting cart but abandoned the scheme just in time to avoid capture because of more stringent security measures. He then changed identity with an orderly working in the prison store but that also came to nothing. The Germans then discovered another orderly standing in for Lieutenant John Hyde-Thompson of the Durham Light Infantry and his plan was scuppered.

In mid-April Flight Lieutenant Norman "Brickie" Forbes and Lieutenant Airey Neave visited Thorn-Podgorz where a British medical officer was resident as a dentist. By previous crafty arrangements they changed identity with two soldiers from Neave's own army company and were smuggled into their sleeping quarters. Sent out on a suitable working party, they easily escaped from that and set course on a long march to Russia, reasonably disguised and with a fair stock of food. Their phoney ID documents had been provided by our expert, John Mansel, back at Thorn. After many hardships and close calls with suspicious Nazis, Neave and Forbes were caught and given a rough time at the hands of the Gestapo who accused them of being spies. Luckily for them they were eventually believed and returned to Thorn, where Scarface locked them into two disgusting cells in the moat. About the same time, Auntie Paddon and Big Steve from Barth were caught trying to escape in a dust cart which led Auntie to tell a particularly objectionable German NCO his fortune. This contributed to one of the charges at a court martial which he eventually had to face.

Meanwhile, the indomitable Eric Foster—still under an unserved sentence from Spangenberg—had prepared a bedsheet rope and manufactured a scaling ladder with a large hook at one end. One night in mid-May he managed to lower himself into the moat, but as he prepared to start hauling himself out the other side, one of his ladder chains broke with a loud clatter. The wandering searchlight exposed him and guards started screaming, with the predictable unpleasant results. Foster thought his end was nigh.

As a result of all this escape activity the German security department had tightened things up. Our orderlies had to live in our prison so that there could be no more simple identity swaps, and any guard escorting prisoners out of the fort had to have a signed and stamped pass authorising him to do so. Escaping from Thorn had become much more difficult. I had foreseen it would, and for this reason I had set in motion the manufacturing of a complete guard's uniform, with rifle and bayonet for a more complicated effort. Once fit enough, I began planning my next attempt, this time with our best German speaker, John Milner, who, as a bogus guard, was to march me out of the fort as an orderly on some chore. The camp escape committee, though, thought this too good a scheme to be left to the pair of us, and fastened upon us an expanded party of other "orderlies". These were to be Geoff Dodgson, the irrepressible Pissy Edwards, and two army officers I hardly knew. My heart sank as this would be stretching the odds somewhat, but it is best to be gracious and public-spirited about such things, so Milner and I agreed to give it a go. We planned to split up into three pairs and go our own ways, if and when we managed to get out of the fort.

Then, in the late spring of 1941, with our preparations well advanced, something happened which affected our personal fortunes. This was the dramatic flight to Scotland of the deputy Führer of Germany, Rudolf Hess. A painfully loyal but not very bright devotee of Adolf Hitler, Hess took it into his head to fly to Britain and negotiate a peace agreement that would free Germany to concentrate on the imminent attack on the Soviet Union. For some reason, he seems to have believed that this would be a fairly simple task to accomplish. At all events, his flight was an extraordinary one. Borrowing a twin-engined Bf 110 long-range fighter, he flew nearly 1,000 miles, evading several British fighters sent up to intercept him, and baled out in the dark just a dozen miles from his intended destination. Needless to say, the British, treating him as the lunatic he undoubtedly was, declined to enter into negotiations. An embarrassed Hitler was forced to announce publicly that Hess had gone mad. Germans suspected of being in the know about his half-baked mission were arrested and a great fuss was made about illegitimate use of Luftwaffe aircraft. Security was to be intensified and seen to be so, and that is how things stood just as John Milner and I were ready to attempt to steal an aeroplane from Graudenz. Donaldson's attempt to do the same thing two months previously hadn't helped either, but we were still determined to have a go.

"Millie" and I formulated detailed plans for the airfield. Because any notices in the cockpit about "do this and don't do that," would be in German, we agreed that Millie would be first into the aircraft to do the starting up and take-off. Meanwhile, I was to stand by to deal with anybody who tried to interfere at the very last moment, or who was actually in the aircraft we wanted to take.

The question of when and how much violence to use was a tricky one. There could be no question of using violence unless we were certain we were away for good. When a man's life is spared to make him a prisoner of war, it is understood that he is bound by international law to forsake all violence against his captors which, if committed, becomes a criminal act—or so we were told. To kill one of them was, legally, to commit murder for which death was the penalty. I suppose that is really quite reasonable—not that our Nazi captors were always concerned about what was "reasonable".

Millie and I agreed that over the Baltic, I was to take over the controls so that we should share the exhilaration of flying our way to freedom. The likelihood of German fighters being scrambled to intercept us did not bear thinking about—so we didn't! If one always worried about the "what if" factor, nothing would ever get done about anything.

The new forgery department under John Mansel had produced a copy of the normal pass for working parties to go out through the gate. This would, if necessary, be flashed by Millie at the guard on the bridge leading out of the fort. We still had neither German money nor the identity documents which successful escapers were to have later in the war, so our way out of Germany was essentially by air or not at all.

While such final niceties were being perfected, we all became excited by the heavy train traffic on the railway line just outside the fort. Trains by the dozen were rumbling westward empty and those going eastward were loaded with troops and military supplies, not least of which were lorries and tanks galore. During daylight hours, we counted the trains and estimated their contents. It was obvious that something very big was afoot and we were desperate to know how to get detailed information about this back to England. We had the means by codes—mine to Ann being one of them—to get short "telegrammed" messages back, but such a wealth of information called for something more detailed.

I thought of this very seriously and had a brainwave. The Germans took photographs of us which they sold at high prices. We were permitted occasionally to sew a photograph onto a letter for home. The army officers' mail took about a month each way, but the Luftwaffe insisted that the mail of RAF officers should be censored by them as well. This meant our mail had to go through the Luftwaffe Intelligence Department in Berlin and resulted in it taking about twice as long.

My idea was to take two postcard-sized photographs, carefully sandpaper the face side off one to half thickness and the reverse side of the other one down to half thickness, place a message in plain language between them, and stick the two halves together again round the edges. It turned out to be not merely as simple as that and I had to develop quite a process so that nothing showed even if the photograph were looked at with a powerful light behind it. For testing, I made a box with an electric light in it and a piece of glass from a broken window.

I found there was no way I could make my miniature writing invisible over the light except where the photograph was black. I therefore eventually selected a photograph of some Royal Navy officers taken at the funeral of one of their number who had recently died in the Spangenberg Lower Camp. The naval uniforms provided plenty of black. I also found that if the two halves of the photograph were glued together only at the edges, it was just possible for the two halves to bow outwards and this would not do. It had to be glued at as many points as possible.

Eventually, I took a piece of flimsy translucent toilet paper and faintly traced out the black areas. Within these areas I wrote my message with a pencil sharpened to a needle point. I got my writing down to microscopic size and was able to write nearly a hundred-word message in plain language. I then cut out all the areas of the bog bumph which were not written upon, placed the paper against the back-side of the photograph, carefully and very lightly glued the unwritten areas and the edges of the card and pressed the reverse side of the half thickness postcard into place. This was then put under pressure until it was dry and a minute amount was trimmed off the four edges with a razor blade, effectively obliterating all signs of a join.

The finished article tested over my light box revealed nothing at all. Those of us in the know, including my new army friends, John Mansel and "Scotty" Scott-Martin who had given me every encouragement, were tremendously excited. We knew it was a risky business because this was espionage, and it was not known where a prisoner of war stood if caught out at that game. We all supposed there was a chance it could mean a firing squad and our excitement was considerably tempered with apprehension.

The matter came up about air force mail taking much longer to get home than army mail, and Scott-Martin made what I consider was a very gallant offer under the circumstances, permitting me to send the letter with his name printed on the back as the *Absender*. I agreed to this on the following conditions: that it was all done in my handwriting which could be identified if it came to the crunch; that he would send his full quota of legitimate letters for that month and that my quota would be one short; and that the letter had to go to one of my correspondents who would know to pass it on to Ann, who would decipher the coded letter giving instructions about the photograph.

That meant that Scotty should be absolved of all blame if there was a misfire. In reality, although I insisted that I would take full responsibility if anything went wrong, I doubt if the Germans would have been very fussy about whether they shot one or two of us if they were angry enough. I therefore maintain that Scotty's offer was a gallant one and deserved recognition—not that either of us got any in the end.

I sent the letter to my old nanny, Edie, because nearly all mine went to Ann, and it was just possible that her name might have rung a bell in the mind of some alert censor. He might wonder why Captain Scott-Martin was writing to Flying Officer Tunstall's fiancée, and become suspicious. The letter would be gibberish to Edie and the photograph a mystery, but the letter did say "please show this letter to Auntie Ann". She would twig that bit. Ann would see my indicator that there was code and the coded message was "with extreme care, split open this photograph".

In the event it all worked out perfectly, and this was only the first of several such messages I sent home, all of which were received by MI9. I was told after the war that they had been quite excited about this new development and were recommending me for an award. I still have in my possession that original postcard which was returned to Ann by MI9. The others, I believe, are in their museum.

As for the value of our information, it was only a drop in the bucket. But it is the accumulation of drops from various intelligence-gathering sources that lead eventually to the acceptance of a belief upon which decisions are made. We now know that our drop arrived in the bucket at the very time Winston Churchill and his colleagues were trying to decide whether Germany intended to invade Russia. The main flow of information on this subject no doubt came from the interception of German wireless messages which our cryptographers had broken. The problem with code messages, though, is that one never knows whether the enemy has tumbled to the fact that their code has been broken. If they have, they are liable to continue using it to feed false information. That is why confirmation sources like ours became desirable, if not essential.

Our intelligence activities behind us, the day for our big break arrived at last. Our greatest worry was that Scarface might stick his nose into things at the crucial moment, and it was arranged that another officer in my room, Captain Earle Edwards, whose German was coming on well, would collar Scarface on some urgent pretext and take him off to a remote corner of the fort during the vital period. John Milner and I both had our Luftwaffe working uniforms under our outer clothing—Millie's excellent German army uniform with belt, bayonet in its scabbard and rifle slung on his shoulder, and Tunstall in his British army orderly's khaki greatcoat and field service cap.

In the fort's main exit tunnel we assembled quickly and Milner rapped out the order to "*Marsch!*" Out we went towards the bridge, laughing and joking in a very relaxed manner, until Milner, bringing up the rear, barked harshly at us, "*Maule halten*" ("Shut your traps"). The guard on the bridge heard and saw Milner and started to unlock the gate.

This time, thanks to Edwards, there was no sign of Scarface. The guard opened the gate and we had passed through when he yelled, "*Halt!*" We were now outside and Millie, following behind us, was face-to-face with him. They started talking and I saw Milner bring out the pass. Not far ahead were some trees and bushes by the side of the road and several of us started to edge towards them. "*Halt!*" screamed the gate guard and let fly a string of German invective. Milner went on talking to him. Then, to our tremendous relief, the guard began to shut the gate and Milner strolled nonchalantly towards us and told us to get on. We gladly did so, rounded a bend, and ducked into a wood where we laughed off some tension. We changed into our final rig, shook hands all round, wished each other good luck and dispersed on our various adventures.

"What was biting that Goon on the gate?" I asked Millie.

"Nothing. He just wanted to pass the time of day."

We had walked out of Fort Hermann von Salza in the mid-morning and by early afternoon we were outside the barbed wire fence surrounding

Graudenz *Flugplatz* just outside the town of Thorn itself. There was all the usual activity of a Luftwaffe base, but the increased number of sentries patrolling the perimeter since my last visit immediately impressed me. Where aircraft were parked at dispersal points, more sentries strolled to and fro while mechanics worked on the machines, thanks to Herr Hess (and also, as we later learned, Herr Donaldson).

We felt vulnerable as we walked round the outside of the wire looking for an entry point. We would be less conspicuous and attract less suspicion once we were inside and could mix in the general activities. Eventually, we came across an overgrown ditch running under the fence. Choosing our moment when patrolling sentries were reasonably far away on their beat, we crawled along the ditch, under the wire, and when we figured nobody was looking our way, we stood up from the weeds and started to walk briskly round the inside perimeter.

At the first opportunity, we picked up a couple of ground markers and carried them as if they were due for re-painting or replacing. At least this made us look busy and purposeful. For the rest of the afternoon, we walked about the airfield, picking up and carrying one thing after another from here to there and back again. It must have taken the Luftwaffe a week to find half the things we moved around that afternoon.

At last we chose our aircraft. It was a Ju-F.13 standing close by an air raid shelter which would provide us with a hiding place until we were ready to make our bid. Moreover, a ground crew was running the engine by which we knew the thing was serviceable and the engine would be already warmed up for us. This meant we could leap aboard, start up and belt straight off, whereas to do this with a stone cold engine could easily be risking an engine cut on take-off. We slipped into the air raid shelter and watched events in a state of great nervous excitement.

Matters worked out better and better. When the mechanics finished testing the engine to their satisfaction, and ours, they refuelled the aircraft for which we were also duly grateful. Everything was going our way and our hopes were as high as our excitement. Then the mechanics got out of the aircraft, which had a cabin door—not a cockpit canopy—and did not lock the door after them. It was about 5.00 pm and we noticed that our mechanics were not the only ones to start walking off towards the hangars and technical site. Others were doing so from other aircraft. It was obviously knocking-off time.

The sentry in his steel helmet and with rifle slung on his shoulder continued to make a regular beat from one end of this line of several aircraft to the other. He was doing this regularly and his movements had become predictable. As he passed our air raid shelter heading away from the direction of the hangars, I whispered to Millie, "Now! Let's go!"

We ran out very quietly behind the guard and made it to the aircraft. In the distance towards the hangars, we noticed another sentry approaching. He was far enough away not to worry us if we were quick. Millie opened the door of the F.13 and climbed aboard. I was about to climb in after him when our sentry broke his routine and turned back early. He came back towards us and approached quite casually. If he made trouble now, should I clobber him or not? Millie hesitated by the door; we knew it would take us minutes to sort out the starting procedure; and there could always be a bit of a trick about it that would delay us. Some aircraft are like that. The guard was still approaching from the hangars and was much nearer.

If we clobbered this one and the other guard noticed, the game would be up at once. At least we would have a rifle, but a shooting match would obviously alert the whole airfield. If we killed one or both and the engine didn't start, we would both be hanged for murder quite legally under the Geneva Convention. If the engine had been running, I believe neither of us would have thought twice about it—but at this stage, no, it was better to play it cool. We could move off and try again. That guard had no idea how his fate had been hanging in the balance as he strolled up to us and called in a friendly manner:

"Haven't you chaps finished yet?"

Millie, as arranged, did the talking and I have no criticism of the way he handled everything.

"*Ja*," he said, and with the air of a man brushing his hands together at the end of a job, he added, "Just finished."

It was our cue to jump down, close the door of the aircraft and start walking back to the hangars as all the others had done. The other guard was now almost upon us and we realised why ours had turned short. This other guard was his relief. As we walked away, the two guards met and exchanged greetings. They then went through the German set routine of handing over a guard post. They stood facing each other. They then stepped round each other like stiff dancers so that although they still faced each other, they had both re-orientated through 180 degrees. We supposed this was their method of delineating the moment when "I'm off, you're on."

By this time, we were twenty or more yards away and going at a brisk pace. It was a long walk to the hangars and once there, we knew we could conceal ourselves and make another plan. Unfortunately, the relieved guard was a normal human being. Why walk all that way on his own when he could have company?

"Hoi," he shouted, and in an almost injured voice, then added: "Wait for me!"

What could we do? I had confidence in Millie's German and could always play the strong silent type. We let the hurrying guard catch up with us with little option, running would have given the game away completely. I suppose Millie could have called back to the guard something quite friendly like, "Sorry, mate. We're late already. We've got to get a move on." We waited for the guard. He was a chatty fellow and as we walked along, Millie kept him going quite happily. Then, because he didn't recognise us, he asked quite amiably:

"Which *Kompanie* are you chaps in?"

A German *Kompanie* in the Luftwaffe was the equivalent of one of our Flights in the RAF and are lettered A, B and C. What came over Millie at that moment, I will never know.

"Number Two," he said.

"Number Two?" said the guard in surprise. "There is no Number Two." Then he looked at us more closely and suddenly the penny dropped. He jumped aside from us, unslung his rifle, slammed one up the spout and shouted, "*Hände hoch!*"

Sick at heart, we put up our hands and he marched us to the hangars, bringing up the rear with his rifle at the rabbiting position. Others saw us coming and ran out to see what was up. I had thoughtfully taken my Luftwaffe hat off. Millie had not and was clouted for it.

Contrary to what might have been expected, nobody took a sporting view of the matter, probably because they had stopped such a rocket over the Donaldson attempt. They were hopping mad and we were frankly apprehensive about the outcome. We were told that what we had attempted was sabotage and that we would be shot. Don Donaldson and the others having disappeared, we didn't know whether to believe them or not.

Chapter Eight

"What's the plan?"

John Milner and I were separated, and on return to Fort 15 at Thorn our treatment was unpleasant. It is something to be said for the Germans that we were never actually beaten up, but we were pushed around and bawled at quite a bit, which is dangerous. I have never resented having a strip torn off me by a senior officer I admired and respected, but I will not be shouted at by my inferiors. Nor will I be manhandled with impunity. I am not a brawler, largely because I do not like getting hurt. But if oafs push me around or shout at me, I am liable to cut loose, which is why such provocative treatment is dangerous. Maybe it was calculated to provoke us into conduct which would justify being beaten up or killed. It is quite possible.

I saw nothing of Millie for days. Meanwhile, I was slung into the most disgusting hole I had ever seen. It was at the bottom of the moat close to the open ditch and was, literally, a hole in the outside wall. It had a curved brick arch for the roof and a similar inverted arch for the floor. The iron bed stood across the bottom of the arch, cutting off the segment of a circle. The door was a heavy wooden one, and in the brickwork on each side of it there was an open rifle slit. What was left of the straw litter from the bed had been stuffed into the rifle slits by a previous occupant, probably Airey Neave or "Brickie" Forbes, presumably to keep out the cold. It also kept out the light. It was very chilly, especially at night, so I left the straw where it was and lived in the semi-darkness. Sanitation was the usual jam tin and this had not been emptied. It was half full of old faeces and mould. Once a day, a guard came with some slop and a hunk of bread, and twice an officer came who ranted about sabotage and the prospect of shooting me. I was not allowed to wash and spent most of the time shivering from a mixture of cold and apprehension.

173

I had never been very religious and my ideas about the whole subject were pretty muddled. It therefore seemed to me a despicable thing to start praying for deliverance as if one had really enjoyed faith all along but had only just realised it in the nick of time. On the other hand, here was a situation that demanded no stone be left unturned. If God was there, standing by just waiting to be asked for a helping hand, how could I possibly address Him? After all, you couldn't expect to con God even if you wanted to—which I did not. I pondered the situation for a long time and eventually decided to give it a go. I remember the substance of my prayer quite clearly.

"God, if You are there, I know that You will at least give me marks for honesty and that You will be too big to refuse me help just because I haven't joined the club. I need help desperately, but if I am to remain honest with You, I cannot make bargains. Maybe the Germans don't really intend to shoot us anyway. And if I get out of this now, how will I know whether it was with Your help or not? Even if I survive, I will not say to others it was because I prayed. Lots of survivors say that, but the non-survivors say nothing! If You will help me on this basis—thank You. If it should come to the worst, please give me strength to meet the end bravely."

It was all I could do and I have never said my survival was even partly due to prayer. I still do not know. If God were indeed there listening to my plea, I suppose He did give me a few marks for honesty, but how He must have smiled with pity at the arrogance and pride that still burned, even in those extreme moments. Perhaps it was my pathetic lack of humility that saved me. Perhaps He decided to give me some more rope.

Quite suddenly, the situation changed. I was taken to a reasonable cell at the outside end of the iron bridge and Millie was in an adjacent one. We could talk to each other quite easily. Millie had a good voice and we spent many hours singing lustily, including German songs which Millie taught me. This was good for our own morale and puzzled the Germans no end. After about ten days, we were let out, returned to the camp and nothing more was said about our escape. It was all rather mysterious until a German officer confided to me:

"You were very lucky," he said. "The *Kommandant* of the prison camp and the *Kommandant* of the *Flugplatz* had been in so much trouble over Donaldson's attempt that they decided to hush yours up."

"What happened to Donaldson and the others?"

"They have gone to a special prison."

This was cheering news. He was referring to Colditz, of course, and I met Don and the others there a year later. At the time Millie and I thought we were lucky not to have been sent to Colditz, but later I regretted that we had not.

I realised that our mistake at the aerodrome was waiting until everyone had finished work and deserted the aircraft. We should have made our bid during the hustle and bustle of the day. It was usually the way with escaping. One learned slowly by mistakes and bitter experience. I was certain that if I could have one more chance at the *Flugplatz*, there would be no mistakes, so I decided to have another go. I asked Millie if he would like to join me again, but he decided to give it a rest for a while. I resolved to go solo this time and to make a full Luftwaffe uniform rather than the simple fatigue rig. Wearing a formal uniform, I could give myself some worthwhile rank which would possibly help to keep inquisitive sentries at bay.

I had figured another possible way out through the moat and set to work on my new uniform. It was progressing nicely when we were told, without warning, to pack for another move, and the escape preparations were wasted. I could not even make a quick break through the moat for an unprepared run because such a scheme depended upon watching the movements of the sentries over a considerable period. A viable moment for the attempt would occur only occasionally and the opportunity would have to be seized there and then.

There had been two main purges of "bad boys" to Colditz. The first was in mid-April 1941 and consisted of my erstwhile fellow-escapers to the Thorn airfield, "Errol" Flinn, Don Thom and Don Donaldson. A second purge to Colditz a month later, just before the rest of us were all moved out of Thorn, included Airey Neave, "Brickie" Forbes, "Big Steve" Stevinson, and Auntie Paddon.

Having been ordered to pack for a move, I was not at all sorry when I learned that we were returning to Schloss Spangenberg. I had had more than enough of Thorn. Despite the opportunities it presented for getting beyond the wires and walls, it was the most desolate place I had ever been in or ever would. The peeling lime-washed walls of those dim vaults spoke only of war, of killing and destruction, of iron discipline and the misery of men away from home and all forms of tenderness.

Spangenberg was different. It was mellow, had marinated for centuries in all of life. Generations had lived their full existence here. There had been lovers and laughter, hopes and disappointments, striving and achievement, creation in the frescoes faded on the dining room wall, craftsmanship and artistry, and something left for me to feel like a living pulse. I felt I could take Spangenberg much longer if necessary, provided there was some glimmer of hope provided by escape attempts or the war ending—with all that promised of a new life with the lovely young woman who was waiting for me. The other grim places, I feared, would gradually dull my senses, and I hated them.

Kassel is situated in central Germany which was a disadvantage, but there was a military airfield near the town which was handy. The nearest neutral frontier was Switzerland, some 260 miles south, my preferred destination. Sweden to the north was more distant, and no way was I going to fly westward with a German aeroplane and try my luck against our own Fighter Command in an enemy aircraft.

The least-complicated aircraft to start up and fly were the slower ones, and I always had my eye on a Ju-F.13 or a Ju-52 rather than the faster types like the Messerschmitts or Ju-88s. A slow aircraft from Kassel to Switzerland, to be sure, meant a two-hour flight over enemy territory which would give the Germans plenty of time to scramble fighters for an interception. There was no answer to this hazard, so I dismissed it. We—if I could enlist a crew—would have to take that chance, and I toyed with the idea of trying to take some German mechanics with us as hostages so that fighters could not shoot us down without killing them too.

Arriving at Spangenberg again, we met up with a new contingent of RAF prisoners, one of whom was the tiniest thing on two legs I ever came across in the Royal Air Force. I doubt if Dominic Bruce was much over five feet nothing. He objected strongly to being called small, and insisted that he was "medium-sized". Nearly everyone in prison camp had a nick-name, most of them rude, and Bruce was often referred to as "the medium-sized man", but to me he was always Bruce or "Brucie".

PDT in Spangenberg Castle, 1941.

His record was already remarkable. He had enlisted as a boy apprentice in the RAF in 1935 and trained as a wireless operator. He volunteered for aircrew duties and became one of the renowned Wop/AGs like dear old Keating. While still in the ranks before the war, Bruce earned himself an Air Force Medal, the other ranks' equivalent of the Air Force Cross awarded to officers (an unnecessary form of discrimination, I have always felt). Flying at night in one of the lumbering old Handley Page Harrows in bad weather, his aircraft wound up in a thundercloud and things got very bad very quickly. An engine iced up, so did the airframe, and the radio went on the blink. Being the determined little devil he was, Bruce got the

177

radio going again with the aircraft steadily losing height and everyone in a state of controlled panic. He managed against the odds to get out an SOS. The crew had to drag him away from his set when it came time to bail out. They opened the escape hatch in the floor of the aircraft, which hinged upwards and inwards. So here these chaps were with the escape hatch standing vertically open, the Harrow losing height rapidly and everyone standing around the hole politely saying, "After you."

Bruce was persuaded to go first, so putting the palms of his hands together like a pixie about to dive into the magic pond, he took the plunge. His parachute harness caught on an obstruction inside the aircraft, down slammed the hatch behind him and there was Bruce, hanging by his back, under the Harrow like Peter Pan in his pantomime flying sequences, and his anticipation of the aircraft's first contact with the ground extremely distasteful. Meanwhile, the other chaps were straining to get the hatch open again with Bruce's weight hanging on it. At last, with a final tremendous heave, they succeeded. Brucie reappeared on board like the Demon King coming up through the stage floor. This time, he took a clean dive through the hole and everybody else followed. The whole air force had a damn good laugh and Dominic Bruce won his AFM. Later he retrained as a navigator and once again was forced to descend by parachute, this time over Germany from a flaming Wellington bomber. Brucie was extremely proud of being the only man known to have bailed out three times and to have landed only twice.

Such a man was an obvious candidate for my new crew. By this time, I believe I was the leading RAF escaper in Germany. Other officers were asking if they could join me on my next attempt on the assumption that I would be cooking another scheme up—which I always was. So when I made my initial approach to Bruce, he knew very well I was serious about it.

"Brucie, I am going to have another go for an aircraft from Kassel Aerodrome," I told him.

"And the best of British luck!" he said.

"The destination will be Switzerland. I need a good navigator. What about it?"

"You're bloody mad!" he said. Then his impish face crinkled into a big grin: "I'm on. What's the plan?"

"What's the plan?"

I told Bruce one plan which I thought was a cert, and another possible. Number one was a very little tunnel—short and sweet. There was one potential snag, though, and it was partly for this reason that I had recruited the little (I beg his pardon, medium-sized!) man. For an hour every day, we were allowed to take exercise in a small gymnasium which, in contrast to the rest of the establishment, was beyond the boar-filled moat and separated from the exterior by only a single stone wall. This enclosure had wooden floors and contained various kinds of exercise equipment, including an old box-style vaulting horse. My idea was to park this device a few feet from the exterior wall; insinuate Bruce within; and have him dig a short tunnel of ten feet or so from this point of concealment. It would be a relatively simple matter to cut out some of the floorboards and put in place a suitably camouflaged trapdoor to give access.

Making it easier still was the fact that the two German guards who accompanied us during our exercise period usually did not come inside the gym. With plenty of noisy activity inside, we could cover up the sounds of gentle sawing and trapdoor construction. Loose spoil from the tunnel could be loaded into sausage-like bags down our trouser legs and scattered later into the moat from the ramparts when sentries' backs were turned. Once the trap was finished, the tunnel should go quite serenely barring accidents or solid rock, especially as we should not have to shore it up. I hoped we might be out in three or four weeks.

The day arrived to begin cutting the camouflaged trapdoor entrance for the tunnel. We enlisted the help of a slick team under the leadership of Flying Officer Sammy Hoare who was promised second go at the escape if we could pull it off successfully without its being discovered. They positioned the wooden horse about four feet from the outer wall of the gym and smartly lifted the top layer of the horse off while one of us popped inside to cut the trapdoor. Meanwhile, another of the team kept watch at the door of the gymn to give the alarm if any nosy German approached.

Bruce and I took turns at the simple carpentry and all went well for a few days. Then came the very thing I had dreaded. Somebody on the German security staff must have been one jump ahead of us. Instead of only two Goons standing outside, another one was to be positioned at the door of the gym to watch what was going on inside. Another ruse was urgently needed to neutralise his presence.

Fortunately, one of our friends, whose name I have sadly forgotten, was quite an accomplished acrobatic tumbler, virtually of circus standard. He agreed to put on some spectacular performances for a minute or two just outside the gym door, one at the beginning of the exercise session and another a few minutes before the end of it. I would loiter near the door at the critical times, draw the new guard's attention to the spectacle and ensure that he was suitably engaged. Simultaneously I would give the sign to whip off the top of the horse and pop a nimble little fellow inside it and drop the top back into place very smartly.

Slowly, the tunnelling began. Then another snag arose. Near the base of the wall of the gym we began to encounter very large stones. The process was becoming more and more dicey. We got rid of some stones by having some chaps, who had suddenly become interested in weight-lifting, bring one or two hefty stones into the gym to do their exercises and take three or four out. But it was now becoming a painfully slow process and complete disaster threatened all the time.

This situation encouraged Bruce and me to persevere with our exploration of every possible nook and cranny of the castle besides working diligently at the production of our Luftwaffe uniforms, which we were determined to have as nearly perfect as possible with proper buttons and insignia including, for me, a pilot's badge which we cast from lead stolen from the castle roof.

About this time we heard that a South African air force pilot had also recently arrived in Spangenberg, He was Captain Eustace Newborn, formerly of South African Airways who had, before the war, flown 600 hours on Ju-52s and 200 hours on Ju-86s. This was music to my ears! Moreover, his uniform included some beautiful field boots and we needed some nice leather to make a pistol holster as part of my German uniform. Eustace was signed on at once. Germany was lousy with Ju-52s and Ju-86s and we would have no more dithering about how to start up with him on board. I suggested to the others that Eustace would be the pilot, Brucie would be the navigator and I would be the air hostess.

By now, my German, consisting of perfectly learned colloquial phrases sufficient to meet most foreseeable eventualities, was the best of the three of us, so it was decided that my rank would be *Feldwebel*, the equivalent of our sergeant, and the other two would be privates. That way, I could do the talking if any were necessary. I even had a couple of medal ribbons.

Our uniforms finished, and work on the tunnel possible for only forty-five minutes a day, Bruce and I set about perfecting alternative escape schemes just in case. This entailed exploring every inch of the castle and to some we became objects of good-natured derision. As a New Zealander called Potts once jibed, "I thought the idea was to get out of this castle, not further into it!"

There was one bit of castle we were extremely anxious to investigate, but it was completely walled off with brick and plaster. It was said to have been the apartment of the principal of the Forestry School. He was now reported to be serving as an officer on the Russian front and his wife had, presumably, gone home to live with mother.

There seemed no easy way into his flat, not only because of the wall but also because a special watch was kept on it by two characters who were proving to be a damned nuisance one way and another. One was the Spangenberg equivalent of "Scarface", a German artilleryman named Mel, the other his civilian side-kick, a sour hunchbacked old creep with an enormous drooping moustache whose real name was Kulmer but whom we unkindly called "Shagnasty". We were told he had been the caretaker at Spangenberg for many years. I always maintained they must have found the miserable old sod walled up in the keep. There being no quick way into the flat, Bruce and I turned our attentions to the attics. These were also forbidden territory and there was no simple way into them either. However, after a while we made an interesting discovery. High out of reach on a landing of the staircase to our dormitory we spotted a little trapdoor in the wall. With "stooges" set to watch out for Mel and Shagnasty, we rigged a sort of ladder, opened the trap and squirmed ourselves into a cramped dusty dark chamber about six feet square and four feet high. Its ceiling was of rough lath and plaster. It was a perfect secret place from which to dig upwards into the attics which were obviously enormous affairs under the high pitched, cathedral-like roof of the castle. In this roof were numerous little dormer windows with wooden shutters painted on the outside with Gothic zigzag stripes.

We closed ourselves into the dark little chamber and quietly began to pick away at the ceiling. It was easy but horribly dusty work, and we nearly choked. Soon, we had a hole big enough to put a head up through. An eerie faint light came down from the attic space but weirdest of all was the ghostly moan of the wind above us, punctuated by doleful clack-clacks from the loose shutters.

In the gloom, I felt Bruce easing himself upwards to put his head through the hole. No sooner was it up than it was down again with Brucie in a state of silent shock which I could sense rather than see. He seemed dumbstruck and pointed upwards silently. I pushed him aside a bit impatiently, put my own head up and had it down again just as quickly. I had met the cold silent gaze of a man standing waiting for us, skulking behind a pile of old junk. His face was pale and there was a deathly look about him. We crouched there waiting for sound of movement, but none came. Then Brucie took another cautious peep and stayed up long enough to take a better look at the silent watcher. He then enlarged the hole and went up through and I followed. There, on a pile of old junk, was a life-size bust of Emperor Franz Josef, or somebody, staring at us with sightless eyes.

The real bonus of our attic exploration was to find a staircase down to the Forestry School principal's flat. At the bottom was a sturdy locked door. By this time both of us were expert lock-pickers and always carried our tools. We were inside the flat in two shakes and looked around in disbelief. We had discovered an Aladdin's cave!

There was so much useful escape material, including a wardrobe full of good-quality civilian clothes and the absent forester's Sunday best Army Reserve uniform, spare rank pips, cap, boots, a Mannlicher-Schoenauer 6.5 mm hunting rifle with boxes of ammunition, and a Luger 9 mm Parabellum semi-automatic pistol with thirty-two rounds. There were detailed maps of the surrounding countryside, an excellent magnetic compass, dispatch cases, and even a box of stale cigars! There was everything an escaper could hope for. Brucie and I stared at each other dumbfounded. We could hardly wait to rub Potts' nose in this lot!

We now hoped we had found another way out of the castle, using that uniform and those beautiful civilian clothes, briefcases and cigars. We didn't know how, but there *had* to be a way. There *must* be. We locked up the apartment; took the Luger but left no traces; pulled some junk over the hole in the attic floor; and returned via the little chamber to our quarters. We couldn't believe our luck and our New Zealander friend had to eat his words, especially when he saw the Luger!

We were now nearing the end of July. The gym tunnel was progressing painfully slowly because of the large foundation stones which had to be dislodged quietly by careful nibbling and levering. We could not risk the noise of chiselling or hammering. We decided to hand the tunnel, lock, stock and barrel over to Sammy Hoare, and to concentrate our minds entirely on a super gate scheme using our newfound wealth. Everything now depended upon our finding a way to break the apparently infallible check system on the gate.

It worked like this. The sentry on our side of the moat bridge had a key to the barbed wire gate into the castle yard. He was forbidden to open the gate except with a direct order from, and in the presence of, the guard commander who was on duty in the guardroom at the opposite end of the bridge. Anyone wishing to come into the castle first reported to the guard commander, identified himself and signed the book. The guard commander then escorted him across the bridge to the gate, and ordered the sentry to let him in. When this person wished to come out, he came to the gate where the sentry blew a whistle to summon the guard commander, who came with his book. Only when the guard commander was satisfied that this was the same person as he had recently admitted, did he authorise the opening of the gate. Then the person had to sign himself out with a matching signature and identification.

The system should have been unbeatable. But there is a flaw to be found in most security systems if one waits and watches patiently. We did, for a very long and tedious time—and eventually we were rewarded.

There were three guard companies at Spangenberg and they worked eight hour shifts. C company was in the charge of a *Feldwebel* whom I knew by sight but whose name I never knew, so for convenience I will call him Schultz. He was a shade less meticulous than his two colleagues of A and B companies. This was revealed whenever his company was on the afternoon shift at the time when our orderlies carried the rotten scraps, peelings and rubbish from the kitchen.

Schultz allowed his gate sentry to unlock for the orderlies without calling him. What harm could there be in that? They went no further than the bridge, from which they tipped the scraps into the moat for the wild boars. The orderlies were then immediately locked back into the castle by the gate sentry. Schultz did not bother to move his backside out of the guardroom for such a trivial routine matter. He was probably far too busy playing cards. The other guard commanders obeyed orders implicitly.

Of course, had anyone else tried to get out of the gate at the same time as the orderlies, they would have been stopped until Schultz came to check up on them. By any ordinary sentry they would. But Schultz had one big dumb ox in his company whom we called "Blockhead" and we figured that if anyone could be persuaded to do the wrong thing, it was Blockhead. He was also the least likely of all the guards to be bright enough to recognise our actual faces and particularly Bruce's unusually small stature.

All we needed for the scheme, which we worked out in careful psychological detail, was C company on the afternoon watch and Blockhead on gate duty at swill-tipping time. As there were ten other perimeter guard posts that Blockhead could be on, we had to play a waiting game—a long and extremely patient one.

I was to be rigged up as an immaculate army *Hauptmann* in his best uniform, shiny field boots, grey gloves and all. Bruce and Eustace would be visiting doctors from Switzerland—very well dressed although, even after tailoring, Bruce's jacket was cut a little on the generous side, and his crotch somewhat droopy. The doctors would be carrying smart dispatch cases, things no prisoner could get their hands on, and one would actually be smoking a large cigar—again, something quite out of reach of prisoners of war.

Eustace would be wearing a rather caddish Tyrolean type hat and Brucie a large black Homburg which tended to sit down on his ears, but he did have very adequate ears. They stood out sideways like air brakes. Underneath all this sartorial splendour, I was to be wearing my full Luftwaffe uniform pilot's badge and medal ribbons, and the other two beneath their civilian clothing had their Luftwaffe privates' uniforms. The briefcases would contain very little food, as we intended to have only one night out before a "shit or bust" effort at Kassel *Flugplatz*. Of more importance, we thought, was a shoe brush, some boot polish, a clothes brush and a razor so that we should not appear scruffy in our uniforms at Kassel. We also carried the detailed local map and that excellent compass.

Thinking of my last effort on Graudenz *Flugplatz*, I had asked the Senior British Officer, Brigadier Somerset, to let me take the Luger and thirty-two rounds. Stuck into the ear of a Luftwaffe mechanic, it could ensure us a hostage for a safe ride south. The SBO absolutely forbade us to take it and said that as soon as the Germans discovered we had escaped, the Luger and the hunting rifle should be handed over to them. Otherwise, he said, we stood a good chance of being shot on sight. He was right, of course, so I did the next best thing. I made an accurate replica with a wooden core covered with sheet lead stolen from the roof, and rubbed down to a flawless smoothness. The barrel and other parts I actually cast. Blueing was achieved with boot polish and the finished article looked perfect. It even handled nicely with a good balance.

All our gear for the escape was hidden in the sick bay. We had no intention of throwing all this magnificent clothing away unless the scheme had a good chance of success, so we decided that on the day—if it ever came—we would first give Blockhead a gullibility test. This was not very difficult. John Milner, with his perfect German, was now our official camp interpreter. Just before swill time, he would go to Blockhead and ask, "Has the German officer with the two Swiss doctors gone out yet?"

This was more than a mere gullibility test, it was a mental conditioner as well, there being no visiting Swiss doctors with a German officer escort in the castle then or at any other time! Blockhead could answer one of two things. Either, "What the hell are you talking about? There are no visitors," in which case the whole scheme was off; or, hopefully, a puzzled sort of "No," in which case he had accepted that there *could* be an officer and two doctors in the camp. Milner was to give us, behind his back, a thumbs-up or a thumbs-down depending upon his judgment of the extent to which Blockhead had been successfully bamboozled.

If it was thumbs-up, the orderlies were immediately to go for the gate with the kitchen waste. Blockhead would—contrary to standing orders— unlock and open it without calling the sloppy guard commander Schultz, and we would emerge from the sick quarters, strut the length of the yard waving a cigar and chatting to the British medical officer, and hit the gate whereupon I was to look at my watch and say my carefully rehearsed piece, "*Du lieber Gott, Herr Doktor, schon viertel zwei. Kommen, wir müssen weitergehen!*" (Good God, Doctor, it's already a quarter to two. Come on. We must get a move on!)

This, we hoped, would introduce the necessary atmosphere of urgency to fluster Blockhead sufficiently to let us through the already open gate— with plenty of bluster and a look from me which would imply "Don't you dare cause us any delay, my man." The whole thing depended entirely upon some good acting and a show of complete confidence and superiority. All the other prisoners were briefed. Those who happened to be in the area, and it was not to be unusually crowded, were to act out their own parts in the pantomime by working themselves up to a semblance of insolent attention as they normally did for a German officer. I, in turn, would grudgingly acknowledge them with a salute or two.

We feared that, even if we managed to get through the gate, over the bridge and past the guardroom, we might have little start time before the alarm was given. Blockhead would be sure to mention the unusual event to somebody else and nobody else was as dim as he was. Or any of the guards standing around might wander into the guardroom and mention it to Schultz, who would immediately blow a fuse. Our plan was that if we got past the guardroom we would charge off into the bushes on the hill and emerge at the bottom. But there lay the difficulty. For two miles there was this long straight open road with no cover whatsoever to the left or right before it reached the thick forest. Once we reached the trees, we knew we would be much harder to find. Before that point, it would be vital for us to know if and when our escape had been discovered so that we could take whatever evasive action was possible. What that might be under such impossible circumstances on that open road we had no idea, but we definitely needed a warning.

Quite reasonably, we assumed that if the Spangenberg guard company suddenly became aware of our escape there would be some obvious reaction such as shouted reprimands and orders, running around and generally jumping up and down. Should this be observed by our chaps, they were to stoke the kitchen fire with a good quantity of wet grass previously gathered from the ramparts. This would send up a white smoke-signal from the chimney such as announces the election of a new Pope at the Vatican. Until we reached the forest, we would repeatedly look back anxiously at the castle on the watch for this unwelcome, and almost certainly fatal, signal.

C company had been on the afternoon shift several times by the end of August, but never with Blockhead on the gate. We were becoming desperate. Sammy Hoare's tunnel was, at last, almost ready to break after tremendous difficulties with the gym foundations. Then the German *Abwehr* officer noticed the scattering of large stones outside the exercise pen and became suspicious. He organised a thorough search of the area and the gym tunnel was discovered.

At the time it seemed a crushing blow. But perhaps our efforts were not wasted. Two years later, in 1943, the same idea of digging a tunnel from beneath a wooden horse was used at Stalag Luft III (Sagan), all three escapers on that occasion getting home after stowing away on ships to Sweden. Escaping being one of the main topics of prison camp conversation, including schemes old and new, I like to think that some of our original wooden-horse workers or watchers, who were then at Sagan, may have mentioned it from time to time, and that perhaps our idea contributed something to the brilliant success of that effort. It is a reasonable hope.

Our own long-awaited big day arrived at the beginning of September 1941. C company was on afternoon duty again and we were thrilled to see Blockhead on the gate. The code word "Claymore" alerted everyone concerned and we quickly dressed ourselves up in the sick bay. I was not usually affected by stage fright, whether it was on stage or before an escape, but on this occasion I was uncharacteristically tense. There was so much superb gear at stake. I did not believe I could get away with more escape attempts without being shipped off to this mysterious Colditz we kept hearing about. Moreover, this time I felt so much more depended upon a first class personal performance. Could I browbeat this sentry into disobeying orders with his guard commander only fifteen yards away?

I proceeded very deliberately to get myself psyched up. I told myself, "I AM Hauptmann Adendorf. I HATE these bloody undisciplined Englishmen out there in the yard. We ARE late. Curse these damn fool Swiss, nattering to the British doctor. We WILL miss their train and

187

Sketch by John Mansel of PDT's "gate job" at Spangenberg.

that idiot sentry had better NOT hold me up or I will see him in hell."

Milner was at the gate talking to Blockhead. Somebody said, "It's thumbs up! GO!"

Exactly as planned, the orderlies came out of the kitchen halfway down the Hof and headed for the gate. As Blockhead started to open it, I remember I coughed nervously, took a deep breath and stepped out into the yard, followed closely by Dominic Bruce and Eustace Newborn.

"What's the plan?"

I then strode down the middle of that yard as fast as was reasonable. The orderlies were at the gate and, as briefed, were making some sort of difficulty with Blockhead who was arguing with them. Behind me, I could hear our medical officer importuning the "Swiss doctors" who, I learned later, were palming him off, little Brucie in particular, with airy waves of his beautiful big cigar. Some officer prisoners, lounging about the courtyard, sullenly heaved themselves to their feet and stood more or less erect. A giant South African friend of mine, Jimmy Imrie, was gazing at the sky— whether as a sign of implied insolence, or because he didn't trust himself to look at me without laughing, I don't know. I saluted left and right as though it pained me to do so. We were almost at the gate.

It was a hot day and I was wearing two suits of clothes. I was sweating! Then Bruce, a non-smoker, swallowed some cigar smoke and started to cough and choke. We were at the gate. It was open. Blockhead looked flustered. Our medical officer was saying goodbye to Brucie who was still choking. Blockhead opened his mouth and looked from me to the guard room and back.

"*Du lieber Gott, Herr Doktor, schon viertel zwei. Kommen, wir müssen weitergehen!*"

Blockhead put out a staying hand, palm towards me, and opened his mouth as if about to protest. I glared him straight in the eye. His resolve teetered for a moment and then he sprang to attention and gave me a smart-heel clicking salute. I cursorily acknowledged it and stepped onto the bridge. The others were following, Brucie now under control. We were halfway across. But then we had to run the gauntlet of the men of C company who were sitting having a last drag at their cigarettes. These were not Blockheads. They knew us, certainly little short-arse Bruce. Only one thing for it—bluff to the end. I drew myself up another half-inch and glared straight in their direction. As one man, they leapt to their feet. Cigarettes were out of mouths and eight hands snapped up to a smart salute. I acknowledged with arrogant dignity, and with a strong voice called, "Heil Hitler."

We were over the bridge, turned right on the path down the hill, dived into the bushes and almost collapsed with silent hysterical laughter as we tore off the outer garments and converted ourselves to three Luftwaffe men.

189

We rolled up my army uniform and the civilian suits into small bundles and hurried through the bushes down the hillside. We wanted to hide that uniform and civilian clothing really well so that they might be available to anyone, maybe even ourselves, escaping later.

Little did we know that long before we reached the bottom of the hill, pandemonium had broken out at the guard room. Somebody must have mentioned the outgoing party to Schultz and he nearly exploded. He was immediately on the phone to the *Kommandantur* at the lower camp in Spangenberg town. His men were running in and out of the guard room shouting orders at each other and the white smoke billowed up from the kitchen chimney. Unfortunately, we were not yet out of the scrub on the hill and could not see it. We stuffed the escape clothing up a large old overgrown dry-looking drainpipe and soon emerged from the scrub at the bottom of the hill. We brushed ourselves down to get rid of any twigs or leaves, checked each other's appearance as smart Luftwaffe men and set out hopefully up that long two-mile stretch of open road with no cover to left or right. We were completely unaware that the white smoke had already billowed out of the kitchen chimney and dispersed. Nor did we know that in the lower camp German troops were kicking motorbikes with side cars into life or piling onto open lorries. They were after us!

As we set off up that road, myself leading and the other two abreast behind me, we kept glancing back at the castle.

"Whacko", said Brucie. "No smoke!"

I could hardly believe our luck. Delighted, I said, "I can understand Blockhead keeping his mouth shut in case he dropped himself in the shit—but all those others!"

"Well, there's still no smoke!" said Bruce, and Eustace added something like, "Bully for us!"

We pressed forward at a pace which was nearly a run and must have been nearing the halfway-mark to the forest when we heard the motorbikes and lorries of our pursuers.

Eustace said in a somewhat resigned voice, "Don't look now, but I think we're being followed."

I took a glance backwards and realised the game was up. This was the pursuit squad, no doubt about that. Knowing that the situation was really quite hopeless, I said to the others, "Just keep going. Swing those arms like Goons, across your body. We might as well play it out to the end. We've nothing to lose by it."

The first motor-bike roared by, then another, then a lorry load of troops who cheered and waved to us. We waved back. Then another lorry load, and as it roared past, somebody yelled something about some prisoners escaping from the Schloss. We waved back at them and they were gone at full speed. They were looking for three escaped prisoners dressed as a Wehrmacht officer and two civilians. They were not interested in three Luftwaffe men.

Considering our extremely short start, the Germans obviously threw their cordon far too wide, probably in compliance with a standing order in the event of an escape. At any rate, they allowed us to reach the woods with nothing worse than acute anxiety. It was a wonderful relief to plunge into the cool silent depths of the forest where we felt relatively secure in its subdued half light. We flopped for a short rest to gather our breath and our wits. Then we set off for Kassel on a compass course set by our expert navigator, Dominic Bruce.

Our only fright at that stage of the journey came from a herd of wild boars standing in our path as we pressed along a fire break. Their leader was a bristly old male with menacing tusks who stood defiantly before them eyeing us malevolently and tossing his head with his hackles raised. Being born cowards and thoroughly brainwashed about wild boars by the Spangenberg security staff, Eustace and I were all for skirting around this lot. The indomitable little Bruce, however, picked up a bit of dead stick and, drawing himself up to his full five foot nothing, advanced on them like Admiral Lord Nelson—bloody, bold and resolute. As he approached really close to them, while we admired his pluck from a sensible distance, they suddenly fled. Our little hero then waited for Eustace and me to slink up to him while we sheepishly discussed the terrible slashing damage known to have been caused to heavy-duty tyres by irate warthogs in Africa.

Sometime before dusk, we were surprised to hear the muffled roar of engines on a steady continual note. Compelled by a dangerous curiosity, we altered course slightly towards the noise which gradually increased to a thunderous roar that had all three of us completely puzzled. Then, from our secure cover in the trees, we saw ahead of us a boundary fence almost as formidable as the one surrounding Barth. Under the trees stood a row of sheds with small gauge railway tracks leading into them. Here and there, we saw a purpose-built trolley supporting a huge internal combustion engine. From within the sheds came the steady roar and it became immediately obvious to us that this was an enormous camouflaged plant where mighty engines were being tested and run-in, presumably before being fitted in tanks, aircraft or even, perhaps, submarines.

In the vicinity of this installation, we made careful note of several landmarks including a prominent overhead power line running through the forest along a wide fully cleared lane like a firebreak. With these and our compass bearings, we pinpointed the position as accurately as we could as a possible potential target for Bomber Command. Later, if we failed to get home, I intended to send this information back to British Military Intelligence in a split photograph and, in fact, I did so.

As the fine September evening was fading into darkness, we reached the far edge of that part of the forest nicely on track, and there, below us, lay Kassel. Beyond to one side, we could discern the airfield. We retreated some way into the dense forest and found a hollow in which it would be safe to light a small fire which would not be visible beyond the rim once darkness covered the smoke. Having no utensils, we could not cook or brew up, so we ate half our meagre escape rations and made comfortable soft beds in the pine needles.

The silence, peace and lovely resinous smell of the forest after the harsh clamour and stinks of a prison camp affected me deeply with a rare contentment. Despite the chill of night, we rested well but slept only fitfully as we took turns to sit on guard. In the morning, we finished our rations which had been limited for the sake of appearances and because our intentions were such that success or recapture seemed inevitable before the day was out. We spruced ourselves up with careful brushing, combing, shaving and polishing and re-capped our plan.

We would again march, myself leading, the other two abreast behind me. I would carry the briefcase. We would march openly with confidence straight towards the airfield where we would skirt around in an effort to spot an easy way in. Once inside, we were certain we should find a Ju-52 or a Ju-86 as both these types were extremely common. We firmly resolved not to risk taking any other type of aircraft, lest we waste Eustace's invaluable experience. Although we had no maps, once airborne we intended to hit the Rhine about Frankfurt and follow it down to Basle. Switzerland should be unmistakable with its Alps and lakes.

On entering Kassel, we found it was alive with Wehrmacht personnel— army and Luftwaffe. We were a bit nervous about this at first, until we realised their numbers helped to render us quite inconspicuous. We soon became accustomed to throwing salutes to officers with that proud upflung German head, and to receiving them from all ranks below mine of *Feldwebel.*

By mid-morning, we had located the Luftwaffe airfield which was surrounded by a formidable wire fence. There seemed little hope of breaking through unobserved. We were delighted to glimpse beyond the buildings an odd assortment of aircraft, which was promising. Following the fence round, we came to some more important-looking buildings and then we saw the two main gateways. In front of the guardroom amidst the traffic and personnel going in and out, stood one of the most imposing figures I have ever seen in uniform.

He was an enormous heavily paunched gentleman of the *Feldgendarmerie,* or military police. His helmet was set above two massive bushy eyebrows beneath which his piggy eyes flitted restlessly over the throng. A bulbous nose, veined like Gorgonzola cheese, was set above a magnificently upswept Kaiser Wilhelm moustache which bristled with importance. The folds of a massive neck hung uncomfortably over a tightly fastened collar, and on his chest, hung by a chain, the shining kidney-shaped breastplate, which is the *Feldgendarme's* badge of office. A broad leather belt supported a cutlass-type sword and a more business-like semi-automatic pistol. Breeches and shiny field boots completed the ensemble.

What surprised and encouraged us beyond our wildest hopes was that nobody seemed to check in or out at the guardroom and the flow both ways was unhindered. Most people using the gate simply gave the policeman a nod and he nodded back. I muttered to the others, "This is a piece of cake. Don't worry about the Kaiser—he's all piss and wind. Now, march as if you owned the place."

We went for that main gate in great style. The Kaiser gave us a casual glance as we approached, but as we went past him, with a voice like a flak-burst, he exploded one word. "*Halt!*" Without slackening my pace, I looked back at him to try a rank-pulling technique and was horrified to see him gathering his bulk as if for propulsion in our direction. "*Herr Feldwebel,*" he roared. "*Wohin gehen Sie?*" (Where are you going—who are you—I don't know you!)

Our over-confidence had underestimated the Kaiser and this was the pay-off. I quickened the pace and threw at him one of my well-practised German phrases for all occasions: "*Ja, ja. Jetzt hab'Ich keine Zeit… Ich komme wieder.*" (Okay, Okay! I'm in a hurry—I'll be back in a moment) and with that I turned a corner to the left and we went at a near-trot. I last glimpsed the Kaiser staggering at the cheek of anybody ignoring his authority, saw him apparently recover and prepare to accelerate into a charge.

"Quick! Follow me, chaps," I said as we rounded the corner and I opened a door in a building on the side of the road, let the others in and closed it, hopefully before the Kaiser drew a bead on us. There were several uniformed clerks in the office we had entered, who looked up enquiringly. Fortunately, there was another door opposite. We smiled at our surprised friends and shot through the other door, doubled back towards the guardroom, then round a technical building into a hangar and out the other side onto the airfield. We had lost the Kaiser at the cost of considerable adrenalin and a much-increased pulse rate.

We now repeated my previous performance at Graudenz, carrying things around and looking busy. We searched every part of that airfield with falling spirits as we realised there was no Ju-52 or Ju-86. There were Ju-88s and Heinkel 111s, but nothing unguarded or unoccupied that was not picketed down, chocked and covered. After all the effort we had put into the escape, it was hard to accept such foul bloody luck. For two pins, I could have wept. I mean that literally, I remember it so well.

Several times, our resolve weakened as we eyed a Ju-88, but in the end, we decided to stick to our plan, encouraged by the ease with which we had mingled with the populace throughout the morning. At that rate, we could head west for Belgium 150 miles distant and call in on any airfields en route until we found what we wanted.

After nearly three hours at Kassel *Flugplatz*, we regretfully slid out through the main gate—no Kaiser this time—and headed a little south of west. If we could skirt to the south of the Ruhr industrial area and get across the Belgian frontier, we could hope to deliver ourselves into the hands of the Resistance which had become more organised in helping RAF aircrew who had bailed out of crippled aircraft. And, of course, we intended to call in on all airfields en route looking for a Ju-52.

We were not then aware of the lengths to which German security had gone to ensure our recapture. A signal had been sent to every military and police unit in the whole of German-occupied Europe with instructions that it was to be brought to the notice of every individual serviceman. It contained a detailed description of each of the three of us: name, age, height, hair, complexion etc., and the fact that we were dressed as a German Army *Hauptmann* (Captain) and two civilians. This, of course, was wrong. We were now three Luftwaffe men.

Our biggest problem was food. We had none, and no money. Fortunately, it was the best time of the year to try to live off the land, although having to do so would undoubtedly slow our progress and increase our risks. An immediate priority was to pick up a tin can which would serve as a stewpot, and a bottle in which to collect drinking water. These had to be small enough to conceal in the briefcase.

We resolved to travel only by day and to march openly, choosing as far as possible roads on which we would not appear out of place. This meant, if possible, no quiet country lanes. At the other extreme, we knew that walking on the Autobahns was forbidden. Hitch-hiking was out because of the language problem, but we would look for an opportunity to steal bicycles if this might be done without leaving a trail and generating another hunt. We would lie up at night rather than try to make furtive cross-country forays which would ruin our uniforms and, if we were challenged, nullify their advantage. A senior NCO pilot of the Luftwaffe was something no farmer expected to find in his stockyard in the middle of the night.

It looked as if our staple diet would become apples, pears and plums stolen from wayside trees, and such root crops as we could grub out of the ground. Bellyaches loomed as distinct possibilities. Places to lie up for the night must always be selected well before nightfall because what looks very secure and well hidden in the dark, is sometimes horribly exposed in the cold light of dawn. With all these factors, we reckoned we would be lucky to make straight-line progress of twenty miles a day. That meant, at least, another eight days to Belgium.

We were lucky to have no rain at any time, but the days were long weary plods with hunger gnawing at our guts and, worse still, abominable thirst. We found a tin for cooking and a bottle on a rubbish dump, but suffered one irreplaceable loss. Brucie, being a navigator and a perfectionist, was meticulous when taking compass bearings to see that no deviation was imposed on the compass needle by any magnetic material on his person, and he did have a very magnetic personality! To make sure about this, he set the compass on the ground and stood back while it settled down. Then Brucie would set our direction or choose our road and say, "That way," and off we would go. Two hours after one such occasion, poor little Brucie realised he had forgotten to pick up that superb stolen compass!

Eustace and I were commendably restrained over the matter. We felt rather sorry for Brucie who was disconsolate. Luckily, we had clear skies so again Scout training paid off and I used my watch and the sun by day and, when necessary, the stars by night. We had no navigational problems—except the absence of a map. And that was indeed a bit of a problem.

There were other complications. My ankle injured over Rheims soon began to play up but I managed to keep quiet about it and, sure enough, our diet soon produced gripes and intestinal squitters despite our hot vegetable stew of potatoes, turnips and an occasional onion each night. What we missed more than anything was bread.

On our second day out from Kassel, we struck the River Eder and came upon the magnificent sight of the Eder Dam which was built in 1914 to prevent winter flooding and to improve navigability for barges on the River Wesel. It also generated hydro-electricity and supplied water for the industrial Ruhr Valley. As we, in Luftwaffe uniform, walked along the bank of this vast dam, enjoying the scenic beauty and tranquillity, it never occurred to us that we were looking at the future scene of one of Bomber Command's most famous exploits. A year and a half later, my friend Guy Gibson would lead the Dambusters raid and destroy this massive edifice, having already breached the Moehne Dam some sixty miles away. It was a triumph of technical ingenuity, precise airmanship and supreme courage for which Gibson was awarded the VC and half his crews gave their lives.

That night, as we settled into a hide-out, a problem arose from a most unexpected quarter. Eustace turned difficult. We had made good progress that day and were becoming hopeful that slowly but surely we would reach our goal. Our disguise was apparently perfect and so long as we gaily exchanged salutes and "*Heil Hitlers*" with the natives, it seemed that no one would ever suspect us. But Eustace, an intelligent, honest, thoroughly likeable man who would become a medical doctor after the war, had gone morose on us. He was giving us only monosyllabic replies and was obviously having a first-class sulk. Brucie and I were puzzled. Brucie looked at me and I shrugged my shoulders. Then Bruce asked him kindly what was the matter. His vehement reply staggered us.

"There's too much 'Heil Hitlering'," he said. "I'm sick of it. 'Fuck Hitler', I say!"

Our mouths dropped open as we stared first at Eustace and then at each other. I remember our reply to this amazing outburst was delivered fiercely:

"Listen, Eustace. We all say 'Fuck Hitler', but you will 'Heil Hitler' with the rest of us or we'll fuck *you*!"

Eustace looked sheepish, thought about it for a while and mumbled himself to sleep. Next day, he had cheered up and became a model Nazi again.

We all had our failings and mine seemed to be lack of stamina. Whether this was because I had been on a prison diet much longer than the others, because the nagging ache in my ankle was getting me down, or because they were simply tougher, I do not know. But when the going was really hard, I was the laggard, and wiry little Bruce was the pacesetter. Although the days were warm, our sleep at night was fitful because of cold. This meant that our hardships during the day were thirst, hunger, tiredness and footsoreness in that order. The latter was a particular worry for me because of that damned Rheims ankle. Blisters had burst and our feet were toughening up, but thirst, with only one small bottle between us, and rare opportunities to fill it, was sometimes particularly unpleasant. We dared not go to houses or farms to beg, in doubtful German, for water. It would arouse suspicion and any human contact leading to conversation and questions had to be rigorously avoided.

On the next occasion, I was the odd man out and fiercely angry with the other two who just laughed at me. Ravenously hungry as usual early one morning, we marched purposefully into a tiny village which had hardly woken up to the new day. The only activity was outside a largish building round a horse-drawn van which was being loaded with loaves of bread fresh from the baking oven. The smell was torture to us!

We had not gone far before we heard the clip-clop of the pony approaching from behind and the van passed us by, again trailing that tantalising scent of newly baked bread. The driver, an elderly man, sat in a relaxed posture on the seat, leaning against the side of the van in such a way that he could as easily look back into his load of warm bread as look forward over the pony to the road ahead. Then he stopped outside a small shop. As we approached the van again, the driver and another fellow were unloading some bread. Agony a third time as we walked by!

It was too much for flesh and blood to stand, and I made a plan. We were now leaving the village and it looked as if the van might overtake us yet again because it appeared to be on a delivery round, presumably to local grocery shops in that area.

I briefed the others. As the cart went by, I would bob down behind it, bent almost double, so that if the driver looked back, he would not see me behind the tailboard. Also, I would coincide my footfalls with the clip-clop of the pony. I would also screw my head around to try to look backwards—a bit of a contortion for a doubled-up runner—and they must give me a thumbs-up sign when they could be sure the driver was looking steadily to the front. Thereupon, I would straighten up, grab a loaf and throw it laterally into the ditch.

I had not realised what an unnatural, strenuous, exhausting performance I had committed myself to. It was exacerbated by having to take inordinately slow, exaggerated, prancing steps to keep up with the cart while coinciding my footfalls to the slow clip-clop of that lugubriously addle-pated Teutonic pony. To do this, all doubled up and simultaneously twisting my neck so that I could look backward while I pranced forward was a performance I never want to attempt again. However, being the heroic sort of chap I am,

I managed it and looked back at my so-called friends to see if they were giving me the vital thumbs-up signal.

They were not! They were tottering about with uncontrolled mirth, neglecting their duty entirely. I could have gladly murdered them both. Eventually, after what seemed like an excruciating delay, they pulled themselves together; gave me the signal; and a loaf went sailing into the ditch, then another, then another. I then staggered to the side of the road in a state of collapse and fury.

When they reached me, I vented my wrath on those two idiots with every expletive to which I could lay my fairly experienced tongue, but they continued to laugh. Brucie said he thought he would never see such an undignified Luftwaffe *Feldwebel* who was all "bum and boots". That did it! And the bread helped. I started to laugh too as we devoured two of the loaves like wolves and, with extraordinary forbearance, saved the third one for later.

For once I was a hero—but the next episode in my role as "escape Führer" negated all my painfully acquired respect. It was the end of another hard day's slog, dusk was falling, we were exhausted, but worse than that, desperately thirsty. We were on a road running through a dense wood. It was time to settle down for the night. We went down the bank into a little valley, over a moist patch and up the opposite slope, and found a pitch to bed down in good cover. Our thirst was raging and our bottle was empty.

Pulling the "gallant leader" stuff, I said, "You chaps fix up the hide for tonight and I will see if I can find water." As we had crossed the moist soggy patch, I thought I had heard the tinkle of running water off to my right. It was almost dark as, clutching our empty bottle, I made my way back down to the "moist patch" and by the time I reached it night had fallen. I again heard the faint tinkle of water and gingerly trod my squelchy way towards it. I was quite impressed to discover I was right as usual.

Groping around, I came across an obviously man-made stone cavity with water trickling into it and leaking out of the lower lip. Eureka! Feeling around in the dark, I roughly confirmed the layout, filled our bottle, drank it dry, and re-filled it for my companions. I made my way back to them and basked unobtrusively in their gratitude and admiration. After all, what the hell is a leader for! We ate some raw bits and pieces we had filched from fields and orchards and settled down to a fitful slumber. The weather remained dry.

Next morning, we spruced up as usual and still feeling quite pleased with myself, I adopted a "Follow me, Men!" attitude and decreed we must first re-fill our water bottle for the next day's march. The underlings agreed with proper respect and off we went. I knew where to go and soon found the little stone water trap. Yes indeed—there it was! There was only one snag. Floating in it, upright, with its paws up as if begging, was an enormous, dead, bloated, gangrenous, decaying rat.

It was our ninth day out from Spangenberg. The first two days had been lost to the flying plan. The country we had traversed since then between Kassel and the Rhine was rural and not really suited to our disguise. We estimated we had made 150 miles or so since leaving Kassel and should soon reach the Rhine somewhere a bit south of Cologne and Bonn. We had been constantly on the lookout for aircraft obviously on an airfield circuit or an approach but had seen none, so we just had to plod onwards.

We were becoming a bit gaunt, having lived almost entirely off the land and so often desperate for a drink. My ankle was nagging at me but I thought it best to say nothing about it lest it detract from morale all round. We were not certain of our position having no map but navigating by the sun, which fortunately shone brightly throughout, and my watch. I kept us on a course approximately WSW with the aim to skirt south of Cologne and the huge industrial area, and find the Belgian border on a rough heading for Aachen or Liège.

We expected we would hit the river Rhine or a tributary any moment and the border on the tenth or eleventh day at the latest. We were sure we would make it even if we should collapse as soon as we were in the care of our allies. We knew how we intended to make our first cautious approach to them. Our hopes were very high.

We were extremely tired after a bad night when, feeling better for stolen bread, and coming across a lovely grassy river bank, warm in the sunshine, we decided to rest awhile. We found a more or less secluded spot, took off our boots and socks and gratefully dabbled our feet in the water. In two shakes, Brucie and Eustace were fast asleep and I was about to follow suit when I sensed a presence. There, smiling down upon us, was a toothless

"All bum and boots": stealing bread near Kassel. (See p. 199)

old hag and a comely rounded wench with a baby in her arms. They looked like field workers who wanted to pass the time of day with three of their gallant boys in blue.

The old woman started to cackle away in a country patois, which made my poor understanding of German even worse. I nodded my head and shook it and smiled and looked grave with now and again a "*So!*" or "*Ach, so!*" but I knew it would be my turn to hold forth and then the game would be up. I was desperate to get rid of them. She was saying something about the girl's husband who was in the Luftwaffe in *Frankreich* and I thought I was making the right happy rejoinders with a big smile all over my face until I realised the point of the story was that hubby had been killed there. I switched facial expression smartly and threw in a "*Pech*" (bad luck) and knew I wasn't going to fool anybody much longer.

Brucie and Eustace had woken up and were looking anxious. Finding me rather a dull conversationalist, the old girl then turned to Brucie and gave him an earful while he, quite uncomprehending, smiled at her like a dazed owl. It was time for action. With all the blustering authority I could summon in bare feet, I shouted at the woman, "It is forbidden to speak with them!" Her eyes widened.

"*Warum*?" (Why?)

"They are under arrest!"

Brucie understood that one all right. The women's eyes opened wider.

"*Warum*?"

Brucie had caught on quickly. He did the finest brutal-and-licentious-soldiery act you can imagine. He looked from one to the other of the women and drew back his lips in a lascivious leer while something between a growl and a drooling gurgle escaped through his clenched teeth. Both women took two involuntary steps backwards, put forced hesitant smiles on their faces, wished us a hurried "*Auf wiedersehen*" and were gone!

Our footwear was on in a trice and we were gone in the opposite direction. One way and another, I was very unhappy about these pastoral perambulations and was glad that in another day or so, we should be back among the crowds where three men together in uniform would be less conspicuous on some sort of duty. In the professional flying game, one is taught not to think in terms of luck; similarly with escaping—this is an activity in which average good luck is no use at all. Without excellent good luck all the way, one is normally lost. One slice of bad luck is usually fatal.

On our tenth day out, we were heading along a secondary road which passed through a village where, we later learned, the Germans had set up a small subsidiary prison camp. These were known as *Arbeitkommandos* and were for prisoners of war working on local farms. In the village street, there was an off-duty guard from the camp. He was unarmed, leaning on his bike and chatting up a village lass. As we approached, he sprang to attention and saluted me with a resounding click of his jackboots to which I responded appropriately.

"See how that Goon looked at us? I don't like it!"

The others had noticed nothing unusual and said so. They also suggested I was getting jumpy about being in the countryside. That was true. Nonetheless, I thought it might be an idea to play safe and disappear into the woods. On discussion, it was finally agreed that this was contrary to our agreed *modus operandi* and we should stick to the road and be brazen. Our uniforms were still surprisingly presentable although our faces were looking pretty haggard.

We made another quarter of a mile when we were aware that our German friend was now coming after us on his bike and he had another soldier with him, both with rifles slung on their backs. They were accompanied by an old civilian with a large white Franz Josef moustache. Having reached us, they all dismounted and the two soldiers saluted me which was nice of them, but I didn't feel so good. However, with a brusque air, I demanded "*Was wollen sie?*" (What do you want?)

"Please, *Herr Feldwebel*, may I see your papers?"

My stomach turned over. It was obvious to me the game was up, but putting on my best superior air and acting offended, I blasted at him, "Papers! Papers! Why?"

"Excuse me, *Herr Feldwebel*, but I demand to see your papers."

"You demand! I am a *Feldwebel*. You are a *Soldat*! Dear God, man—are you mad?"

At this stage, the two rifles were off their shoulders and the bolts slammed two rounds up two spouts. Now, the deference went out of the soldier's voice.

"Your papers. At once! I believe you are *Engländer!*"

I swore at the man for insulting me, but knew I was only prolonging the agony.

"*Hände hoch!*" (Hands up!)

Slowly, we raised our hands. The guard jerked his rifle towards me and said to the old man, "Take his pistol." The civilian fumbled nervously at my holster and extracted the dummy pistol and then covered us with it. I was thankful if was not a real one. He was trembling so violently, I was sure it would have gone off.

We were marched back to the *Arbeitskommando*, and a little later, a large open Mercedes arrived to take us off, escorted by a German NCO and the soldier who had arrested us. The Mercedes had extra occasional fold-up seats and he rode in the back with us. As Germans sometimes tend to do, he waxed sentimental and kindly.

"*Ach, Krieg ist schlecht, nicht?*" (War is rotten, isn't it?)

"Yes, worse for some than others," I replied.

"I have not seen my family for five months," he said.

He produced several photographs from a wallet, all so typical of any soldier's family. How many millions of such wallets were there in this sad world? How many millions of such photographs? How many millions of anxious fathers, mothers and children?

"*Ja, Krieg ist schlecht*," I replied. "No, and I haven't seen mine for a year, and I will not!"

Then he waxed even more sentimental,

"See—I have here a photograph of my family—my wife and children."

Having got the chap nicely mellowed, one thing was essential. We must discover what had given us away. There were so many fatal mistakes one could make—swinging the arms incorrectly; walking on an *Autobahn*; smoking an English cigarette which smells so different from the continental ones, eating Red Cross chocolate when the Germans had none. What had we done to arouse this man's suspicion? I had to know for next time.

"You did well to catch us." He looked pleased and nodded.

"You will probably be given the *Kriegsverdienstkreuz* for it." He looked even more pleased.

"*Ja, es ist möglich.*" (Yes, it's possible.)

"But tell me, how did you know?"

"Ach, it was simple. When the *Feldwebel* walked past, I knew I had seen him before. But where was it? I asked myself. When I was training? No. In Poland? No. In France? No. Then I remembered where I had seen you before. You see, until three weeks ago, I was a guard at Schloss Spangenberg. I have often seen you on the other side of the wire!"

In escaping, one slice of bad luck is so often fatal.

Chapter Nine

The only remedy, escape

Our escort was unwilling to tell us where we were bound in the big open Mercedes, and we knew only that we were travelling northeast. It was maddening to see the miles flashing by that had been so laboriously plodded in the opposite direction. Eventually, we drew into the minor town of Frankenberg on the River Eder, some fifty miles from Kassel. Taken to a building which had none of the usual trappings of either a police station or a military headquarters, we were obliged to sit for some time in an austere office rather like a waiting room. Our guards seemed on edge.

At last it seemed somebody was ready to see us and we were ordered down a passage. Our NCO escort led the way followed by Newborn, then Bruce and myself with our friendly sentimental captor behind me. We filed towards a room on the right and as I entered, the NCO was making a brusque military report to somebody seated at a table. The next moment, my friendly guard took me by the shoulder and propelled me forward with a mighty shove which sent me stumbling into the room. In a split second, he had transformed himself from a sympathetic human being into a good Nazi. For a moment I was shocked and puzzled, until I saw the cold fish-eyed civilian creep sitting at the table. Gestapo!

I knew far less about the Gestapo in 1941 than I was to learn as the war progressed, but I had heard enough about the breed to know one when I saw him. His malign presence also explained the anxious behaviour of our escort. Everybody in Germany feared them and their sinister powers, there was no doubt about that. Whether the ordinary German knew about the detailed horrors of the concentration camps or not, such expressions as "You'd better be careful what you say or you'll be going up the chimney" were becoming more commonplace.

Standing there in Luftwaffe uniform, my own reaction to the situation was that it had to be played very cool indeed. The immediate objective was to get out of the clutches of this character as soon as possible. I tried no old buck with him and was thankful that we had a military escort which meant that the Wehrmacht knew where we were. That made it less likely we could quietly disappear. I answered the softly spoken questions from our interrogator promptly and respectfully. Almost apologetically, I explained why I could not give information which it was my military duty to withhold.

Newborn and Bruce were looking at me sideways almost in disgust and disbelief. Then, to my horror, when they were required to answer questions, they seemed to go out of their way to demonstrate to me how it should really be done for maximum insolent effect. Fish-face was not amused and even our escort seemed aghast at their temerity. Our guards' expression did not imply outrage, as they would if the victim of the insolence had been one of their own officers, rather they were looks of pain, as if we were all in the same boat and they too wanted to get the hell out of it.

The ordeal was terminated by a phone call which we gathered came from the General of Area Military Headquarters. We were to be returned to Spangenberg forthwith to await his pleasure. The Gestapo man looked like a vulture deprived of some entrails and we went on our way relieved, if not rejoicing. When they were informed of the identity of their interrogator, Newborn and Bruce were considerably chastened. Had the same situation occurred two or three years later, the outcome would quite likely have been fatal.

Back at Spangenberg we were segregated. I was put into a civilian cell in the town, although I knew there were cells available in the castle with the others. Separation was always worrying because anything could happen with no witnesses around. The first interrogations by the *Abwehr* officer concentrated entirely on the whereabouts of the army officer's uniform we had stolen. I refused to say where it was. Then I was visited by a tall, thin *Feldwebel* interpreter who had a flat scarred face. He had been a prisoner of the British in the First World War and was always most considerate to us. With no malice intended, he was known as "Frankenstein".

Frankenstein had brought me some mail from home which included letters from Ann with photographs attached. He watched as I eagerly opened them and he saw I was obviously affected by the pictures. He smiled kindly.

"You are foolish, Herr Oberleutnant. You had much to live for, is it not? Your escapes have been gallant. This last one was brilliant. We all say so and I personally congratulate you. It is a pity that some think you should be shot for it. Be careful—be very careful."

I thought his use of the word "you *had* much to live for" was no more than his imperfect English and his warning that I should be careful was no more than a generality about my defiant attitude as a POW. Still, one does tend to take this kind of announcement rather seriously and the stomach does a slow roll. What really worried me was that it came from Frankenstein, who was a good old boy. It was not in his nature to invent a threat toward a prisoner. I therefore concluded that he had heard something. I had already established that the Germans did not shoot us as a matter of policy for using German uniform. They could not possibly have known about our visit to the Kassel airfield, although considering my record, they may have guessed. They had no means of knowing that we had spied on the engine testing plant. No—I did not believe there would be a formal trial and a firing squad. Then what was in Frankenstein's mind?

Later in the day I realised what Frankenstein was getting at and I firmly believe he intentionally warned me and perhaps saved my life. He had given me a veiled tip-off which was as direct as he dared to make it. It was after I had eaten my midday bowl of slop that the bolts of my cell door slammed back and the door opened on two evil-looking specimens, each carrying a Schmeisser. Adrenalin! I have a quick imagination and immediately thought of the Princes in the Tower. Enter the assassins! They said one word: *Spaziergang!*—Walk.

Perhaps I should have declined their offer, but I did not think of it. Exercise during a period of solitary confinement was prescribed by the Geneva Convention, but it invariably took the form of marching up and down for an hour in a small yard within high walls. There was such an exercise yard outside my cell, but I was herded out of the yard and into the road.

"*Los!*"—Get on—the Germans shouted and urged me forward with jerks of their Schmeissers. They wanted me to head out into the countryside towards some woods in the opposite direction from Kassel. My heart began to thump. We had all heard about this one often enough. "Shot while attempting a further escape." They ordered me to leave the road and head towards the trees. I did so but stuck very close to them so that they were almost treading on my heels. When they slowed down, so did I. I was determined that if they did shoot me, there would be powder burns on my body, and I knew the Senior British Officer would demand to see it.

"*Los! Los!*" they yelled and jerked the Schmeissers again. "*Weitergehen*" (Get a move on). I was petrified and reckoned it was time for a good ploy. I pretended to be more angry than frightened; stopped dead and turned to face them.

"Do you think we British are stupid?" I asked them. "We know what you want to do. I was warned and have sent a written message into the Schloss for the Senior British Officer. It gives him my word that I have no intention to escape from you. If I am shot today, at the end of the war you will be tried for murder and you will hang at the end of a British rope. It is your choice." I accompanied that threat with a rather graphic performance of a man choking with a rope around his neck.

The two uglies stared at each other for several seconds, and when they spoke again their tone was entirely different. I demanded that we return immediately to my cell, and that was what we did.

Back in the town cell, the *Abwehr* continued their efforts to prise out of me the hiding place of the uniform, and again they used the shooting threat which was now old hat. Then the *Lageroffizier*, a decent intelligent English-speaker, tried a different tack. The ex-principal of the Forestry School as a Reserve officer was now on the Russian Front. The uniform was the one he had worn at his wedding and had great sentimental value for his wife. She asked if I would please let her have it back. I am a sucker for a good sob story, but in this case there were overriding considerations.

"Please tell the lady I am sincerely sorry about that, but the uniform could be useful to us again and it is my duty not to reveal its hiding place. I have a duty the same as your husband has. I am sure you will understand."

Next day, the same officer came back with another story. For a long time, the Senior British Officer (SBO) had been asking the Wehrmacht to move us out of the castle because of the confined space and lack of exercise facilities. I knew this was true. Now, the German officer continued, the Wehrmacht had agreed to move us within a few weeks, provided the SBO gave his parole that there would be no further escaping from Spangenberg. The SBO, he said, had agreed, so please could the poor lady have her husband's wedding uniform back? I asked if the bit about the SBO's parole was true on his word of honour as a German officer. He said it was. It was quite false and I should have known better, but later that day I showed him where the uniform was hidden.

The next day, the same officer, accompanied by guards, escorted me to the Schloss cells. On the walk up to the castle, he was chatty. He came out with the old hardy perennial about us being brother Saxons. We should not be fighting against each other, but against our common enemy and that of civilisation, the Russian communists. I told him I thought there might have been some truth in this, except that the Germans seemed to have some fairly selective ideas about what was civilised. I asked him if he thought the merciless persecution of the Jews fell within their definition. I also asked him if the German expansionist programme and the armed take-over of neighbouring states was also their idea of civilised conduct—the rape of Poland, Czechoslovakia, the bombing of Rotterdam and Coventry. He came back with the injustices of the Treaty of Versailles and I admitted that in retrospect it didn't seem all that clever. I assured him nonetheless that the Germans could forget the idea of the British joining forces with them against the Russians. Churchill had made the point plain enough. He would join forces with the Devil, if necessary, to see the end of Nazi tyranny. Back came another hardy perennial.

"We did not start this war but, thank God, we shall finish it!"

I told him I did not agree with either half of that statement. He closed the discussion with another observation, the truth of which I little realised at the time, nor do I think he understood the reasons for the truth of it.

"Whoever wins this war, you or us, it will mean the end of the British Empire."

Our Spangenberg escape and the treatment I received as a result of it marked a turning point in my attitude towards the enemy and captivity. Why I was not sent straight to Colditz I do not know, but from this time forward, I was officially labelled *Deutschfeindlich,* meaning "definitely anti-German". What they thought all the other chaps were, goodness only knows. As a *Deutschfeindlich* individual I was to be grabbed on any possible charge, real or contrived, and thrown into solitary confinement. In the Colditz guardroom, when the German garrison capitulated in April 1945, they found photographs of seven of us prominently displayed with instructions to all German guards to do just that. Perhaps this was intended to break our spirit or upset the balance of our minds. It had the opposite effect on my own spirit and I became increasingly intransigent and provocative.

Back once more in Spangenberg Castle, I was put into a cell adjacent to those of Dominic Bruce and Eustace Newborn. These cells were in a part of the attics and were reached by a long stone spiral staircase which went up to the cells and nowhere else, as all other doors off the staircase had been bricked up. My cell had a little barred window which overlooked the scene of our recent escape triumph, the bridge over the moat and the guardroom. We were not sentenced for our escape, but held in "preventive arrest" as if the Germans were cooking up something special; perhaps a court martial, which could award sentences in excess of the *Kommandant's* twenty-eight-day limit. The *Kommandant* assured us that the time spent in solitary would count off our eventual sentence in accordance with normal military practice. He obviously thought the cooler was the best place for us—or for his own peace of mind.

Our treatment in the cells varied from one guard company to another. Companies A and B were apparently taking the mickey out of company C because several of them had sprung to attention and saluted us on the way out. The upshot of this was that A and B treated us with reasonably good humour, and C company was far less gracious. Particularly bloody-minded was an *Unteroffizier* friend of Blockhead's, who was now doing his own stint in a cooler for having let us out through the gate. Blockhead's mate—I call him "Poface"—was a sour character who enjoyed shouting and pushing us about. He also took every opportunity to search our cells, an excuse to throw things around and leave our meagre belongings in disarray.

In solitary confinement we were not allowed Red Cross food nor cigarettes, although, as we were under only preventive arrest, they should

"Poface" objects to PDT's consumption of tobacco.

not really have been denied us. There was a small iron stove in each cell and we were given a miserable little ration of fuel for these. In the centre of my cell, near the stove, there was a hefty wooden pillar, part of the structure of the castle. Against the pillar stood a small table. Each cell had an electric light with a screw-in type bulb under the familiar round metal shade, green on top and white below, hanging from the ceiling by a fly string.

Every day, we were taken down the staircase and out over the bridge to the exercise pen where we marched up and down for an hour. Returning to the cells up the long spiral staircase, we went ahead of our guard, usually an elderly man, who followed behind laboriously puffing up the eighty or so steps. It was usual for us youngsters to disappear ahead of him round the bend of the spiral. This gave me an idea for smuggling in some food and maybe even cigarettes which really do seem to alleviate the pangs of hunger to some extent.

Next time I was taken out for exercise, I dropped a note in the courtyard with a wink to another prisoner who was standing around there. The note requested that a tin of cigarettes, matches and some food be placed near the top of the staircase. This was done while we were exercising. On our return, I disappeared from the guard's view round the bend in the spiral staircase on the way up; rushed ahead; snatched up the contraband, concealed it on my person; and then allowed the guard to catch up. In the cell, I fashioned a hiding place for the cigarettes by making three flat cardboard hooks which just slipped over the top hole in the light shade and on these hooks, I laid rows of cigarettes so that the top of the sloping shade was partially covered with them.

I took care not to smoke for some time before an expected visit by the guards, but one day Blockhead's mate, Poface, came up looking for trouble as usual. As I heard his clomping footsteps approaching the top of the stone spiral staircase, I threw my dog-end out of the window and frantically waved my arms about in an attempt to disperse the smoke. When Poface entered he sniffed then screamed, "You have been smoking!" and immediately turned my cell upside down to search. He dragged the straw out of the palliasse, threw rations about and emptied a small tin of sugar onto the floor in a vindictive orgy.

212

Furious at not finding the cigarettes, he eventually stomped off down the staircase. I was fuming angry too. I waited for Poface to appear on the bridge to the guardroom, gave him a shrill whistle from my heavily barred window, and as he looked up I nonchalantly took a good draw on a cigarette and in full view, blew out a cloud of smoke to the sky.

Poface tore back up the staircase and arrived panting and screaming to repeat the search while I sat and smiled at him. Dusk was upon us and he switched on the light to aid his search. Foiled again, he thought of a clever reprisal. He would leave me in the dark for the whole evening by removing the bulb from my light fitting. He started to unscrew the bulb, during which process the shade was jiggling about. I realised it was a matter of seconds before my cigarettes would shower down upon him.

They did, but precisely at the moment the unscrewing broke the electrical contact. I saw them begin to fall at the moment the light went out and probably because he was in such a vile temper, Poface did not feel them pattering on his shoulders. Raging and swearing, he left me. I had no light and that put him one up, so I resolved to equal the score.

With outright malice, I planned my revenge. Next day, I took an empty round cigarette tin with its lid on (we used them as little containers for anything) and stood it on a plate in a prominent place on my table and watched the bridge for his expected approach. When I saw him coming, I set my trap. There stood the tin on the table with its lid on. As he entered my cell, I was lying on my bed. I feigned waking from a deep sleep with surprise and alarm. Just too late for clever old Poface, I leapt up from my bunk and made as if to go for the tin. With a shout of triumph, he beat me to it and grabbed it firmly in his right hand. His scream was a mixture of pain and fury. I had just filled it with glowing coals from my stove!

Poface dropped the tin and the hot coals began to smoke and scorch the wooden floor. He clasped his blistered fingers under his armpit. I had gone too far and the situation turned very ugly indeed. It was very obvious Poface couldn't take a joke. First he took a swing at my face with his heavy bunch of keys which I blocked with my forearm. Then, with his left hand, because his right hand was too sore, he whipped out his bayonet and faced me. He was white-faced and trembling. His chest was heaving and his lips were drawn back tightly from his teeth. He lunged at me with the bayonet and I side-stepped the thrust. Screaming abuse, he came at me again. I dodged behind the oak pillar and little stove. There followed a grim ring-a-ring of roses round the pillar and the stove. I was extremely frightened, but considerably more agile than he was. The hullabaloo was terrific, what with him and me shouting and Bruce and Eustace joining in. He nearly got me against the pillar and lunged again, but I managed to dodge his bayonet as it thumped into the wood. Fortunately, the screams and shouts were heard by other Germans and there were soon footsteps pounding up the staircase. Poface was still screaming hysterically when a *Feldwebel* and a private burst in through the doorway.

They had to restrain Poface physically and gradually order was restored. The smouldering floor was stamped out and the little cinders were scooped up. They took Poface away and he was never seen in our cells again. I felt very satisfied with the outcome which caused much merriment throughout Schloss Spangenberg, and I knew I would get a few more days' solitary.

I must stress that the importance of such incidents was the one-upmanship it afforded us in our oppression, the healthy laughter it generated and the blow to German morale when it was forced home to them, time and time again, that no matter what they did, they could not

After burning his hand, "Poface" goes in for some bayonet work.

get us down. The excitement and satisfaction of such activities in between escape attempts helped to preserve at least a modicum of sanity.

Our protracted stay in the Spangenberg cells was quite bearable now that we had organised illicit tobacco and Red Cross food. It became even less tedious when Dominic Bruce had his lock-picking tools smuggled in and proceeded to let himself out of his cell using a table knife to slide back the bolts. Having done this, he liberated Eustace and then unlocked my door. We decided my cell was the least austere of the three and gathered there each evening for a sociable chat once we were reasonably sure there would be no more routine visits from our jailers.

All good things come to an end, however. During one of these evening socials, we were all sitting on my bed with our feet up and steaming mugs of cocoa in our hands when we were startled by footsteps on the staircase. After a moment of panic, we realised there was no time to disperse, so we sat back again and, with intense interest spiced with a dash of foreboding, awaited events.

The cell door was pushed open by a German *Sonderführer* interpreter from the Censorship Department. The fact that the door was not locked apparently did not register with him and he entered the cell intent upon reading me a charge sheet and the award of ten days' more solitary for damaging the cell floor with hot cinders.

We sat there wordless and smiling benignly as the *Sonderführer* cleared his throat, adjusted his steel-rimmed glasses and read from the charge sheet which I was obliged to sign. Having completed his chore, he turned to leave the cell, reached the doorway and, with his back to us, suddenly froze. He slowly turned to face us again, his mouth hanging open with incredulity. He stared, blinked and said quietly, "But there are THREE of you here!"

We smiled and nodded as if according full marks to a child for mastering a difficult test of comprehension. Then, as if suddenly electrified, he broke into a high-pitched torrent of protest and shouted for help from my window overlooking the guardroom while we calmly drank our cocoa as if there were no disturbance at all.

Eustace and I were each sentenced to a further five days' solitary, and Bruce was to be court-martialled on the serious military charge of breaking free from arrest. I gather he got away with it by arguing that getting out of a cell was part of escaping, and "escaping" was not a court-martial offence for a POW according to the Geneva Convention.

After nearly eight weeks in the cells, we had received no sentence for our escape. There had been no more talk of shooting, but the delay was ominous and we expected a court martial and removal to the dreaded Colditz *Straflager* (Punishment Camp), rumours of which had been circulating for some time. Finally we were let out of the cells and told to pack our simple belongings. The whole camp was to move. This was a blow because Bruce and I had by now formulated two more escape schemes. With the *Kommandant*'s reassurance that the time already served in solitary would count against our eventual sentence, we were herded out of the fairyland castle which we saw for the last time.

I have no firm recollection of our journey from Spangenberg. I believe there was the usual flurry of activity by the train jumpers and it was the normal depressing and uncomfortable experience, although mercifully quite short. Our destination was an enormous hutted camp, Oflag VI-B at Warburg, about forty miles northwest of Kassel.

Warburg accommodated 3,000 prisoners and was soulless, bleak and unfinished. Washing facilities were a row of taps surrounded by a sea of mud and the pit latrine, or *Abort*, was a thirty-six-holer serving our end of the camp, where the RAF and the Fleet Air Arm had two or three huts to themselves. The remaining huts were occupied by army officers.

The main gate was at our end of the compound and, as at Barth, let into a German compound housing the administrative offices of the *Kommandantur*, the punishment cell block, Red Cross clothing store, German barracks and *Abwehr* headquarters. Close by the brick buildings at the far end was a secondary gate with a permanent guard situated very close by a machine gun and searchlight tower on stilts. This gate let out into the wide world—an extensive plain without cover.

Immediately upon arrival, Bruce and I picked any old adjacent beds in the RAF block and without waiting to unpack any gear or bother about domestic comfort considerations, we were off to case the joint and formulate escape plans. I firmly believed the essence of success was to get in first. What interested us most was the secondary gate which we observed was used occasionally to march out guarded working parties of our own orderlies. These were never allowed through the gate without the escorting guard producing a pass, apparently issued from the main guardroom. However, the identity check on individual Germans passing through appeared lax, certainly much slacker than the gate security system at Spangenberg. We immediately formulated a plan, registered it with the escape committee and set to work on two German army uniforms.

From these preparations I spared time only to send off another urgent split photograph to MI9 in London. This contained a description and the position of the engine testing plant we had discovered on our last escape, and some hot information about U-Boat operations and German installations at the port of Saint-Nazaire in France that had come our way via a recently-downed bomber crew whose captor, a U-Boat captain, had been foolishly garrulous.

Our Warburg escape plan suffered a number of setbacks, and the first of these was the German security officer himself. Major Rademacher was a particularly unpleasant, very efficient, and thoroughly unprincipled Nazi. This specimen became a byword among the prisoners for callousness and provocation. Several apolitical Germans hinted that they disliked him as much as we did. Some even apologised to us after a particularly destructive search when an elderly British major was hit in the teeth with a rifle butt. All our belongings had been thrown out of the hut windows by the Germans and, together with our bedding, were scattered in the rain while we were body searched. The apologetic Germans excused themselves by saying Rademacher's orders had been "Destroy, never mind searching." This man, having perused the prisoners' crime record sheets, which had just followed us from Spangenberg, sought me out. He came looking for trouble.

By my bed, I had stuck a sheet of brown paper on the wall and on this I had pasted all the photographs I had of Ann—my lifeline in those dreary days. Rademacher leered at the photographs, made a dirty gesture with his hands followed by a coarse remark about my nice bed companion. He also remarked about how comely she would be for the German troops when they occupied England. Luckily my friend Pissy Edwards saw what was coming and grabbed me before I could hit Rademacher. Pissy hissed in my ear, "Don't be a bloody fool, Pete. Can't you see that's exactly what he wants you to do?" Rademacher would probably have made it an excuse to shoot me on the spot. I cooled down, but Rademacher now knew he had found my Achilles heel.

He ordered me to turn out my belongings. As I did so, his eyes lit up when he saw Ann's carefully packaged letters to me, all of which bore the stamps of German censors. The clever bastard snatched them. "I am taking these for censoring." I pointed out to him that every letter bore the censor's rubber stamp and begged him to let me keep them. He smiled with his head to one side.

"I am taking these for further censoring," he said. "If you behave, you may get them back. And one thing more, you will not be a nuisance to me here as you have been elsewhere. Here you will not get the chance. I shall see to it that you and your friend, Bruce, spend most of your time in the cells."

He then told me that we were soon to begin serving twenty-eight days solitary confinement for the Spangenberg escape. He said the sentence had just come through. We pointed out that we had already served much more than twenty-eight days and had the word of Spangenberg's *Kommandant* that this time would count against sentence.

Rademacher smiled nastily. "I am not responsible for the promises of fools," he said, "You, Bruce and Newborn be ready for the cells at nine o'clock tomorrow morning." He pronounced our names as Toonshtaahl, Brookeh, and Neffborn. He then swaggered off with Ann's letters in his hand and subsequently, whenever I asked for their return, I was told that they had been lost.

With the prospect of a twenty-eight-day stint in the cooler to impede our escape plan, it looked as if Rademacher's threat to keep us out of action would be made good. We immediately went to the escape committee with our problems, only to find that they had made a decision which complicated things still further.

One of our particularly bright orderlies had managed to take a good look at a working party's pass for exit through the secondary gate. He had described it in detail to John Mansel, our old friend from Thorn. John had now developed his art and at Warburg trained others so that he soon had a well-organised forgery department working to his high standards. As

Warburg split up later, and officers dispersed to other camps, they took Mansel's perfectionist training with them and I think it fair to say that he was the British master forger of the Second World War.

With an opportunity to produce a working party's gate pass, the escape committee now waxed ambitious. Instead of just Bruce and Tunstall getting out, why not use their home-made German uniforms idea to march out a nice big bogus working party? When they told us of this development, our hearts sank. The scheme had now become more complicated and cumbersome, but it would have been selfish and less than our duty not to agree. The committee undertook to have our "Goon skins" completed together with all other paraphernalia made, such as dummy rifles and bayonets, and John Mansel would come up with a forged gate pass to wave at the guard—all this while Bruce and I served our time in the cooler. We still had no German money, maps or personal identity documents and we would have to make our own way through Germany as best we could. Well, we had done it before, so why not again?

Another difficulty holding things up was finding a satisfactory method of dying the pale blue Belgian army greatcoats. These had turned up from goodness knows where and we were tailoring them into German uniform greatcoats, but there was none of the dye the Poles had smuggled into us at Thorn for such purposes.

That night, anticipating more time in the cooler, I lay awake for some time pondering this snag. Eventually, on the verge of sleep, my mind wandered off to more pleasant thoughts of home and Ann. I started to compose a mental invitation list for our wedding. It was a nice dreamy exercise until it came to the name of Hew Watt, a childhood friend. Our family once went to visit him at his father's farm, at Heath Place, Orsett. I was proudly wearing my very first long trousers, part of a brand new white sailor suit. Hew and I had a boisterous romp on their lawn. Sadly the grass was still somewhat damp from a recent shower and I drowsily recalled the scolding I got for all the green stains on it from the grass. Then suddenly I was jolted wide awake. The grass had stained it green *like a German uniform!* Could wet grass be the answer?

I waited impatiently for our hut door to be unbolted and was out with the very early-morning walkers. I am sure some of those early birds must have looked at me sideways with a sympathetic smile. "Poor old Tunstall, he's picking grass now. Pity! Ah well."

Before breakfast, I had soaked the grass and rubbed it into the Belgian blue material. The result was perfect, and we went to the cooler full of good cheer, hoping that we might come out to a well-prepared escape attempt.

Dominic Bruce and I were to be orderlies in the working party and the Goon skins were to be worn by a couple of chaps who spoke perfect German. One, I remember, was an RAF pilot named Stevens who had grown up and been educated in Germany. Being Jewish, he was lucky to be alive and free. The other, if I remember correctly, was an army officer, Lance Pope, who also spoke excellent German.

The big difficulty from my point of view was that I was spending so much time in solitary confinement. Incarceration in the Warburg cells followed a set routine. Each carrying his own bedding and toilet kit, we were marched out through the main gate into the German compound, then into a smaller cage outside the cellblock. In this cage, we waited under guard while the new intake was called into an anteroom, one by one. There, each customer's clothing, blankets, and bits and pieces were searched while he stripped naked and was examined intimately for contraband. There was no question of getting even a hacksaw blade into those cells.

At least we were not forced to suffer the stink and indignity of a latrine bucket in the cell itself. When nature called, we were required to rap on the cell door, a cell guard came, and we were required to say "*Abort bitte*", meaning "Lavatory, please", whereupon the guard opened the cell door and conducted the prisoner to a lavatory and waited for him to complete operations before locking him back in his cell.

By some standards, this was not a bad arrangement, except that a lazy or bloody-minded guard could take his time about responding to the call or even decide not to bother at all. The situation could become desperate. One of the several rigged charges for which I did an extra ten days' solitary at Warburg was, and I quote literally from the charge sheet, "For saying '*Abort bitte*' in an arrogant manner." I had been kept waiting to bursting point. Major Rademacher's gang had been well briefed and served their boss faithfully.

We were fortunate indeed that our release from the cells coincided with the readiness of our escape scheme. The bogus working party gathered in the middle of the camp, our phoney guards appeared from nowhere and we were marched to the secondary gate. Stevens went to the guard at the gate, showed his pass, and an argument followed. The gate guard had found some fault with the pass and insisted that Stevens return to the guardroom and have it put right. Stevens about-turned us and marched us back to the middle of the camp, where the whole party gradually dissolved as magically as it had formed a few minutes earlier—guards and all.

Uniforms, superb dummy rifles and bayonets in their scabbards were all safely tucked away in their respective, very cunning, hides, and we stood by for drastic repercussions, but to our amazement, nothing happened. Stevens told us that there had been something irregular about the way the pass had been stamped and while this was being sorted out, I served my further ten days' solitary for asking to go to the lavatory in an arrogant manner. Again, my release from the cells was well timed for the next attempt and the performance was repeated.

Again we were held up at the gate. This time, the objection was apparently that the pass had not been signed by the guard commander in person. After a fine exchange between Stevens and that gate guard including expletives such as *Du liebe Gott, Scheisse* and *Befehl ist Befehl* (Good God! Shit! Orders are Orders!) Stevens again about-turned us and again we melted into limbo to await the storm when the gate guard should mention the story in the guard room.

Again, by some miracle, nothing happened and I served another stretch. This was for insulting the German nation. While being searched by one of Rademacher's men for entry into the cells on the "*Abort bitte*" charge, the searcher who was being meticulous yet jocular had said to me, "Fucking Chermans, *ja*?" Thinking he was merely airing his knowledge of barrack-room English, I had replied "*Ja*" in an uninterested way, meaning he had got it right. The new charge was, "Insulting the German Nation by saying 'Fucking Germans'"! Quite obviously, Rademacher and his crew could go on like this forever and clearly they intended to do so. The only remedy was escape.

Once more out of the cells, our scheme was poised for another attempt. After the two previous failures, the tension was acute. This time, it was known that the rubber stamp was right, it was known that a senior NCO named Braun was to be the duty guard commander for that day, and what was more, a specimen of his signature had been obtained and carefully forged on the pass. There could be no mistake. For the third time, we marched up to the gate and Stevens presented his pass.

The gate was opened. As we began to pass through, the guard called up to the machine-gunner in the Goon box.

"Hey, didn't *Feldwebel* Braun go on compassionate leave yesterday because his mother died?"

"Yes, that's right," said the machine-gunner.

"*Halt!*" screamed the guard.

How could a pass be signed this morning by a man who went on compassionate leave yesterday? Pandemonium followed. Considering the total lack of cover outside the wire, there was no question of our making a bolt for it with a machine gun and several rifles having a go at us.

A few moments of chaos ensued with prisoners and guards, some real, some phoney, dithering and running in all directions. A few shots were fired which fortunately hit nobody, and the next minute there was a headlong flight of bogus orderlies, followed closely by bogus guards, hotly pursued by real guards towards the elderly gentlemen's brick barrack block close by. There, in blissful ignorance of all these goings-on, some stuffy old senior Pongos were deeply engrossed in a rubber of bridge.

Imagine the irritation caused to one such bridge school as it was described to me afterwards. Just as somebody had decorously bid "two hearts", the door of the room suddenly burst open and a British orderly, without apology or explanation, rudely tore across the senior officers' room and dived out through the window. It takes a lot to dislocate a dedicated bridge school, however, and those worthies looked at each other with raised eyebrows and a comment or two of gentle amazement before somebody said "two spades". At that moment, a breathless German guard—a real one—barged into the room, glared around and crashed out again. Hardly had he departed, and the bid had gone up to "three hearts", when there was a further upheaval at the door and another dishevelled guard, complete with rifle, appeared, slammed the door shut and, breathing heavily, leaned against it. The bridge players stared at the German in dismay, their confusion absolute when he panted, with a perfect English accent,

"Don't just sit there with your bloody mouths open. Hide me!"

Not one of the escape party was caught. The German uniforms, civilian clothes, forged papers and dummy rifles were stowed away in the hides where they had been previously kept and these were camouflaged at emergency speed which does not make for thoroughness. The whole camp was tense in expectation of a German onslaught which we knew must soon follow. The place swarmed with all available German troops who carried out an immediate search.

Under the circumstances the search was not well organised, with Rademacher and his crew storming around directing a panic operation. There were a few nasty incidents, but nothing of very great value was lost. My own security measures were among those at fault. In the rush, I had carelessly left among my scant belongings a small scrap of the cloth I had experimentally treated with wet grass to make it German-uniform-green. It was found and handed to Rademacher who was delighted.

Rademacher shouted he had known all along that Toonshtaall and Brookeh would be behind the whole thing and I soon found myself before his office desk in the *Abwehr* headquarters. Meanwhile, overnight, our hides were better secured; a wise precaution, for the search continued for several days. Rademacher's main anxiety was that the prisoners had acquired rifles. These were so perfectly made that it never occurred to the guards who had seen them that they were dummies.

Rademacher stormed at me and threatened furiously until eventually I could take no more. I broke down and agreed to do a deal with him. I told him it was my duty to give no direct information, but if he would please release me from this intense and distressing interrogation and return my fiancée's letters to me, I would give him a helpful tip. He eagerly agreed at once. I extracted from him a promise on his word of honour as a German officer that he would never let the British know I had squealed. He became almost conspiratorial and friendly. I seriously doubted if the bastard had any honour, but he was delighted with the information I gave him. Ann's letters were immediately found and I was escorted back to our compound by one of Rademacher's henchmen. I must have looked very downcast to him because he no doubt knew of my betrayal of my comrades. I warned my friends to stand by for some repercussion the next morning and soon enough it occurred.

Looking out at the German compound from our quarters it seemed as if every soldier who was not actually on guard duty round the wire was falling in on parade. Obviously something big was afoot, like a massive search or worse.

The German officers and senior NCOs were going round the ranks with clipboards and lists and carefully looking at every man's rifle. The process went painfully on for a very long time. And when the guards on duty round the wire were relieved they joined the strange process on the German parade ground. It was as if every man's rifle was being checked against a list from the armoury, and that is exactly what was happening. The information I had so reluctantly spilled to Rademacher was that I understood two guards had been subverted and had procured a couple of Mauser rifles for us. I had suggested that he should have every man's rifle checked against the armoury's records of issue and inventory.

This prodigious waste of time had not yielded the desired results, and I soon found myself in Rademacher's office again where he was jumping up and down in great form. I told him it was not my fault if his bloody NCOs couldn't check their own records properly. We could hardly believe our eyes when the next morning, the whole process started all over again. Needless to say, this was followed by Bruce and I being marched off to solitary yet again. The extraordinary thing was that we were still not shipped off to Colditz, but were eventually back with the rest of the prisoners and hatching a new escape scheme.

About this time at Warburg, we occasionally had the harrowing experience of seeing Soviet prisoners marched along the outside of our wire. These broken people were in an incredible state of ragged starvation. The Germans considered them *Untermenschen*—animals who deserved no human consideration whatsoever. The USSR was not a signatory to the Geneva Convention and therefore treated German prisoners as they saw fit. The Germans did likewise. The plight of these haggard scarecrows rendered quite believable the stories we heard later of dead prisoners being propped up on *Appell*, to be counted so that their meagre rations would continue to be issued and, worse, rumours of cannibalism within their dreadful camps.

It is now known that Soviet prisoners died in their millions, the largest single category of Nazism's victims with the exception of the Jews. Seeing these poor shuffling wretches at such close quarters made us realise that, hungry though we were, we had much to be thankful for—especially our supply, intermittent though it was, of Red Cross food parcels. When we threw anything over the wire to the Russians, the Germans objected violently. However, we continued to do this whenever we could, despite threats that we would be shot at for doing so.

It was at Warburg that I first met the legendary Douglas Bader whose prowess as a fighter pilot with two "tin" legs was already well known. We had heard on the grapevine that he had collided with a German fighter during a dogfight over the French coast and had to bail out in August 1941, thus becoming a POW. Even the Germans regarded Bader with some awe. They had every reason to do so, not only because of his personal combat successes and leadership against the Luftwaffe, but because of his totally intransigent attitude to his captors from whom he made attempts to escape, legs or no legs. These included a descent from a high hospital window down knotted bed sheets. He got away but the Germans made a panic search of the locality and he was recaptured.

When not trying to escape, Bader led them on one dance after another. He may not have been briefed as I was by Squadron Leader Evans to be "as big a bloody nuisance as possible to the enemy", but he was, nonetheless. In any case, a man of Bader's spirit and decidedly autocratic attitudes could hardly be anything else if subjected to captivity. I am sure the Germans regretted that his collision with a German fighter ever put him in their charge.

Douglas was soon enquiring about the possibilities of escaping. Someone told him Pissy Edwards and Pete Tunstall were the two front-runners at that stage of the game and he sought me out to talk about it. We did so at considerable length and, perhaps unwisely, I told him about my "split photographs". Whether, in the long run, my association with the great man was for better or worse I will never be quite certain. In Bader's biography, *Reach for the Sky*, it says that he and I became "a natural team", but I believe that where Dougie was concerned, it was more a matter of a leader and followers. You had better follow the leader implicitly or else, and any "cock-ups" would usually be attributed to the followers.

On first meeting Douglas Bader, one was forcibly struck by the power of his personality. Woe betide any young cock who thought he might share the roost. Mind you, had he not been so self-willed and egotistical, it is unlikely that he would ever have overcome the loss of his legs in a pre-war air crash and then bulldozed his way, against all opposition, back into the cockpit of a wartime fighter aircraft where he vied with the best. It was said of him that he had no pity for himself, so why waste it on other people?

Such a man is not a normal specimen and it exasperated me when some people judged him by normal standards and were irritated by his overbearing manner. On the other hand, there were many of us who admired Douglas tremendously and tempered our judgment accordingly. I did not believe that such a character could possibly go through life without exciting critics and making enemies of the less flamboyant.

In no time, we had our heads together on aspects of an escape plan which he and three others were urgently contemplating. His companions were Pete Gardner who had arrived from Lübeck with him; an army lieutenant, David Lubbock; and a commando, Captain Keith Smith. The idea was that these four were going to join a party of POWs going under guard to the clothing store on a routine visit, at the conclusion of which the prisoners were marched back again into our compound. The Germans did not bother to count them. They took them all in and brought them all back again and that was that. However, in the clothing store there was a securely locked office to which the prisoners had no access.

Pete Gardner, though, had become a very fair burglar, and the plan was for the four escapers, with the help of a diversion by the other prisoners in the store, to pick the lock, slip into the office and lock the door after them. The other prisoners would eventually be marched back into the main compound with the guards no doubt thinking they had them all because there was no one left in the store. The quartet would wait until it was dark, when they would quietly exit by a window into the German compound. This was surrounded by a barbed-wire fence which would not be too difficult to climb over because it was an unlit single wire fence, like the one I climbed over at Barth.

"How could legless Douglas Bader do that?" you may ask. My answer would be: "The same way that he could fly a Spitfire and play a very fair game of golf or even squash." The others would no doubt give him a hand. The snag was that the clothing store was very close to our floodlit, well-guarded perimeter fence and could be seen from the nearest Goon box with its searchlight and machine gun. The fence guards and the machine-gunner needed to be distracted by something else while the four escapers slipped out of the window and into the deeper shadows. Furthermore, they needed to know if the coast appeared to be clear by receiving some sort of noisy signal from a watcher in our compound.

I undertook to create the necessary diversion with enough noise to give the "all clear" signal. During an afternoon in January 1942, the four hopeful escapers went with a large party, under guard, to the clothing store. At some pre-arranged stage the whole party became rather unruly and under cover of their obstreperous behaviour, Pete Gardner picked the lock into the adjacent unoccupied office where Douglas Bader and the three others quietly hid themselves, locking the door after them. The purpose of the visit completed, the German guards ushered everyone out and, thinking they had emptied the place, marched the remainder back into camp, as usual without counting them. So far so good.

I had decided to create my noisy signal and diversion carrying a sack half-full of empty tin cans while pretending that I was either drunk or round the bend. Having chosen the moment for their break when, so far as could be seen, the German compound was quiet for the night, I slipped out of a barrack block window and staggered out clattering the tins then weaved up to the dreaded warning wire, singing lustily, and promptly fell over it, scattering tins in all directions. Guards shouted in alarm as they ran towards that part of the wire and the searchlight in the machine-gun tower obligingly swung my way while I yelled in a panic that was not altogether feigned, "*Nicht schiessen, nicht schiessen!*" (Don't shoot!) I am very glad to say nobody did.

The diversion worked well enough. The four escapers heard all the commotion and quietly slipped out of the building. They made their way successfully through most of the German compound. Then, by sheer bad luck, they eventually bumped into an off-duty German soldier who was wandering around for no good reason. He gave the alarm and only Smith, the commando, managed to climb over the German compound fence and get clean away for five days, at the end of which, despite warm clothing, he was almost dead from winter exposure. Douglas, Pete Gardner and David Lubbock were arrested.

The story has a droll ending. A popular trick with some Germans arresting escapers was to thump them on the toes with their rifle butts—which really hurts! Never one to convey despair, Bader was a bit truculent in the German compound and one of the guards decided to teach him manners with a good hefty thump on the toes. He was amazed at the prisoner's apparent indifference to pain, so he thumped again—harder. Bader laughed at him. The infuriated guard was about to try again when one of the others, recognising Bader, pointed out that he was the "Wing commander with wooden feet!"—but *auf Deutsch* of course. Bader really enjoyed this little episode.

Diversion duty done, I managed to extricate myself from the tin-spilling performance and sneaked back into the barrack block before the riot squad arrived, thus avoiding another confrontation with my friend Rademacher. There had already been far too many of these, what with their contrived charges and our own unyielding reaction to their persecution. There had been other incidents such as my trumpet voluntary on parade on Christmas Day which had caused chaos, amusement and umbrage, and on another occasion, when a bloody-minded German officer had enjoyed keeping us on parade for a long period on some pretext or other. Soon becoming fed up with this, I had done a spectacular parade ground faint and was carried off by three giggling chums, equally delighted to avoid further tedium.

It all went on and on and I forget many of the minor high jinks, not even remembering some of them when ex-POW friends have tried to recall them to me. But the result was that Bruce and I were spending very much more time in the cooler than out of it and had little or no opportunity to join in the "legitimate" camp activities, such as lectures, courses or dramatics. Worse still, our escape preparations were hampered, which was

Colditz, den *18. Feb.* 1943

Dem

Brit. Hptm. Tunstall 25?

Zu Ihrem Strafvollzug von . *10.* . Tagen geschärftem
Stubenarrest am *18.2.43* um *14* . Uhr im Hof ein-
treffen.

Nach dem Appell dem Arzt vorstellen.

Reichmann
Feldw.und Arrestaufseher.

One of many: a typical punishment slip awarding PDT ten days'
solitary in the "cooler".

Rademacher's primary aim. We therefore decided that our next escape
attempt would be from the cells themselves.

The cell block was in the German compound and if we could get out of it,
we would be in as favourable a position as Smith, the commando captain,
who had so recently made a five-day run. He had jumped a goods train
at Dössel which was close by the camp. Of course, we would be unable to
take any disguise nor even a minimum amount of gear into the cells with
us because of the meticulous search always made of each new customer on
the way in. We therefore decided to follow Smith's travel pattern and make
for France.

The cellblock was of heavy timber construction and there was no
question of breaking out of it without adequate tools. This was our one
major obstacle—how to get the necessary tools into the cells with us. We
were due in any day now, awaiting vacancies. Then it snowed. Suddenly I
remembered the nonsense at Thorn when I had been pretending to hide
treasure charts and rude "intelligence messages" in the soft sand. Why not
do the same with a roll of tools in the snow outside the cell block while

queuing to be searched. The tools could be recovered from the snow later when we were let out into the same pen for exercise.

Bruce and I made a selection of essential home-made tools and wrapped them into a small bundle. Then we waited eagerly for our next stretch of solitary, praying that the snow, a good six inches deep, would not thaw. It did not, and we were ordered in for another spell together with four or five others.

The cells were in constant use and filled to capacity, but every few days there was a turnover of customers. It was like moving day with each prisoner carrying his bedding and such belongings as were permitted bundled into his coarse bed sheet and slung over his shoulder. The new intake arrived at the main door of the cell block. By arrangement, another chap pushed himself forward for the first search inside. Meanwhile, the rest of us stood about in the snow outside under the eyes of two other guards. Then two of the other chaps started an argument and as one wound himself up to give the other a haymaker on the chin, the guards stepped in to restore order. As they did so, I scraped a rut in the snow with my foot and Bruce neatly dropped the tool roll into it. I then quickly kicked some snow back over the hole and stood on it—all done in a flash with a look of cherubic innocence on our faces in well practised manner.

The next day, as we piled out for one hour's statutory exercise, I created another diversion and Bruce scraped up the tools and, at the end of our exercise took them into his cell where he hid them in the wood shavings of his mattress. The Germans would never think to search for contraband in the actual cells. We planned to start working on the break the next day.

In the morning we woke to that dead hush which means another fall of snow. We had cherry red noses and there were ice crystals where our breath had frozen on our blankets. Looking out of our cell windows, our spirits fell. There appeared to be inches more snow with a frozen crust sparkling on top. This was no escaping weather and we reluctantly decided to wait for improved conditions. The tools were now safe where we wanted them and we could pick our moment. If the weather did not improve during this stretch, we had no doubt we would soon be in for another. The weather remained severe and then the blow fell. Bruce and I were ordered to pack our belongings. Just the two of us were going to another camp and we had no doubt at all which one that would be. Colditz!

There was little time for farewells, but enough to comply with an order from Douglas Bader to teach Pete Gardner my split photograph technique. I was not entirely happy about this because if either Gardner or I had a split photograph discovered by the Germans, there would be no way to warn the other that the method had been "blown". The censors in all prison camps would be alerted to watch out for any other such secret messages and we could both end up on an espionage charge, and there was no knowing what the consequences might be.

When I met Douglas Bader again a year later at Colditz, he told us a successful break had been made from the Warburg cells using our tools, so at least our effort had not been in vain. He also told me that Pete Gardner had sent some split photographs home successfully. I gathered that all such messages had to have the preamble "Message from Wg Cmdr Bader". Our Douglas was never loath to gather the limelight.

My last farewell was to Pissy Edwards. We wished each other "good escaping" and wondered which of us would have chalked up the most attempts by the next time we met. If we were going to this Colditz place, I had no doubt he would soon follow.

Alas, it was not to be. Pissy was moved to another Luftwaffe prison camp at Schubin. One sunny day, while sitting with his room-mates, he said quite unemotionally, "I've had enough of this bloody place." He then got up from his chair, walked calmly out of the room, across the compound to the warning wire, stepped over it and began slowly to climb up the barbed wire fence in full view of several guards. They shouted "*Halt!*" but he slowly and deliberately climbed on. Shots rang out. My friend clung for a moment, and then fell. That was the end of a great escaper.

Sadly, he was not the last of my friends to decide he had had enough of the misery of captivity. Some could accept it more easily than others.

Chapter Ten

Colditz

Our train journey on 15 March 1942 was eastward, deep into the middle of Germany. The escort of three privates and an NCO had been carefully briefed about our propensity for escaping and were under threat of severe retribution if we eluded them. They, in their turn, had tapped their weapons and reminded us they were trigger-happy and just waiting for trouble. They gave us no chance. We knew we were headed for what the Germans called the *Sonderlager* (Special Camp) which was by now described by prisoners as the *Straflager* (Punishment Camp). Nobody knew much about it except that it was at a place called Colditz and was probably an old castle or fortress.

Our time in the train was spent carefully watching for an opportunity to make a break and in speculation about our new prison. I had rosy visions of another Spangenberg which were to be horribly shattered. We arrived at Colditz railway station after dark and established that we were somewhere between Dresden and Leipzig—as plumb centre in Germany as we could get. This was bad for escaping, being 400 miles in any direction from the nearest unoccupied territory. Since my last bombing target had been near Leipzig, though, I felt I had come full circle.

As we stepped out of the station we saw a fantastic sight. There, beyond the town and apparently floating in the black night sky, was an enormous fortress bathed in the glare of floodlights. The grey walls, almost white in the fierce lighting, were pierced with rows of small black windows. The pile was topped by a jumble of high-pitched roofs and the odd rounded tower with one ornate domed top reminiscent of a minaret. The vertical walls rose some ninety feet above ground level and from its suspended appearance, we correctly assumed that part of it must be perched on a more or less sheer cliff.

There was none of Spangenberg's fairyland charm about this one! It was a forbidding sight which left us speechless. Our reaction was not lost on our escort who smiled and nodded at us with a knowing satisfaction. It was a long tramp from the station near the River Mulde, through the town and up, ever upwards, towards the dominating presence of the huge fortress. At last we saw our first Colditz guard standing at a stone arched gateway, like the entrance to a tunnel through a huge stone watch-house. We then found ourselves on a wooden bridge spanning what had once been a wide moat. At the end of the bridge, we came to a building with a clock tower. In this was a cavernous archway closed by enormous heavy wooden doors with huge iron studded hinges. We were obviously expected and under observation through a spy-hole, for as we neared them, one of the huge doors swung open. Behind them were two armed guards who heaved the door shut behind us and secured it with a dramatic thumping and clanging of iron bolts and bars.

From the tunnel through this inner guard house, we emerged into a large courtyard, entirely surrounded by gaunt grey buildings several storeys high. Some of this courtyard was under turf and flowerbeds and was, we learned later, the *Kommandantur* for the Colditz garrison. In this courtyard, there were guards gazing up at the buildings ahead which were floodlit. These apparently abutted on to some of the prisoners' buildings and were therefore constantly watched. Next, we came to yet another building with a tunnel through it, also closed by hefty iron-bound doors. These opened as mysteriously as the others and were clanged shut behind us by more guards. This was a longer tunnel and on the left were small heavy doors which, I was to learn, opened into what was known as "the lower punishment cells". Out of this third tunnel, we found ourselves on an upward-sloping cobbled carriageway. Beyond the high building on our right was a smaller stone archway, also closed by heavy studded wooden doors with a spy-hole and a sentry standing close by. This, we guessed correctly, was the entrance to the prison. Straight ahead, facing us, yet another stone arch marked the end of the road. Its doors, we soon learned, were the entrance to the guardroom.

Outside these doors, we were handed over to the Colditz guard commander. Papers were signed, heel-clicking salutes made, orders barked, jackboots clunked on cobbles, keys jingled and eventually the heavy door in the small arch opened. The Colditz guard commander gestured us towards the archway. Once through that we realised we would be finally and irrevocably in the clutches of this formidable prison, possibly for years to come. It was quite daunting.

On the other side of the door in the archway we saw a floodlit cobbled yard completely surrounded by tall grey buildings with heavily barred windows. The yard was deserted except for two armed guards on duty. By day, this was the prisoners' exercise yard. It seemed like the bottom of a stone pit and indeed was just that. We had been reduced to a state of silent awe for the past few minutes. Now Brucie looked at me with a rather wan smile. When he spoke, I thought he sounded a bit shaky.

"We'll get out of this bloody place too."

"You bet," I replied. I was surprised at how husky my own voice had become.

Through the archway, we were herded up some narrow stone steps on the left and locked separately into two of the "upper cells" where we spent the night in fitful sleep with plenty to think about. To me, home and Ann seemed a very, very long way away.

The next morning, we were meticulously searched and turned loose into the yard where we were greeted by and taken under the wing of the British prisoners' adjutant. Then, under the curious stares and welcoming grins of dozens of scarecrows wearing the uniforms of many different European countries—French, Belgian, Dutch, Polish and even a Yugoslav or two— we were led off to meet the fifty or so of our own countrymen who were already prisoners in Colditz.

There were quite a few boisterous reunions as we met men we knew from our former camps—Don Donaldson, Don Thom and "Errol" Flinn who had disappeared from Thorn after their attempt on the airfield while I was down with meningitis. There was Bill Fowler, who I had last seen at Barth where he coined the name "Goons", and "Little Steve" Stevenson who gave the theory of flight lectures. "Brickie" Forbes, who had escaped with Airey Neave from Thorn, was there but Airey had escaped yet again from Colditz. There were a few others.

Best of all was Auntie Paddon who, since I saw him last at Thorn, had been up to all sorts of capers including escapes and recaptures. Our reunion was short-lived for on 7 June he was carted off back to Thorn under heavy guard to face a German court martial for having been extremely stroppy when rounded up for transfer to Colditz. We assumed he would be returned to Colditz to serve whatever sentence he was given at his court martial and I looked forward to his return. Little did I realise I would never see him again.

The SBO at Colditz when we arrived was Lieutenant-Colonel David Stayner. He had recently taken over from the rumbustious Lieutenant-Colonel Guy German, who had been personally involved in early Colditz escape attempts. Guy German had been sent off to Spangenberg by our hosts who considered him a bad influence and were keen to see the back of him. Unfortunately for them, some months later, Guy was back in Colditz again and I found him a true kindred spirit.

David Stayner, nicknamed "Daddy", was a very different sort, but was a good SBO and quite a crafty old boy. He kept himself clear, as far as the Germans were concerned, from any obvious complicity in disruptive behaviour of any kind and might even appear to them to be aloof from it and almost disapproving, but there was a twinkle in his eye which we all recognised full well. I liked Daddy Stayner and we got along famously—he was a friendly, sympathetic and approachable man, and was appreciated by everybody.

Nearly all the British Colditz inmates had been sent there after only one, or at the most two, escape attempts. Some army officers had been sent to Colditz simply because they were Royal Engineers and therefore presumed, correctly, to be inveterate tunnellers. It made me reflect what a long run I had had for my money and how lucky I had been not to have landed up in Colditz much earlier. I was soon to learn that this was far from the truth.

The British prisoners who had been longest at Colditz were three Canadian pilots who had joined the RAF before the war. Hank Wardle was a long-limbed good looker with a sunny disposition who was destined soon to make a "home run" to England. Then there was Keith Milne, a sleepy-eyed, gangly humorist with a droopy moustache which earned him the nickname "the Breed". And lastly Don Middleton, a softly spoken, sensitive chap who was one of the survivors of Don Donaldson's Hampden crew shot down off Norway. All three had got out of Spangenberg late in 1940, long before I went there. Hank had climbed a barricade on the way to the gymnasium and the other two had pulled off an excellent "gate job" by carrying a ladder and pretending to be German white-coated painters who were about to knock off and to go home. It was their clever, but short-lived, escape which resulted in the very stringent gate security which we had later to overcome. The Germans thought they had made a repeat of that sort of escape impossible.

On arrival at Colditz, those early Canadians had been marched down to the Schloss park and stood against the wall facing an armed squad of Germans. They thought their last moment had come before a firing squad, but it was "only a joke!" They were not very amused.

Before the arrival of any British at Colditz, the only occupants had been eighty Polish officers under General Tadeusz Piskor and Admiral Józef Unrug. They were remnants of those gallant outgunned few who, it is said, had hurled themselves in cavalry charges against German tanks in 1939. These were the stroppy ones who, in continued defiance at Colditz, provoked and ridiculed the Germans when they were not engaged in more serious escape activities. Their defiance and reluctance to salute the Germans had kept the castle cells full. Their court-martialling had been followed by appeals and in the end a sullen compromise had been reached. The Germans did not recognise the Poles as a nation and the Poles did not recognise the Germans as people to be saluted. I have never ceased to wonder at the indomitable spirit of the Polish people.

A few months before Bruce and I arrived in Colditz, there came some Belgians and 250 French officers under General Le Bleu. Most of the French were loyal to the Allied cause and several turned out to be excellent escapers. Others were sympathetic towards the Vichy Government under Marshal Pétain which was, to some extent, cooperating with the Germans who had occupied much of France. The latter were, at least, unreliable, and some of them inclined to be German collaborators. This introduced a spicy element of uncertainty into Colditz, especially where the safeguarding of escape plans was concerned. Fortunately, however, the worst "collabos" (as we called collaborators) had been repatriated to France before our arrival. Separate from their compatriots, in a special little area, the French officers with Jewish blood were segregated. If we had not eventually won the war, I wouldn't have given two pins for their chances of survival. As it was, they were temporarily protected by the Geneva Convention as serving officers, and what a highly intelligent gifted little company they were.

In July 1941, about sixty Dutch officers were consigned to Colditz. They represented all three services with some from the Dutch East Indies and a few with mixed European and Asian blood. They were all men who had steadfastly stood by their Motherland in her time of need, and this was not their only distinction. When the Germans occupied Holland in 1940, there were some Dutchmen who, like the Royal Family, managed to flee to England to carry on the struggle from there. To those who remained, the Germans offered an amnesty in return for the signing of what became known as "the declaration". The signatories had to promise that they would not take up arms or do anything contrary to the interests of the German Reich so long as hostilities continued. Any who refused to sign were to be imprisoned with veiled threats of worse.

The vast majority of Dutch officers signed the infamous declaration, but sixty-eight officers, including the officers from the colonies, and one corporal refused to do so. It was these who, already having proved intransigent, still preserved an apparently polite but totally uncooperative attitude to the Germans and were sent to Colditz. We regarded them as the cream of the Dutch officer class. For the others, a word in fairness must be said. Many maintained that their signatures were obtained under duress and therefore were not binding. They claimed they could do more for their country as free men and that the Colditz "men of honour" were idealistic fools.

Argument about the declaration raged for years after the war and was even referred to Queen Wilhelmina for a ruling. I gather her attitude was "keep me out of this one, boys" and it was never really settled until many years after the war when a re-written Dutch military code forbade the signing of such a document.

The Dutch officers had gone to prison camps with their kit packed and organised so that they presented the only immaculate turn-out in Colditz. Their discipline and deportment matched their appearance. One of the Dutch naval officers, Lieutenant Frits "Bear" Kruimink, was to become

Dutch POWs at Colditz with their dummy "Moritz" (fourth from left),
used to fool the Germans during roll calls.

a close lifelong friend. He retired as a vice admiral. I remember once
ragging Bear about the way the Hollanders deported themselves with such
perfect military dress and discipline on *Appell* while we conveyed a spirit
of defiance and non-cooperation by our sloppy parade indiscipline. I said
something to Bear about the Dutchmen standing there, rigidly motionless
like a lot of stuffed dummies! The joke was well and truly on me when he
confided that on occasions two of the Dutch officers on *Appell* really *were*
dummies to cover up for absentees on some nefarious project or other
or even for escapers. The dummies were named "Max and Moritz" after
two Dutch comedians. The Germans eventually discovered them, but not
before they had done sterling service.

A close second to the Dutch in standards of deportment were the Poles
who had a tendency for dapper heel-clicking with well-polished riding
boots and an indomitably defiant attitude. The French were the epitome
of Latin slovenliness, affecting a superbly eloquent slouch on parade,
preferably unshaven, and even with an occasional Gauloise drooping from
the corner of an insolent mouth. The Belgians approximated them closely.
The British were scarecrows, many of whom did not possess a complete

uniform and anyway elected to dress outrageously with a nice sense of the ridiculous all their own. They treated German parade discipline with utter indifference which obviously irritated our hosts to our entire satisfaction. Now and then, the British flabbergasted the rest of the Colditz community, especially the Germans, by deciding on occasions such as the King's birthday to make the *Appell* a British parade. The suddenly smarter turn-out, the Guards-type precision drill and the cracking cheers on such parades not only boosted our own morale, but also pointed up the dumb insolence of the normal provocative sloppy behaviour.

The marked differences in national characteristics among the POWs caused little or no discord, although the Germans occasionally made efforts to stir some up. No doubt they hoped to divide and rule, but were invariably met with a concerted front against the common enemy. If any misunderstandings did brew up between the national communities who were obliged to live separately in different quarters, it was usually the British who were the most successful peacemakers. National characteristics shone through in all camp activities, especially escaping. The fiercely heroic Poles would go for the intensely daring and spectacular roof schemes; the French for brilliantly conceived and engineered tunnels; the Dutch for a craftily planned surprise which the enemy would never expect from such a well-behaved, apparently staid company; and the British for the outrageously impossible with a deceptive façade of taking nothing too seriously and managing to muddle through. The British plans were, in fact, exceptionally imaginative and meticulously executed, but we thought it more in keeping with our national style to convey the impression that we had hashed them out a few minutes previously on the back of an envelope.

Security was tight within the castle, as well as around its perimeter, and there were many no-go areas for the POWs. The parcels office in the western wing, for example, from which were issued personal clothing parcels from prisoners' families and the all-important Red Cross food parcels, was very highly secured against inquisitive prisoners. There was good reason for this. MI9 was beginning to send in very useful material for escapers such as maps or German currency inside cardboard chess or draughts boards or a tiny compass inside a walnut shell. Red Cross parcels never contained any contraband.

The security was very tight indeed—to the extent that we could not take away a tin of vegetable stew or pineapple chunks in their original containers. All such luxuries had to be tipped out on to a plate. This was because the Germans once unearthed a tunnel in which air was pumped to the working face along a pipe made up of empty tins joined together end to end. Thus the terrible inconvenience to both us and the Germans of emptying all the tins. Meanwhile, tunnel air pipes were made of something else. The hard covers of all books sent to us were likewise slashed open to ensure they contained no maps, money or phoney identity documents from MI9.

All these security measures were in fact a farce because the prisoners had long since found a way to break into the parcels office down through the ceiling, and parcels containing contraband had, by that time, become recognisable to us. All such parcels were whipped out of the office before the security staff had a chance to examine them. Thus the escaping fraternity in Colditz was never short of German money, identity papers, maps or compasses, but both prisoners and jailers suffered much unnecessary inconvenience.

Anyway, before they became available from MI9 I once made my own super little compass in a screw-top cap of a bottle. Tiny compasses like this and other wicked contraband could be made small enough to go inside a small cylindrical tube called a "creeper". This could be reluctantly inserted—preferably with a spot of Vaseline—into one's rectum. A reasonable creeper could also contain a tightly rolled map, paper money and even a false identity document. Thus, even if you were caught in the act of escaping, the Germans didn't realise what you had hidden up your whatnot. Some creepers were made from shortened toothbrush containers. I believe one lucky chap had the opportunity to use a celluloid cigar capsule from a rather splendid tobacco parcel.

When not thrust up unmentionable parts of one's anatomy, such contraband material as forgeries, *Reichsmarks*, maps, and the like, had to be carefully hidden to withstand searches which were very thorough and tended to be sprung on the prisoners without warning at any time of the day or night. Objects were stashed away in cleverly constructed hides. Design and maintenance of these became the responsibility of a separate

MI9 at work: a photograph of PDT with Alex Gould at Spangenberg...

security department falling under the overall supervision of the escape officer. Initially they were simply under a floorboard or such, but as the Germans became more thorough and expert searchers, the prisoners had to create more sophisticated hides. Initially, a hole could be knocked into a solid wall, a frame made and plastered in with a perfectly fitting hatch. The whole thing could be lightly plastered over and coloured to become quite invisible. Such hides were safe for a while, but as time passed they had also to be what we called "knock-proof" so that if searchers were tapping along a wall, they would not sound different.

One very clever hide existed in my forty-man dormitory where a huge plastered beam ran across the ceiling from one wall to the other. On the wall at one end the beam rested upon a large ornamental supporting cornice. For some unknown reason there was no corresponding cornice at the other end, so we made a hollow and removable one to match absolutely. The Germans never noticed the architectural improvement and that hide was never discovered. Because of its elevation, it did not even need to be knock-proof which would have been necessary had it been lower down.

The ambience in Colditz Castle was desolate—all grey stone walls, grey cobbled yard, black iron bars on all the windows and hefty timber doors. A bit of creeper was growing up one wall with no other living plants

...and the "civilianised" version smuggled back into the camp
for use in forged identity documents.

to be seen. There was perpetual noise throughout the day of voices and
clomping footsteps on bare-boarded floors with much laughter and very
little grizzling. The worst noises of all were the sudden clamour of the large
electric bell or, sometimes, the factory hooter-type klaxon horn to call us
to *Appell*. I hated that hideous noise which made me feel like a fly trapped
in the soundbox of a gramophone. *Appell* was normally twice a day, but
when escaping hotted up, or we were being particularly uncooperative,
there could be more. The most I remember in one day was seven. Also
fixed to one side of the building was a loudspeaker which could thunder
its message to the reluctant listeners. Its main use was to relay to the
unreceptive prisoners the occasional radio broadcast *Sondermeldungen*
(Special Reports) of the latest German victory on land, or at sea—Rommel
in North Africa or the successes of German U-Boats sinking thousands of
tons of British registered shipping in the Atlantic or elsewhere.

The objective of forcing the *Sondermeldungen* into our ears was quite
clearly to subdue our spirits and remind us who the conquering heroes
were, but we quickly learned how to nullify their effect. We would gather
in the cobbled yard and listen to the dreadful news with rapt attention, and
as it finished we would all cheer madly and throw our caps in the air in

apparent ecstasy. The poor German guards would look on in open-mouthed bewilderment and soon we were deprived of the *Sondermeldungen* and the loudspeaker was removed—but not before some bright lad had stolen a useful electro-magnet or something out of it which came in very handy in the manufacture of an alarm system for tunnellers. It was all part of trying to stay one jump ahead of our jailers, ensuring that our morale never sank too low and we remained more or less sane.

Completing the west wing, in the corner abutting the gate house, was a "de-lousing shed" and a shower room in which we were allowed to have a short sharp warm shower once a week, if we were lucky—once a fortnight, if not. And there were lavatories with no doors which was fortunate for one poor chap who tried to hang himself in one of them, but was spotted and restrained. We also had a tiny kitchen in which we could knock together a more appetising evening meal consisting of delicacies from Red Cross parcels like Spam or bully beef bulked up with left-overs from our midday German issue of vegetable slop.

In the southwest corner of the castle was a theatre containing a large enough auditorium to hold an audience of a hundred or so and a stage with a graceful proscenium, curtains and all. Gracing the cornices of the walls of the auditorium were many stone or plaster ornamental shields erected to the honour and memory of famous German composers such as Mozart and Beethoven. Some of these plaster tributes had been erased and defaced. It was clear that these had originally been erected to famous contributors to German *Kultur* who had been Jewish and subsequently assiduously defaced to comply with the new Nazi desecration of anything Jewish.

The theatre had, long ago, been a part of the German aristocracy's enjoyment and patronage of the arts. Now, the different nationalities were allowed to use it for their own presentations, produced with German approval and, by invitation, a German presence at the opening performances. The Dutch had put on a colourful musical with a strong East Indies flavour and Hawaiian-type music. The best and most well remembered British show had been a musical called *Ballet Nonsense* with the largest, brawniest, most heavily mustachioed officers dressed in flimsy tutus, prancing around like wild elephants high on marula fruit. Most of the music was composed by an army officer, Jimmy Yule, who played the piano in our "orchestra", and the words were by anyone with the wit to write them. By all accounts, *Ballet Nonsense* was hilarious and I was sorry it had happened before my time in Colditz. The theatre was useful to the Germans as well as it was something they could withdraw as punishment whenever they felt like it, which they frequently did.

More serious dramatic presentations were produced by Territorial "part-time" officer, Teddy Barton, who had been a professional producer before the war. Under his direction, I was destined to play two "character" roles, Mr Doolittle, the cockney dustman in *Pygmalion*, and Shakespeare's Falstaff. I have always preferred playing "character" roles.

Unfortunately, I was dropped from any further Colditz productions because I could never be depended upon to be available on opening night because of my very frequent and lengthy stints of solitary confinement. But that is running ahead somewhat and, in my opinion, none of my performances have ever excelled my portrayal of a pompous overbearing German *Hauptmann* when we blustered our way out of Spangenberg Castle. For me, that will forever remain one of the greatest moments of my existence.

The only other so-called privilege the Germans could take away from us was our one-hour, heavily guarded, daily visit to the park in the castle grounds. The park was surrounded by an eight-foot barbed wire fence and, beyond that, a formidable wall, all guarded by armed sentries. The hour for exercise was, in fact, not so much a privilege as a requirement of the Geneva Convention, which the Germans respected insofar as it suited them.

The last aspect of Colditz which was of vital importance to all prisoners was the food, which became a principal subject of conversation. Prisoners talked about food; the end of the war; food; women; food; escaping; and food. I suppose it will always be thus with any company that is desperately short of it.

Our British medical officers tested the calorific value of our German rations and concluded that they were just sufficient to support life if one avoided all exercise; in other words, if one stayed constantly in bed. For all those years as prisoners, we never once tasted fresh milk nor saw an egg, nor even sat on a chair with a cushion, arms or a back. The only exception was a production in the theatre when, for the purpose of setting a particular play, the stage managers built a wooden armchair. Bizarrely, there was sometimes a little queue of chaps asking to sit in it for a few minutes "just to remember what it felt like". As for the rest of us, we each had our own four-legged stool and often carried it around for convenience should we wish to sit down and chat.

What saved us were the Red Cross food parcels. Ideally, the intention was that each prisoner should receive one parcel each week, but this was hardly ever achieved. Very occasionally indeed, the supply would be sufficient to meet this ideal for a short spell, but normally we were glad to receive half a parcel regularly. There were times when the supply fell below this and other times, especially towards the very end of the war, when we received nothing.

Most of our Red Cross food parcels came from Britain and occasionally from Canada. While in solitary confinement, the Germans would not allow us any Red Cross food. Our mates were always kind, however, and saved our share up for us. Then, when we came out of the cooler, we had a glorious bash.

At Colditz I renewed my reluctant acquaintance with the hideous German jam ("for POWs only") which was handed out to us in dollops once or twice a week. It was so utterly disgusting that, our intense hunger notwithstanding, we all put it down the loo and pulled the chain. We took it only because presumably somebody had to make it, which was better than them making armaments. Eventually, however, the German jam came into its own.

Some clever lads found that the dried fruit in Red Cross parcels, if mixed with water and a little yeast—obtained by bribing a German guard—and allowed to ferment, could later be distilled to make a drop of alcohol known as "Fruit Alc". Likewise, we found that the jam could be similarly mixed with yeast for a like purpose. I always said that this stuff did not ferment. Rather, it festered. Still, the resulting product could also be distilled to make "Jam Alc" which, on earliest attempts, looked murky and smelled and tasted like burnt rubber. But it did have the desired effect if you could swallow the awful stuff. Later, it was improved somewhat by double distilling and filtering through charcoal. Despite our best efforts, it was still pretty "eugh!"

The *Kommandant* was responsible for giving our disgusting Jam Alc a new name, which it bore forever more. Distilling was *streng verboten*, partly because the construction of stills required the theft of bits of piping and an occasional *Kübel* (cooking pot) from the Germans. One night on a snap search, the Germans caught two British officers sitting in a dark corner like old witches huddled over a bubbling still and were so delighted that they telephoned the *Kommandant*. He chose to grace the occasion with his august presence. At the scene, he demanded a cup to taste the brew. He spat it out and shouted, "*Jauche*" (pronounced Yowkher). From then on, Jam Alc was always known to us as Jauche, even before we knew what it meant, and even after we learned that Jauche is the liquid slurry that drains out of the gutter behind cows in a milking shed. I always thought it was a reasonable name for the stuff.

We strove to have two meals a day, not counting a bit of bread and something for breakfast. There was the midday German slop, some of which we might save to cook up in the evening, laced with Red Cross food and cooked in our own little kitchen. I once cooked a superb apple pie using Red Cross apple purée with a discreet dash of Jauche and a crust of boiled potato, slightly browned to perfection and served hot. Yummy!

The British company was a fine, high-spirited band of brothers, whose wry sense of humour soon dispelled most of my initial depression about the escape prospects for a newcomer and the claustrophobic environment. If they could be so cheerful, some of them after two years inside, what had I to be miserable about? I soon regretfully came to realise that there was no question here of getting in quick with a basic or even sophisticated escape plan. Apparently every feasible idea had been used long ago and "blown", or was booked.

Most of the inmates were hard-core escapers. But the *Abwehr* staff were no less security specialists with the full support of the OKW, or German High Command, which was determined to make Colditz the escape-proof fortress it was meant to be. Certainly, there was no other prison camp with anything like the same proportion of guards to prisoners. Even at the escape-minded Luftwaffe camp, Stalag Luft III (Sagan), where, on the personal orders of Hitler, the Gestapo eventually shot fifty out of seventy-three recaptured British aircrew after the Great Escape of April 1944, there was a German strength of only 280 to keep tabs on 11,000 prisoners. Here at Colditz, throughout the war, there was always very nearly the same number of Germans as prisoners (counting German orderlies, bottle washers and such). This made things very difficult for us, but at least we had the satisfaction of holding down an almost equal weight in enemy manpower. Under the circumstances, it is remarkable that Colditz claimed more "home runs" than any other prison camp.

To us newcomers, the international flavour of Colditz was refreshing. Even among the British, there were men from all over the Empire, including an Indian doctor, "Jumbo" Mazumdar, as well as Polish and Czech air force pilots who had escaped to Britain and joined the RAF as their countries were occupied by the Germans. Another refreshing aspect of Colditz was that here, as in Warburg, we prisoners were from all three services—army, navy and air force—which provided a wider range of reminiscences and attitudes.

An exotic element was the *Prominente* contingent, retained by the Germans against the possibility that they might later come in handy as hostages or human shields. Among their number was Captain, the Earl of Hopetoun, son of Lord Linlithgow who had once been Viceroy of India. Charlie Hopetoun was one of the nicest and friendliest men in Colditz, a great humorist whose talents made for much theatrical fun. He also shared my doubtful privilege of being officially branded by our keepers as *Deutschfeindlich*. After the war, Charlie inherited the family title to become the Marquess of Linlithgow. He and I remained very good friends for years afterwards.

The Germans missed a trick when they sent Sub-Lieutenant Michael Wynn, RNVR, to Colditz. He was soon to become Lord Newborough. They caught Micky during the successful commando raid on the French harbour at Saint-Nazaire on 28 March 1942, which put out of commission the only Atlantic dry dock capable of handling their battleships. This was a suicide mission if ever there was one, nearly two-thirds of the more than 600 men who participated in the raid being killed or captured.

The Germans managed to sink by gunfire the motor torpedo boat Micky

A religious service in the courtyard at Colditz.

was commanding, but not before he had fulfilled his mission to help blow up the lock gates to the important dry dock. They later picked poor old Micky out of the water with one eye hanging out of his skull, attached only by the optic nerve. He told us that they shoved his eye back in, but not very cleverly, which explained why, when Micky turned up at Colditz, he had one eye that seemed to be looking out sideways. It had a positively sinister appearance and he became "Wicked Wynn" to the loving Colditz mob for evermore. It was entirely typical of him that when he died about fifteen years ago, he had himself cremated and his ashes shot out of an eighteenth-century cannon.

I suppose it afforded a measure of uplift for very ordinary fellows like me to hob-nob so intimately with such noble companions. I also hope it did them some good to hob-nob with us ordinary chaps! For most, we went our separate ways after the war, but Charlie Hopetoun and Micky Wynn became my firm lifelong friends and the Colditz bond never failed any of us.

This, then, will give the reader a general idea about what life in Colditz was like. Now let's see how the prisoners lived that life, the essence of which was laughter, good-natured ragging and making sterling friendships that would last a lifetime. When you have a very well-defined and positive enemy there is little point in silly little bickering quarrels. We got to know our close companions far better than our own brothers.

There were lectures, classes and various activities in most prison camps to which a majority of people might well devote their attention. All these diversions existed in Colditz too, but I believe the concentration of most inmates seldom strayed far from escaping or keeping the Germans in their place no matter what the personal cost. Apart from renewing old friendships, my immediate aim—like that of my crafty little apprentice, Dominic Bruce—was to get out of the bloody place.

Knowing that Colditz was a different kettle of fish where there was little chance of "getting in first", we realised it was essential to acquaint ourselves with exactly what had been tried before and then, if possible, think up something new. Upon showing an interest in escaping, we were immediately briefed that on no account were we or anyone else to poke around freelance because there were so many plans already afoot that could be compromised by blundering into somebody else's scheme.

So, we first made a study of all the previous escapes and attempts. It was a fascinating subject which filled me with admiration for my fellow prisoners but some depression for my own chances.

All the different national groups were equally escape-oriented. At first they had vied secretly against one another for successes. This led to some initial snarl-ups with one plan cutting across and compromising another. Co-operation and co-ordination were necessary and had soon been established, especially after one hare-brained attempt had fouled up another more serious plan. It also became policy for one group to invite selected escapers from another to participate in their schemes on a reciprocal basis.

This arrangement was of particular value to the British when posing as a travelling slave labourer or collaborator from one of the occupied countries. As a French or a Dutch worker with forged identity papers, it was helpful to be travelling in company with a genuine Frenchman or Dutchman who, when necessary, could do all the talking. Such mixed escape teams scored some outstanding successes.

The curtain had not really gone up on escaping from Colditz until the spring of 1941, by which time the contingents of various sizes from all the European allied nations had arrived in the castle. It is at this embryo stage that I would undoubtedly have best employed my own talents had I been there. It would have been castle-probing all over again and I probably would have qualified for a place on one of the schemes of 1941/42. This was the year of successes with newly acquired German money, forged identity papers and continental travelling companions.

With all those facilities there would have been been little reason to be shivering under frozen cabbage leaves or riding on trams with no money for the fare. Instead there would have been a nice quick rail journey through Germany almost to the Swiss border—and a known way of crossing it with a fair chance of avoiding detection.

It became clear to me that my long-delayed assignment to Colditz had not been fortunate after all. On the contrary, I had obviously missed a number of very good escaping chances and I began to wonder whether I would ever have an opportunity to make another run for it with the aid of all these new and essential advantages. Now I was a new boy in Colditz and it seemed I would have to stand in line. I felt I must comply with the local order of things and, meanwhile, see what I might be able to do to help others.

There were certainly plenty of recent successes to celebrate. Airey Neave and his Dutch partner, Tony Luteyn, had made a brilliant escape in uniform barely two months before our arrival and news had recently come through that they had made it to Switzerland and thence to England. They followed in a long line of intrepid escapes. As far back as mid-April 1941, a Frenchman, Lieutenant Le Ray, had been the first to escape successfully from the Schloss and soon after him, Lieutenant Odry followed. At the time nobody seemed to know exactly how they did it, but my guess then was that it was something to do with the park. Usually, we were allowed to kick a ball about for one hour per day there. This exercise area was much smaller than a football pitch and a scattering of trees made for interesting complications in the soccer rules.

Access to the park was through our prisoners' gate into the sloping approach yard, and after that along a steep, narrow cobbled lane with a high wall on one side and a barbed-wire fence on the other. Still, the march to and from the exercise area had had been subject of many escape attempts, some of them successful. My own "chameleon" trick had been used several times with interesting variations. Bear Kruimink had collapsed by the roadside under a blanket sewn with leaves and debris to become a heap of rubbish. It looked perfectly good but a guard dog sniffed him out and he was thrown into the cells.

On another occasion a French officer, Lieutenant Boulé, had worked a superb "chameleon" into an excellent disguise as a woman, hoping to be mistaken for the wife of one of the German guards. He stepped out of the column and started to walk back the other way. Regrettably, the British had not been informed that this attempt was about to come off. As Boulay effected his metamorphosis into a woman and wheeled around, his wristwatch strap broke. As he was passing back down the column, with everyone including the guards thinking he was a *Frau* from the German married quarters, the watch fell from his wrist. Auntie Paddon, who was in the column, saw this happen. Picking up the lost item, he called to a German guard pointing to the woman who had just dropped her watch. The guard ran after her and, engaging her in conversation, saw through the disguise. This very unfortunate incident was one of several which exemplified the need for closer and more trusting cooperation between the international communities of prisoners. On another occasion "Lulu" Lawton joined up with a Frenchman and, changing identities with two of our orderlies, went to work, under guard, in the park. Both escaped but were soon caught.

The Dutch successfully exploited a deep-water conduit in the park which, at one point, had a heavily bolted manhole cover over it. An extremely clever Bible study group organised by their escape officer, Captain van den Heuvel, chose to gather round the cover and somehow managed to pop two men down the hole under the very eyes of several guards whose attention was, of course, cleverly diverted for a few moments. The hefty manhole cover bolt was then replaced with a cleverly manufactured replica made of easily breakable glass. Somehow, probably using their two excellent collapsible dummies, the Dutch fiddled the count in the pen. The exercise hour finished and everyone safely departed, the two inside the drain pushed the manhole cover upwards to smash the glass dummy bolt, climbed out, cleaned up the glass splinters, replaced the real iron bolt and got away over the wall.

Two pairs of escapers worked this plan and all four made it to Switzerland. A bright guard, alas, spotted the third pair going into the hole, despite the diversions and contrived obstructions. These escapes were typical of the Dutchmen under van den Heuvel, known to us affectionately as "Vandy". Dear old Vandy was killed shortly after our war, fighting revolutionaries in the Dutch East Indies (today's Indonesia).

Don Thom and Bertie Boustead, a long streak of aristocratic, drawling, good-natured humanity, also tried a "chameleon" on the park approach as two *Hitlerjugend*—the uniformed Nazi Hitler Youth. Their disguises were good, but the Nazi salute they gave the German NCO on their way back down the column was not and they were caught. Captain Harry Elliot and a Pole, Lados, dodged the column into an air raid shelter, but were discovered by a search party when one of the frequent counts suddenly indicated two were missing. They were thrown into the cells from which Lados escaped and reached the Swiss frontier where he was caught. He had made the journey with a broken bone in one foot, injured after dropping from his cell window after cutting the bars.

The most spectacular and heroic escape from the park was made by a persistent French escaper, Pierre Mairesse-Lebrun. A dashing young cavalry officer, he had already made one previous successful exit from the park. On the first occasion, a tiny Belgian officer was smuggled down on the walk under the voluminous cloak of a giant Frenchman. Then Mairesse-Lebrun hid himself in the rafters of an old open-sided pavilion in the park and the count in the pen was compensated with the addition of the little Belgian. The Germans were satisfied and did not search the park carefully. Unfortunately, Mairesse-Lebrun was arrested at a railway station while tendering out-of-date German currency.

Mairesse-Lebrun's epic and most spectacular escape from the park came later, in July 1941, and was accomplished while serving twenty-one days' solitary for his previous escape attempt. At that time, exercise for those in the cells was provided down in the park with its six-foot barbed-wire mesh round it. Mairesse-Lebrun was an athlete and one of his fellow countrymen, Pierre Odry, also in the cells, was another. On exercise in the park, these two made a habit of running round the perimeter just inside the wire, leap-frogging over each other. One day, at a signal from Mairesse-Lebrun, the other fellow turned to face him, crouched slightly with his fingers linked, so that his hands formed a stirrup a little above knee height. Mairesse-Lebrun tore towards his companion and sprang to place his right foot into the stirrup. With a circus-type "hup," the strong man heaved upwards and Mairesse-Lebrun went sailing clean over the fence. He landed and sprinted the twenty or thirty yards to the main ancient wall of the original and larger park. That wall was about twelve feet high and could be scaled only by clambering up the wire fence where it joined the wall. Meanwhile, Mairesse-Lebrun came under fire from two sentries who proceeded to empty their rifles at him. The story goes that the Frenchman knew he would be an easy target if he slowly climbed up the wire, so he deliberately ran back and forth at the foot of the wall, counting the shots as bullets whizzed past him. When he reckoned the two magazines must be empty, he briskly climbed up the wire, reached up for the top of the wall, heaved himself over and was away.

Mairesse-Lebrun was wearing only shorts and a shirt, but he made his way south on stolen bicycles and successfully reached unoccupied France where he did some sterling work with the Resistance. Later he crossed over the Pyrenees into neutral Spain where he was caught and imprisoned in another fortress for a while. After this escape, the Germans added two feet to the height of the barbed-wire fence round the cage; put a door in the park wall so that guards could more easily pursue a fugitive; and discontinued exercise in the park for prisoners serving a stint of solitary confinement in the cells.

By the time Bruce and I reached Colditz, every conceivable trick had been tried on the walk to and from the park and from within it. The German precautions had tightened up to such a degree that nobody was allowed to carry a blanket with him, and all greatcoats had to be held open during the count.

On first arriving at Colditz, I went on several walks to the park to sniff out opportunities and came to the sorry conclusion that, for the immediate future, none remained. I was right. No more attempts succeeded for twenty-seven months, by which time the Germans had become less vigilant. Even then, the fugitive had little getaway time and was caught within minutes, close to the castle.

For myself, having concluded that there was no escape from the park walk, I never went there again for two reasons. First, I so hated the counting and re-counting and jostling and herding, which I found had a most depressing psychological effect. Secondly, the Germans maintained the walk was a privilege which they repeatedly withdrew for various reasons as a punishment. My reaction to this was always the same—they could stuff their privileges! I wanted none from them and when I had none, they would be denied the satisfaction of having something to take away.

For more than three years, I never set foot outside the cobbled yard enclosed by our high buildings except when I was marched down to the town cells or carted off to courts martial or once to a military prison in Leipzig. Any sorties outside the confines of the Schloss I viewed as achievements, for they presented possible escape opportunities. Furthermore, the courts martial wasted considerable German effort, organisation and manpower, while providing escape opportunities for my witnesses as well.

In those earlier days at Colditz, while these excitements enlivened the park, schemes were also underway in the Schloss itself, where the Germans had not yet taken the most elementary precautions against workings. By "workings" I mean tunnels or just breakthroughs from prison quarters into German buildings where these backed upon each other. By the time Bruce and I arrived in March 1942, these German security omissions had been made good with sunken microphones to detect digging noises and electrical warning wires on the German side of vulnerable walls.

As matters progressed, the prisoners would be working on tunnels which, by their anxious probings in the vital area, the Germans obviously knew about, but could not exactly locate. Entrances were very carefully camouflaged and seldom on the ground floor where they would be expected. One entrance to a wonderful French tunnel was near the top of an old clock tower in the northwest corner which had once accommodated massive suspended weights to power the mechanism. The prisoners' security systems were cunning and stringent and the Germans' probing was relentless. For the tunnellers, the situation was sometimes, "We know they know, and they know we know they know! It's now a race between their finding the tunnel and our breaking out."

Sadly, no "mass escape" tunnel ever did break out at Colditz although the magnificent French effort came very close to it. A sudden unexpected *Appell* was designed to reveal if any chaps were missing down a hole somewhere. The prisoners eventually devised an antidote to this too. A couple of British officers volunteered to become what were called "ghosts".

Ghosts disappeared from the Germans' sight by their being led to think the prisoners had escaped. Thereafter the ghosts never appeared on *Appell* but were hidden somewhere, sometimes even down a hole if one was being dug, or they stood in for chaps who were already working down a hole and did not have time to get out of it when the sudden *Appell* was sprung.

The ghosts had another very important function. If a couple of chaps really *did* escape, the ghosts stood in for them at *Appell* in order that the absconders should have a good start before the hunt was on. Such a start could make all the difference between success and failure. Why did the Germans not recognise the ghosts standing in for somebody else? Because, on *Appell*, we paraded five ranks deep and the Germans counted bodies rather than checking identities. They were not looking at faces, and anyway a ghost would be in the rear rank, collar turned up and probably blowing his nose at the crucial moment to hide most of his ugly mug!

In the event, the Germans discovered a total of twenty tunnels at Colditz. A few more existed for a time, but were abandoned as hopeless before they were blown. Some are probably still there, undermining the stability of the building, while heavy soil, secretly packed into the eaves of attics, must have imposed a bit of a strain on some of the ancient timbers.

I mentioned earlier that the Poles were lads for spectacular and daredevil schemes which even some of the hardened Colditz escapers considered crazy. Typical of their breed was little, gamin-faced Miki Surmanowicz, and none was more enterprising than he, nor a better lock-picking, cell-breaking Houdini. One night, he made a pre-arranged break from the upper cells where he was doing time for a previous escape attempt and where Bruce and I were to spend our first night after arrival at Colditz. When the castle was quiet with everyone locked in their quarters, Miki let himself out of his cell, then released another Pole, Chmiel, from his. Miki then lock-picked his way on through the main door of the whole cell complex and they were in the yard where there was no night sentry and no floodlight. Accomplices lowered a rope of knotted bedsheets from a window in their quarters above, and the two Poles climbed this until they reached a perilously narrow ledge, about six inches wide, which ran along the side of the building. With their backs to the wall and high above the stone cobbles of the dark deserted yard, the two heroes perilously edged their way along to the end of the building where it abutted onto the guardroom block near the main gate. They took the rope with them.

Stretching upwards, they managed to reach the guttering of the guard house and pull themselves up onto its steep roof. In the roof was a skylight and the two climbers broke their way into it and took their rope with them. They then made for an outside window of the unoccupied guardhouse attics and attached their rope for the 120-foot descent ending with the stone precipice on which the castle stood. Down they went, Miki Surmanowicz first with his plimsolled feet silent against the stone wall in which there were windows of the sleeping quarters for officers of the duty guard squad. Chmiel followed, wearing hefty marching boots which made such a rasping clatter against the wall that a German officer was awakened. He rushed to his window, pistol in hand, and found himself face to face with Chmiel who smiled politely but, reasonably enough at eighty feet above the rocks, declined the excited invitation to put his hands up. There was a hubbub and the two Poles were caught.

The attempt resulted in more lights including some in the prisoners' cobbled yard, and more sentries including one in the yard all night. Catwalks were built outside the castle and other avenues of escape were blocked. It was the same old story with every escape attempt making the business very much more difficult for those who came afterwards.

Our study of the Colditz escape history also threw interesting light on typical German attitudes to duty and loyalty at that time. The canteen guard was apparently subversion proof. True, the Germans were then riding on the crest of a victorious wave and they were not yet disillusioned about their Nazi masters by defeats and the aerial hammering administered to them later by Bomber Command. Even when they were, they remained, on the whole, steadfast to their nation's cause if not so much to the Nazi cause, and there was a difference!

Whatever one may feel about the Teutonic character, especially the arrogance of the jackboot as applied to the barefooted, there is no doubt that the German is an outstanding warrior, a most worthy foe, and must be one of the most reliable allies in a war. I know I would rely upon them on my flank if it came to the pinch in a battle.

It was interesting to examine the situation as this applied to the Wehrmacht-POW relationship. It did not compare with the brutal SS-concentration camp victim relationship. The latter was downright calculated sadistic cruelty of unimaginable horror. We in Colditz knew all about this as time passed because occasionally an escaped prisoner would be caught by the Gestapo, rather than the civil police or Wehrmacht. When this disastrous situation occurred, the prisoner could well find his captors chose, I repeat chose, to disbelieve in his POW status and would not bother to verify his claims. He could then find himself an inmate of one of the many concentration camps for Jews or German political prisoners. Then, God help him! His only salvation was to smuggle word out to the Wehrmacht by hook or by crook and they, normally, would try to have him returned to their fold.

We were, therefore, not in a state of ignorant euphoria about the schoolmaster/schoolboy relationship with Hauptmann Paul Priem, the chief security officer at the castle, but knew quite well what lay in store for the more recalcitrant prisoners in the event of an ultimate German victory or by pushing them beyond the breaking point of their tolerance. We knew we were playing a dangerous game with our lives—but that's war after all, and as I was to learn a bit later on, life can become so miserable that it doesn't seem to matter much anyway.

Much has been said about the German lack of humour. Hauptmann Priem, an ex-schoolteacher who at that time was jovially drinking himself into an early grave, was a delightful denial of this concept. He appeared to see himself as the headmaster of a lot of very mischievous schoolboys who, provided they were treated right and with humour, would be naughty but not too nasty. He was a wise and likeable man and it is a pity his ebullient attitude was not shared by more of his brother officers, many of whom were extremely critical of him.

An amusing incident occurred when Pat Reid and Hank Wardle were caught in a forbidden room whose lock they had picked for the purpose of crafting a camouflaged trapdoor for a new tunnel. Fortunately the Germans never realised this. The pair pretended they had sought seclusion to do physical jerks or something, and Priem locked them in, intending to let them stew for a while. Friendly help was standing by, however, and almost immediately the lock was picked again.

Then the door was lifted off its hinges and paraded round the yard, shoulder-high, followed by a long procession, acting the part of mourners. Priem arrived on the scene and was handed a polite note pointing out that imprisonment without trial or sentence was contrary to the German Military Code of Justice and therefore contravened the Geneva Convention. He laughingly suggested the gentlemen return the door to its hinges, which was done. Everybody saluted everybody else, the German heels clicked in appreciation, and the whole affair was forgotten. More marks for Priem, a man who never engendered ill feeling.

Not all of his colleagues were as levelheaded. Several members of the German staff at Colditz openly advocated shooting. They reckoned a few corpses in the courtyard would persuade the prisoners to better order, and they may well have been right. Had their methods been tried, however, there would have been a tremendous hullabaloo through various international channels and perhaps reprisals against German prisoners, even though their sense of rigid discipline made the latter, generally speaking, less difficult captives.

Despite all that is known about the German concentration camps, I must admit the Wehrmacht usually treated its prisoners from Western countries, at any rate, with some forbearance, and the restraint of individual Germans when provoked was sometimes quite remarkable. The other side of that coin, though, was that the same innate discipline seemed to smother individualism and, frequently, consciences as well.

I did not see enough of Priem before he left Colditz and I understand the demon alcohol finally took him off. He was eventually succeeded by Hauptmann Reinhold Eggers, another former schoolmaster who later made a living cashing in on the international interest in Colditz generated by the bestselling book (and film) written by the British escape officer, Pat Reid. Eggers' self-serving accounts, *Colditz: The German Story* and

Colditz Recaptured, were both published in English rather than German, an indication of how thoroughly the Colditz myth became entrenched in the English-speaking world.

In his books Eggers portrays himself as an equable international humanist, just and good, a somewhat anti-Nazi German loyalist. Perhaps he was. But many of us saw Eggers as a cold-blooded fish, a man of heartless logic, little human understanding and a pedant. Like most other prisoners, I could not like him, nor trust him. His humourless smile was slimy.

It is certain that on my arrival at Colditz, Eggers read my exaggerated "crime sheet", concocted by Rademacher to get rid of Bruce and me to Colditz, and there was no doubt whatsoever that he personally disliked me from the start. There is no doubt either that he soon realised I reciprocated his feelings. In his book, Eggers, referring to the saving graces of the British, punctuates his points with "even Flight Lieutenant Tunstall", as if that dreadful fellow was the most intractable of all the dreadful *Deutschfeindlich* fraternity. Generally, we prisoners did not trust him and felt he was inclined to run with the fox and hunt with the hounds. Perhaps that was precisely his brief, but he stuck to it even after the war.

I knew life could be less unbearable with more Priems around, but he was the only one. The humour he shared with us, and his occasional alcohol-fuelled antics that were not so very different from our own, made for a peculiar kind of togetherness which under the circumstances was a precious thing. Prisoners, even *en masse*, are in some ways very lonely creatures.

Eggers was always at a distance. There was no warmth whatsoever that might make one feel first a prisoner, then a man. His assistant, Hauptmann Püpcke, was different again. He was not trying to be anything but a soldier and a decent one. He was a simple human and therefore easier to understand and like. In a strange way, I felt sorry for him, stuck as he was with his country's rotten Nazi cause. I tangled with him frequently and I am sure he never suspected that I liked him—until we were released when I told him so.

For the rest, there were good honest men among them, but too many Rademacher Nazis as well. And it was the Rademachers who made the impact and moulded one's attitudes. That is why, on arrival at Colditz, I was becoming bloody-minded in the extreme. The Germans were gunning for me and I was equally gunning for them.

German prison camp policies, dictated by the Wehrmacht, but interpreted locally by the Camp *Kommandanten*, were never very clever. Their response to escapes was always to impose more restrictions which only made life more miserable and escapers more determined. As with most security measures, then or now, in any walk of life, their main effect was to inconvenience and harass the vast majority against whom they were not aimed anyway. Such measures seldom hinder the determined specialist, be his activity robbery, murder, sabotage or escape.

This was entirely true of the restrictions and prohibitions of materials at Colditz and other German prison camps. Ink for the production of certain forged papers was made from indelible pencils, so they became a forbidden item. This meant that all those people who would have used these items for making tidy permanent lecture notes or for writing diaries and letters were deprived of them. But the forgery department was never short of materials and never likely to be.

Tools were forbidden and therefore there were no hobby activities among

The forger's art: fake identity card for a "Belgian worker", produced in Colditz.

the discontented innocent. But the escapers still turned out perfect replicas of rifles, bayonets, metal buttons, tunnel ventilation pumps or anything else. Somehow, they would do it with home-made tools. A carpenter's plane can be made from stool legs and the blade of a table knife. Iron bars can be cut with a hacksaw made from serrated razor blades. Wood saws can be made from table knives or gramophone springs. Prohibit dyes and the theatrical community will suffer but somebody, as I did, will think of grass to dye a Belgian army greatcoat green. Clothing from parcels, which might conceivably be used for a civilian disguise, was confiscated, so prisoners made sports jackets or wind-breakers from prison blankets.

No, the only sensible way for civilised people to run a prison camp is to make it as cushy as possible. This minimises ill feeling and weakens the motivation for escaping. Give the prisoners, within reason, everything they need for as normal a life as may be, and make it impossible for anyone to bluff his way out even if he is perfectly disguised as the Camp *Kommandant* himself. Escapers should be stopped at the wire, not by prohibiting indelible pencils. Indiscipline must be scotched with Priem-ish good humour and understanding, not by screaming tantrums and curtailing so-called "privileges" which the bloody-minded prisoners do not care about anyway. As it was, the Germans ran the prison camp war just the way we wanted it. We had every excuse to blow off steam as very naughty schoolboys always will at inept schoolmasters, and our keepers ensured that escape or defiance motivation was kept at a peak.

As one went into the history of escaping from Colditz, the conclusion I had formed long ago was confirmed. You must get in quick! In Colditz others had already been experienced or were going for every possible loophole in the system that I could see. At every corner, there was now an extra guard to cover this, a new Goon box to cover that, or an additional floodlight or some sound detectors to cover the other. The Germans appeared to have Colditz sewn up tight, and the only possible avenues left had a queue of eager escape specialists with priority bookings waiting to have a go.

I did see several possibilities, but whenever I discussed them with any of the old hands or the escape officer, the answer was the same. "Yes, we know about that. The French tried something there last year. The Goons have put sound detectors in the wall." Or, "No, you can't try that, the Dutch are already working on a very similar scheme. If they pull it off and the idea is not 'blown', maybe you can be in on the follow-up attempt." It was terribly frustrating and my morale, for that and other reasons, was beginning to suffer.

The upshot of all this was that I was involved as a prospective escaper in only two attempts from Colditz. In the first one, a combined Dutch and British affair, I was not required to take a hand in the preparations. These were to have culminated in a ninety-foot descent of a lightning conductor on a dark night. Sadly, the preparations for that one were detected by a newly installed German security system.

The second was a tunnel in which I did only a little work before it was also discovered. It was to have been a short tunnel from what had once been a dentist's room on the ground floor, one of a very few rooms that had heavy plain brown linoleum on the floor. All the other floors in the prisoners' part of Colditz had nothing but bare boards or stone. Before this tunnel had progressed very far Eggers realised that the linoleum was being used to make "rubber stamps" for forged papers and also for making the "leather" belts and pistol holsters for bogus German officers' uniforms for escape purposes. He very wisely decided to remove all such lino from floors accessible to prisoners—our tunnel entrance was revealed, and that was that!

This rather put paid to my escape record, as well as everybody else's. After October 1942, nobody made it home from Colditz, except by repatriation for reasons of mental breakdown—some after attempted suicides, and others who never fully recovered. A few more were repatriated for different physical medical reasons, all but one of which I believe were genuine. One bogus physical illness was very cleverly pulled off by a likeable middle-aged Army officer. I must confess I have always had a personal reserve about the principles involved in faking illness for repatriation, in so far as it could prejudice the chance of people with genuine cases of disability getting back home. Another who was repatriated for mental breakdown subsequently claimed he had also faked it but, closely involved with him as I was, I have very good reasons to believe his case was genuine.

The normal German policy for the British was "once in Colditz, never out". The few who did manage to wriggle out were the odd cases for hospitalisation, and the two padres, of whom Ellison Platt was quickly returned to Colditz and poor J.C. Hobling was, I believe, killed by a stray Allied bomb while a prisoner in Stalag XVIIIA. A Canadian Army Lieutenant, William "Dopey" Millar, managed to escape from a hospital near Colditz in January 1944 and was never heard of again. It seems most likely that the poor fellow met a fate which for some time had been promised by the secret services of Hitler's fiendish Reich—death by shooting at Mauthausen concentration camp.

Chapter Eleven

"O what a beautiful morning…"

An immediate opportunity to work out an escape plan for myself being out of the question for the reasons given in the previous chapter, I put the matter on temporary hold and looked at the other aspects of my life in Colditz. They turned out to be not very cheering.

The mainstay of my existence for many dreary months had been the letters I received from my dear Ann. Now there was none to bolster my morale because I was receiving no mail at all from anybody. This was because of my sudden change of address from the Warburg prison to Colditz. Even when that problem was resolved, I suspected that the ogre of a security officer at Warburg was still taking revenge on me by "censoring" and "losing" some of my letters from Ann. The so-and-so knew my Achilles heel and had already tried to take advantage of it. I did not doubt that he was still doing so.

Gradually other letters began to trickle in to me from Edie, and from my father, brother and sisters. But the flow from Ann was somehow being interrupted. One recent letter from her had said that she felt embarrassed to be working on her own father's property, his orchard, as a member of the Women's Land Army. Eventually a letter told me she was about to join the Women's Auxiliary Air Force, the WAAF, and I have to admit some anxiety at the news. With so many young rapscallions on RAF stations— like me before I plighted my love to Ann and became a totally reformed character—a lovely young woman of twenty would have the lads around her like bees round a honey pot, and heroic pilot types would be two a penny! But I always found solace in her first letter to me as a POW with the line in it, "I will wait for you for as long as it takes," and she was wearing my ring. What more could I ask or wish for?

Thus, contrary to my normal pursuit in a new prison camp, my immediate concern was to find ways to occupy my mind and be of some use to the cause against the enemy who had said to me, "For you, ze Vore is ofer!" Well, it bloody well wasn't and I resolved to let them know it wasn't!

I thought of my brief from MI9 while still at RAF Hemswell. "Your duties are—No.1, try to escape." I had done my best at that with a total of eight attempts, four of them successful breakouts, and I would continue to do so as soon as I could overcome the restrictions on "free-lancing". No.2 was "to get useful information home by code or whatever", and my "whatever" had been outstandingly successful with the split photographs I had devised. So then I thought about duty No.3 as briefed verbatim by Squadron Leader Evans—"Be as big a bloody nuisance as possible to the enemy!"

Yes, come to think of it, if there was no immediate possibility of carrying out No.1, nor any need for No.2, there was no reason why I should not participate in No.3 to some extent, provided there was some purpose to it. The Colditz fraternity was already doing quite well in this department and I felt it would be satisfying fun to join in, especially if it could be instrumental in helping escapers. It caused a tremendous amount of laughter too and that, more than anything else, was the only real tonic for the all-prevailing ills of hunger, confinement, boredom and, let's face it, lack of a touch of tender female affection from mums, wives, sisters or girlfriends.

We all rejoiced in laughter, especially when it was at the expense of the people responsible for our miseries, and more especially when sabotaging an *Appell*. Obviously there was no point in disrupting these only when somebody was missing as this would have given an immediate alarm signal to the enemy. Thus, the more often it occurred, the more effective it was when it really mattered to cover up the absence of escapers or, at least, to delay the discovery of their absence.

I reckoned a fair percentage of the prisoners of all the nations were very good at winding up the Germans. The rest enjoyed the confusion, annoyance and discomfort it caused the enemy despite general reprisals and individual punishments. Even our most senior officers clearly enjoyed it, and even if some did not very obviously partake in it none was ever known to complain or remonstrate. As for my senior RAF officers, Paddon and Bader, they had both been stars at it in their own right, and tended to set the pace.

My serious début into what was to become known as "Goon-baiting" occurred a few weeks after taking up residence in Colditz. It was my first really serious effort to sabotage the smooth running of an *Appell*, with a piquant side motive of taking the mickey out of a detested Goon officer. When I get difficult, I get really difficult and this episode led to my first court martial by the Germans.

Having been a bugler in both the Boy Scouts and in my School Cadet Corps, I was able to sound "calls" on the bugle and also on a military trumpet. At Spangenberg I had seized the opportunity to purchase a proper orchestral trumpet through some Swiss benevolent organisation with the intention of learning to play it properly. One particular German officer who occasionally took the *Appell* parades was a regular pain in the bum. He sometimes appeared to intercept prisoners for the sole purpose of exacting a salute from them. Some chaps had taken to running away screaming like terrified schoolgirls if he appeared in the yard, which was always good for a laugh, and feelings against this individual were running high. One morning in early April 1942, this tiresome fellow was the German duty officer due to take the parade and I made preparations to honour him as befitted such a worthy gentleman.

I lurked in the rear, the fifth rank on the parade, with my trumpet concealed under my greatcoat. When we were called to attention for this horribly tiresome Goon, I started to sound the "general salute" and everyone was a bit startled and wondered what was coming next. The Goon was taken aback, but it was obviously a ceremonial recognition of his (self) importance. Unfortunately, after the first four bars of that resounding acknowledgement of respect and subordination, the trumpet call suddenly collapsed into a resounding discordant raspberry! Laughter drowned out the outraged order from the Goon officer to the several German guards on parade with him to seize the trumpet and arrest the perpetrator. As the guards bore down upon me, I decided to get rid of the evidence and passed the trumpet to somebody else. He, in turn, immediately got rid of the hot instrument to another prisoner and a delightful game of pass-the-trumpet began which would have earned the approbation of any professional rugby coach. German guards were trying to intercept the passes to laughter and tumultuous cheers from the spectators.

The trumpet ended up in the hands of a perfectly docile-looking bespectabled little chap, Kenneth Lee, a lieutenant in the Royal Corps of Signals. He was cornered by two large German guards who demanded the trumpet. Playing the innocent he appeared to be, Kenneth refused to hand it over protesting, quite reasonably, that it was not his to give away. A tug-of-war ensued to more cheering from the crowd and eventually the guards won, to the accompaniment of sorrowful groans from the mob. By the way, the docile, harmless-looking fellow, Lee, was one of the stars of Colditz who spent endless hours making beautifully forged identity documents and travel permits for escapers.

The charge laid against me for a court martial was for "misuse of musical instruments" and poor Kenneth Lee was similarly charged as an accomplice. Neither of us was particularly worried because there could hardly be a death sentence for such a trivial offence and it was the first court martial ever brought within Colditz against a British officer. Furthermore, the experience could turn out to be quite interesting, if not actually beneficial. After all, the court was to sit in Leipzig and that meant we would have to be taken there under heavy guard by train, together with any witnesses we could arrange to have. That meant at least a change of scenery and maybe even a chance to make a break for freedom somewhere along the line. It also meant a waste of a lot of German administrative rigmarole and more hours for senior German officers on the court, and we were quite pleased with ourselves. Everyone and his brother wanted to be a witness, and the whole episode provided a jolly subject for conversation for some time. Our SBO, "Daddy" Stayner, had enjoyed the fun and was not the least critical of our conduct. As for Auntie Paddon, the RAF senior officer, he loved it. He left for his own court martial at Thorn soon afterwards.

The date fixed for my trial was 30 July and for Kenneth Lee 28 August. I got away with twenty-one days' solitary which I had already served in "preventive arrest". This annoyed the *Kommandant* who could himself have given me up to twenty-eight days on his own authority. As for Kenneth Lee, he and his star witness, "Brickie" Forbes, broke away from their guards on Leipzig railway station and escaped into the crowd. They were soon caught, but it was good clean fun. His sentence was quite trivial too.

This was my first but not my only revelation that there was more justice and leniency to be had from a court martial than one could expect from an incensed and irascible camp *Kommandant*. The only thing I did not like about the German courts martial was that, as a preamble to the trial, the crime record of the accused was read out to the court at the very beginning before they had heard any evidence and reached a verdict. This was not very helpful to me with all the nonsense charges that had been trumped up by Rademacher at Warburg to keep little Brucie and me in the cooler. It is a principle of British jurisprudence that the past record of the accused may be revealed to the court only *after* they have found a verdict of guilty. As I stood before several more courts martial, the record sounded worse and worse, but I never felt I suffered any great injustice from it.

There was only one other occasion when my ability as a bugler was exercised with serious intent. That was in August 1942 when we heard of the death of the Duke of Kent, the King's younger brother. The Sunderland flying boat in which he was travelling to Iceland in his capacity as Staff Inspector-General of the RAF flew into high ground in Scotland in bad weather; only one crew-member survived. When we heard of the death, it was decreed that we should hold a memorial service and for this purpose, the Germans allowed us to use the Colditz Chapel. The service was attended by officers representing all the other Allied nations imprisoned in Colditz. A bugle was also made available by the Germans with which I sounded the Last Post. It was, of course, performed with all due dignity and respect, without any improper variations by the bugler.

My anti-*Appell* crusade continued. Another opportunity came my way one morning when I was clomping down the bare stone spiral staircase from our British quarters to the yard. Not being keen to attend these boring parades, I was near the end of the trail of prisoners who were undoubtedly, just like me, looking forward to another dull uneventful day in this grey horrible prison.

As I approached the bottom of the steps, I saw something unusual in the wide enclosed stone area at the bottom of the staircase. It was a huge, but *really* huge, heap of wood shavings which the Germans called *Holzwolle*, meaning "wood wool". These were used to fill the palliasse bags on which we slept and dreamed of better times in better places. I was feeling particularly dull, aimless and hopeless. Then, suddenly, an idea occurred to me. What could brighten our day better than a merry blaze? What better to provide a merry blaze than a huge pile of *Holzwolle*? It could do no real damage whatsoever to our own belongings or even to Schloss Colditz. The staircase would act as a chimney for the smoke and the flames could go nowhere to cause any real damage. Furthermore, how simple it would be to get one going, especially as I happened to have a box of matches in my pocket. Most importantly of all, what a splendid way to sabotage an *Appell* and delay satisfaction for the Germans that they still had all their prisoners safely and soundly locked up where they belonged. The more often we could deny them that satisfaction the better.

I thought no more about it. Time for action! I flicked a flaring match into the heap ensuring that there were only a couple of chaps behind me, and we all emerged into the yard and innocently fell in to the parade.

Almost at once a lively conflagration flared up at the bottom of our staircase. The Germans started screaming; the prisoners all started cheering; and the parade broke up completely. Buckets appeared from nowhere and in no time, prisoners were throwing gallons of water about everywhere except on the fire. The Germans, not realising how harmless the spectacular flames really were, immediately summoned the local fire brigade which responded with amazing promptness but too late to put the fire out because it had already died away. But there was still absolute chaos in the yard, soon exacerbated by sticky-fingered POWs milling around the somewhat antiquated fire engine to see what they could pinch off it to add to our collection of forbidden tools. Chaos continued with prisoners of all nationalities, German guards and firemen all shouting, while buckets of water were now being hurled willy-nilly out of high windows to shrieks of laughter and happy enjoyment.

What a lovely, lively morning that was! The Germans were very angry about the whole episode. They even went so far as to accuse us of arson but our camp wit, Lieutenant "Scarlet" O'Hara had the answer to such a ridiculous charge as usual. He told Hauptmann Eggers, "It was not really arson. It was only arsin' about." Eggers could never see the joke.

One of the results of the international water battle that developed after the fire was another camp order. This forbade anything to be thrown out of a prison window. As for myself, it seemed that I was becoming a Goonbaiter rather than an escaper which was certainly not my basic wish. It seemed to be a role thrust upon me by force of circumstance, but whatever my role, I tried to play it well.

The two categories, of course, were not mutually exclusive. Another who combined both successfully was Douglas Bader, who appeared in the castle in the middle of August 1942. For me, the only surprising aspect of this event was that it had taken so long for the Germans to send him to join us. Douglas very quickly sought me out to re-establish our association. His immediate enquiry to me was "How the hell can we get out of this bloody place?" He also said he wanted to send some secret information home. On both subjects I was a little cautious because the escape scheme in which I was then involved with Bear Kruimink was by no means my own idea, and therefore I had no proprietary rights. As for secret messages, I had sent none home from Colditz for two reasons. One was that, having shown my method to Pete Gardner at Warburg before I left for Colditz, I did not know if it was still secure. Neither did I have a suitable photograph available which had to be predominantly black with naval uniforms. For these reasons I did not immediately commit myself to any undertakings on either subject but told Dougie I would see what I could do about it.

What I came up with was a hairy scheme which entailed the construction of an artfully concealed and camouflaged entrance high up in the wall of the British common room, in which I lived, into the unoccupied attic of an adjoining wing of Colditz Castle. At its far extremity, this wing, which was occupied only by Germans, was well clear of the system of anti-escape floodlights. The plan was to climb out of an attic window far from the lights and make our way—with our backs against a steeply sloping roof and our feet in the gutter—to a nearby robust lightning conductor which, with the aid of some rope work, would allow us to make a descent to ground level. With the addition of a rampart to be scaled at the bottom, this amounted to a descent of about ninety feet. The risks involved were immense, but we hoped to minimise these by employing some of the safety rope work used in mountaineering.

The outline having been decided upon, I set to thinking about how we might be able to assist a man with Douglas Bader's disabilities in the descent. When I had worked out a few ideas to help him I approached Bear on the subject, fully expecting him to be justifiably aghast and completely unreceptive. He was not. I think he agreed with me that an escape by Bader would be such a morale booster all round that it was worth a try. As for myself, I had made a personal reservation on the subject that I did not intend to reveal to either Bear or Douglas Bader. It was that in the event that the wing commander proved too much of an impediment to progress I would insist that Bear should go it alone and leave me to help Douglas. We were, of course, intending to travel mostly by train with plenty of German money and excellent forged identity documents.

I then told Douglas about the idea and asked if he would like to join Bear and me on the roof job and he went for it without a moment's hesitation. Well, he would, wouldn't he—such was the man! We then had to refer the scheme to the escape committee for British and Dutch approval. Having considered the reassurances from Bear and me that we could get him safely off the roof, Bader was accepted into the team and was told that from then on he would be required to be present at all escape-plan meetings to discuss progress and possible problems.

Thenceforth Bear and I were often to be seen with Bader between us, his arms round our shoulders and his legs swinging idly as we practised running around the cobbled courtyard. This caused considerable amusement for the other prisoners, and the guards also found it very entertaining. Little did they realise the purpose of it was to perfect a fast departure from the bottom of one of their lightning conductors.

Then came Bader's first appearance at an escape meeting, attended by such stalwarts as van den Heuvel, the Dutch escape officer; Dick Howe, our own new escape officer; Bear Kruimink and several more. It is likely that the other prisoners expected the newcomer to have very little to say, but they didn't know our Douglas. When the discussion turned to the matter of descending the lightning conductor, everyone fell silent when Bader piped up. It was essential, he said, that we should have good air discipline. I was concerned that everyone might be thinking that Bader had lost his marbles. After a moment's pause Howe respectfully requested the wing commander to enlarge on his suggestion. Douglas replied, "In the event of anybody falling off, no screaming on the way down!" The laughter which followed was far from hearty and I know mine was somewhat forced.

His closest friend: PDT and Lieut. Frits "Bear" Kruimink, Royal Dutch Navy.

Sadly, the whole plan collapsed. This time the Germans were one step ahead of us. They had installed a well-hidden alarm system in the attic which, when triggered, was silent on the spot but flashed an alarm in the *Kommandantur.* The result was that our first reconnaissance party entering the German attic found themselves confronted by German guards and that was the end of that.

The best antidote for failure was to jump right into another scheme. Around this time, the *Kommandant* decided we had too many possessions, especially books, and these were cluttering the very confined space available to us. This situation made the German snap searches of our quarters more difficult for them and therefore less effective. The order was therefore given that much of our "clutter" was to be taken away by the Germans and deposited in a storeroom in the *Kommandantur*. This depository was on the third floor with a single small window high above what had once been the moat. Of greatest interest to us was the fact that this was territory which was not floodlit nor guarded by German sentries.

To facilitate this operation, the Germans supplied a number of plywood boxes which had contained Red Cross food parcels from Canada. These were rather like tea chests, a cube of about thirty inches each side. Dominic Bruce was invited to see if he could squeeze his "medium sized" frame into one of the boxes, and, sure enough, he could just do so. Moreover, there was sufficient room to spare in the box for a good length of very fine closely rolled bed-sheet rope, a few vital rations, some German money, forged identity papers and one of the excellent new silk maps from MI9. Brucie was allowed to practise suffering this cramped position for longer and longer periods inside one of the boxes. Eventually all the boxes were loaded with books and other clutter, and one with Bruce. The lids were nailed on securely, or apparently so, and appropriately labelled.

The Germans were then informed that our orderlies were ready to carry the heavy boxes to the German store room. Guards were detailed to escort them and to see there was no skulduggery. The Bruce box was dumped in a nice position with nothing on top of it, and the orderlies and guards departed with one of the former saying in a very loud voice, words to the effect that "Well now, all finished, and off we all go!" This must have been quite an obvious and unnecessary remark to everyone present, but it was music to the ears of the little fellow inside.

Brucie suffered his cramped condition for as long as he could to give the guards time to get well clear. When darkness fell, he emerged and made his descent on the bedsheet rope out of the window down to the edge of the dry moat. Our little hero had not been able to resist the opportunity to rub salt into the prospective wound to the pride of the *Abwehr Offizier* and left in the store room a farewell note in German which said, "The air in Colditz no longer suits me, so I am leaving. Auf Wiedersehen!"

There was one weakness to this escape which was, I suppose, unavoidable.

There was no way of disposing of the rope dangling from the window which would be in full view of the Germans in the light of day. However, luck was with dear old Brucie once again. As it happened, no member of the Colditz garrison noticed it until it was pointed out to them by a civilian passerby. Even the *Kommandant* had passed nearby with an important visiting German officer without noticing it.

Dominic Bruce was such an unnoticeable little chap in a crowd that he fared very well on his own, especially after he managed to steal a bicycle to help him on his way to Danzig. There he intended to smuggle himself into a ship bound for neutral Sweden à la Paddon. Regrettably, he was caught a week later in Danzig. So near and yet so far! However, his determination was admirable. His next intention was to avoid being sent back to Colditz, so he told his captors that he was a crewman from an RAF bomber recently shot down over Bremen. He was sent to Dulag Luft as all newly captured aircrew were. Alas, on arrival at Dulag, he was immediately recognised by the German staff.

The very morning after Dominic Bruce had disappeared in his box, we had another wonderful morning of riotous exultation and laughter because another six prisoners had escaped. They had been working at night for quite some time inside the locked-up office of *Stabsfeldwebel* Gebhardt, whom we called "Mussolini" because of his fat chops. Our local Musso was the right-hand man of the *Abwehroffizier* and was always out and about in the castle, sneaking around trying to cotton on to any infamous activities. Actually, he was not a bad chap, but a confounded nuisance. Towards the end of the war, when Germany was scraping the barrel for cannon fodder, poor old Gebhardt was killed on the Russian Front.

Musso's office abutted the southern end of the chapel. His day's duty done, his habit was to lock up his office very securely and clock off. Directly underneath the office was a store room whose only door gave on to a guarded and floodlit area. The store contained goods available to our Colditz garrison and another German unit in the town below. That unit occasionally sent a small work party of well-guarded Polish prisoners to the store to pick up some goods. These visitors never had any truck with us nor we with them. They were total strangers because none of us Colditz prisoners ever had any access to that store.

Wouldn't it be nice if a bunch of our chaps could suddenly become a party of Polish prisoners with a couple of Germans as an escort? They could then emerge from the store, carrying some goodies, and walk off with them. But how to get access to that store? Let's think about it. What about a hole through the floor of Musso's office which was directly above? That was it. All that was required was a hole in Musso's floor!

Many of us could pick ordinary locks by this time, and the Dutch lockpicker van Doorninck could even open a cruciform lock with his patent measuring instrument to make a key. Musso's office was stealthily visited one night for a reconnaissance and it was decided that the best place to make a hole in the floor was bang underneath Musso's chair at his desk as the chair conveniently stood on a small mat which would hide the entrance hatch. Perfect!

So night after night, the escape gang entered Musso's office and worked on the trapdoor under his chair. The team consisted of our Dutch friend van Doorninck and my old pal Bill Fowler, plus two other pairs: Lieutenant Geoff Wardle with Dutch Lieutenant Donkers; and Captain "Lulu" Lawton with Dutch Lieutenant Ted Beets, together with engineer accomplices. The enterprise was carefully safeguarded by a vigilant team of stooges who would warn the workers of the approach of any German who might hear their quiet little picking or sawing away at the floor.

Then, one night, when the preparations were almost complete, Hauptmann Priem (yet to be replaced by Eggers) decided to do a clever little unexpected night prowl round the prison with guards and a fellow with keys for everywhere, including Musso's office. Panic stations! The stooges signalled to the workers in Musso's office to be silent and they all held their breath. Priem came along the passage ordering every door to be opened so that he could check what, if anything, especially anything nefarious, was going on inside. He came to Musso's office and told the keys man to open it up and the key was inserted in the lock.

"What is this door, anyway?" asked Priem.

The guard answered, "It is *Stabsfeldwebel* Gebhardt's office, Herr Hauptmann."

"Oh," said Priem, "we don't need to bother about that then. They can't get up to any nonsense in there! Let's move on."

Phew! The boys inside could start breathing again and later carried on working. Meanwhile, two German uniforms had been tailored for the German officer in charge of the escort, who would be van Doorninck, and the German NCO to be played by another perfect German speaker, Ted Beets. Four Polish prisoners' outfits were made for Bill Fowler, Geoff Wardle, "Lulu" Lawton and Lieutenant Donkers.

All was ready on 9 September 1942, the day after Bruce had been boxed up in the attic store. The plan worked perfectly. That night the escapers let themselves down into the storeroom via the trapdoor in Musso's office. Meanwhile accomplices replaced the hatch with the mat over the top of it and repositioned the chair. The escapers then gathered together the stores they would be carrying, did a final check on each other's disguises and waited. Next morning they emerged through the storeroom door just after the guards had all changed for the early morning shift. Thus every guard would think the work party had gone into the store just before he came on duty. The Colditz guards bade them a friendly *Guten Morgen* and opened a gate for them to pass through on their way to Colditz town.

It was essential that their absence should not be noticed during morning *Appell*. Dick Howe was jubilant but worried stiff that the escape was almost bound to be discovered too soon. "Pete," he said to me, "we've got to foul up this *Appell* for as long as possible to give those lads a good start. Are you ready for it?"

"I'm ready, Dick," I said.

"Good lad—we've got to keep this one going forever. Pull out all the stops!"

In my present role of trouble-maker and saboteur of roll calls, I was raring to go and had a handful of accomplices all lined up to join in. I had briefed them where to hide before allowing themselves to be found, one at a time. The Germans would think we were just being bloody-minded again for some reason or other, and would eventually find everybody just as they had after the fire in the staircase. Three chaps would stay with me up in the British quarters, three storeys up, along most of the eastern side of the yard below. A few others dispersed themselves elsewhere and the whole mob on parade below knew what was afoot so were ready to join in with organised indiscipline and milling around. Douglas Bader was, of course, in his element.

The Germans would almost immediately assume that they had yet another rowdy *Appell* ahead of them and would be wondering what had upset us this time. It would not be long before the riot squad was called in to help restore order. At last there was some semblance of a parade and the Germans started to count as usual, one in front and one behind the five ranks, together counting—*"fünf, zehn, fünfzehn"*—ensuring that the five ranks were covering off properly. This was my cue to do something to disrupt the count. We, who were up in the British quarters, had the run of the place, including the little kitchen where there were bowls, a bucket or two, and taps with lovely water in them. I had already filled a bucket with water so my first ploy was to hurl the water out of a barred window onto the British company below. You would have thought they were a bunch of silly schoolgirls! They screamed with horror and milled around with big tough British officers wringing their hands and saying things like, "Oh dear—I'm all wet!" Everyone was thoroughly enjoying themselves—except the Germans, that is.

Hauptmann Eggers and his men now realised there were some prisoners not on parade and the order was given for guards to go up to the British quarters, count the number of officers up there and then lock them inside so that they could be dealt with later and punished for their indiscipline. Rather stupidly, the guards locked us in as ordered but left one outside where he could not keep an eye on us. We then wedged the door to keep him out and unable to interfere with our activities.

Eggers, now suspecting something more might be afoot than mere pranks, ordered the boxes of identity cards with photographs of all the prisoners to be brought in and set out on a small table near the head of the British company. That was nice because it was within easy range of a water bomb. With an excellent lob, which I could probably never do again, I landed it *SPLOSH* on the table and many of the identity cards were scattered onto the ground.

I then ran back to the kitchen to fill another bucket with water and stood by for a target at one of our dormitory windows, peering out at the mob as best I could through the iron bars. Douglas Bader saw me and hand-signalled me to wait a moment until he gave another signal to let go. It was obvious and easily understood. Then, when he signalled "GO", I slung the bucket of water out of the window, which was heavily barred like all the others. I could not see directly downwards, but was rewarded by a roar of applause and much hooting and laughter. Bader appeared ecstatic.

I was not aware that Priem was watching proceedings from a window opposite mine on the other side of the yard. He had seen quite clearly who had thrown the water. Nor did I know, until later on, that Bader's signal had been made with a good purpose in mind. Eggers had been walking along the length of the yard, close into the bottom of the wall of our British quarters. Bader's signal and timing had been good, not perfect, but good enough. The mass of the water landed so close to Eggers as to splash him quite generously and he ran for cover to the laughter, cheers and jeers of the unruly mob.

Gradually, order was restored and after a usefully long delay, the *Abwehr* staff discovered seven prisoners were missing and broadcast the signal to alert all the railway staff and security services close by. But they were not fast enough and our disruptive activities had not been in vain. Four of the escapers from Musso's office were caught eventually but two of them made it to Switzerland and thence on to England. To my great joy, these two were my old chums from Barth days, Bill Fowler and his Dutch partner van Doorninck, the lock-picking wizard.

There is a sad rider to this story. A little later on, Bill Fowler was doing development flying on the new RAF fighter-bomber, the Hawker Typhoon, which had some serious teething problems. He was killed as a result of a technical failure on one of them. Nonetheless, if Bill and I ever meet again on the other side of the Pearly Gates, or in the other place, I am sure we will have quite a celebration together! As for me, I had plenty to laugh about but also something to worry about as well. Having splashed Eggers and been identified by Priem, I was charged for my second German court martial with the following: first, assaulting a senior officer on active service in the field and causing him to take cover (possible sentence—death); second, disrupting a German military parade (also a very serious offence in Nazi Germany); third, throwing water out of a high window contrary to the *Kommandant's* recent camp order.

I was somewhat comforted by the fact that we had a smart young barrister among us in the person of Lieutenant "Black" Campbell. The Germans would not allow him to appear in court but he advised me how to instruct my German *Rechtsanwalt* (solicitor). I was held in solitary for some of the time awaiting trial and was, as usual, allowed to communicate with my solicitor only by letter. These the Colditz *Abwehr* department reckoned they had a right to censor so there was no confidentiality whatsoever. Ah well, it was all par for the course.

While I awaited my trial date in mid-November 1942, there was still time for more shenanigans. A German handyman named Willi Pöhnert was often in and about the castle repairing this, that or the other. Willi, who was in his late twenties, was nearly as small as Dominic Bruce, wore very thick-lensed spectacles, and was obviously unfit for military service. We were sorry for little Willi and tried, as best we could, to show him some sympathy and respect. He responded to this with a shy smile.

Willi was never allowed into our domain without an armed guard whose purpose was to ensure that the predator prisoners, who would pinch anything from a screwdriver to a steamroller, given the opportunity, stole none of his tools. The other purpose of such a guard was to protect the morals of civilian workmen and ensure that they were not subjected to any bribery or corruption or fed any propaganda deleterious to the Nazi cause. One day, one of the chapel windows, which was some twelve feet above ground level, suffered a breakage and Willi came in with a twenty-foot ladder and some tools to fit a new pane of glass, helped by a Goon guard with his rifle. He put the ladder against the wall and climbed up it to measure the broken pane. Then he came down and went out of our yard by himself, obviously to go to his workshop and cut a piece of glass to size. The guard was left to keep an eye on Willi's ladder and tools.

I suddenly felt a challenge. How very useful a ladder would be to facilitate access to an area in our attic, or inside one of the huge hollow buttresses of the castle, where I knew the Dutch were considering descending to start a tunnel at the bottom. Anyway, it was always a minor victory for us to pinch anything. Moreover, the guard standing directly in front of the ladder looked like a dolt and poor little Willi could not be blamed for anything that happened when he was not even there. Two good men were nearby, namely Don Donaldson and Flight Lieutenant "Bag" Dickinson who was a very mischievous fellow indeed.

I whispered to Don, "Can you divert that guard's attention?"

"Sure," he said.

There was no need for explanation. Any POW would immediately know what was required. Don sat down on the cobbles of the yard, leaning against the chapel wall, and began an intriguing performance, making all sorts of strange patterns with his fingers against the wall and on his own face. He looked as if he had gone completely round the bend. The guard looked at him in amazement at this strange performance. Don was really enthusiastic about it. I'd wager nobody could have resisted giving him their full attention. Certainly, the guard couldn't. He was transfixed with his back to the ladder only three or four feet behind him against the chapel wall.

Dickinson and I tiptoed behind him and, without a sound, removed the ladder which we intended to take up the spiral staircase, beyond the entrance to our quarters, and higher to an attic where we knew how to unlock the door. Alas, the ladder was too long to go round the curve of the spiral but a young Australian pilot, "Bush" Parker, had turned up to stick his ever curious nose into what was going on and I knew he had a good set of illegal tools.

"Bring us a wood saw, Bush, as fast as you can!" I said, signalling to Don to keep his idiotic performance going, which he did. In little more than a minute, Bush was back with a bow saw. As quickly as we could, we sawed about five feet off that lovely long ladder and I told Bag and Bush to take the longer part up the stairs.

"What about the short bit?" Bag asked me.

"Never mind about the short bit," I said. "Get the long bit up those stairs and hide it!"

"Right," said Bag, and off he and Bush went with the ladder. I had a jolly plan in mind for the short bit.

Don was still doing his stuff with his very expressive fingers, but I could see that he had nearly had enough. The guard was still utterly entranced. Very quietly, I placed the short bit where the ladder had stood, slunk away and awaited developments.

Don got up, smiled at the guard, and walked off just as little Willi entered the yard with a pane of glass under his arm. The guard still had not looked behind him. Willi arrived on the scene and his eyes nearly popped out of his head as he asked the guard what had happened to the ladder. The guard turned round and was flabbergasted. He said something about "*Poltergeisten!*" and the pair slunk off to the yard gate, Willi carrying his tools and glass and the guard carrying the bit of ladder. By now, the word had got about and a small crowd had gathered to cheer. The guard looked very glum indeed, but we were all sure there was a little smile on Willi's face.

We expected the riot squad to be in almost immediately and a search to be carried out, but nothing happened. Obviously Willi returned to his workshop and said nothing about it, possibly to avoid ridicule, and, of course, the guard dared not say a thing because he would have been in big trouble for not doing his duty properly as the guardian of Willi's tools. The ladder came in really handy and Dick Howe was delighted to have it.

This story has quite a touching sequel. In 1985, the Colditz Association of "old boys" made a return visit to the castle, then in the Soviet-dominated German Democratic Republic, to mark the fortieth anniversary of its liberation. As far as the East German communists were concerned we had been ardent enemies of the Nazis so officially we were treated with considerable respect.

For a formal welcome we were gathered in the Colditz Castle Theatre and there was a nicely arranged reception for us. Little Willi Pöhnert was still living in Colditz Town but we had not noticed his presence at the event. Suddenly he appeared out of the audience, ran up and embraced me and said with a big smile on his face, "You vere such Shentelmen!" It was quite a touching little event and I admit I had to blow my nose! I've always been a bit of a "softie" and it makes life more difficult sometimes.

It wasn't all fun and games, though, not by a long chalk. Like it or not, we were still part of an unspeakably brutal war in which the lives even of POWs remained very much at hazard. I received a grim reminder of this in October 1942. One morning, one of our orderlies who had his quarters in the Saalhaus came running to me with the news that a new batch of British prisoners was in the German courtyard and being photographed. I was talking to "Scorgie" Price at the time and both of us hurried off to the Saalhaus and peeped cautiously through the bars of a first floor window. We were in territory forbidden to officers and therefore hoped we should not be spotted by any Germans and pick up yet another fourteen days' solitary confinement.

There were seven prisoners in the German yard under heavy guard. All were wearing normal army battle-dress, gaiters and boots. Two were officers, both of them captains and both wearing army issue leather jerkins over their battle-dress, one with his right arm heavily bandaged and in a sling. I later learned he had taken a bullet through his forearm. All the prisoners were bare-headed except two of the men who wore knitted balaclava helmets. They mostly appeared to be in their twenties but two looked like tousle-headed schoolboys. The other ranks each wore an empty canvas pistol holster in front of the right thigh and round the waist a six-foot rope issued to commandos with a toggle at one end and a loop at the other.

When several of these were joined, loop over toggle, their primary function was to form a climbing rope, but individually they had a more sinister purpose when the object was to dispose of an enemy sentry with stealth and silence. Why the Germans insisted upon their remaining so well equipped is somewhat odd unless it was to emphasise their existence as "prize commando prisoners".

They were commandos all right, and apparently a small unit as opposed to a hotchpotch of random prisoners who had, by some misdeeds, qualified for removal to Colditz. This unusual circumstance excited our curiosity and at the risk of revealing our presence to the German guards, I felt compelled to make contact with them which I proceeded to do with a few furtive "pssts".

The lads in the yard were quick on the uptake and did not react in an obvious way that would have revealed our presence. Instead, they spoke to us as if they were addressing each other. We learned that they were commandos who had been captured after a recent highly successful sabotage action in Norway. We were struck by their rather subdued manner which lacked the normal façade of "old buck" put on by most prisoners for the benefit of the Germans. This was soon explained.

These remnants of the initial twelve-strong commando raid were being shuttled around from pillar to post with no sign of settling down in any normal prison camp. The Germans were hopping mad about the success of their mission, which had been to blow up a hydro-electric power station in Glomfjord on the Norwegian coast that had supplied all the power for an important aluminium factory. To the commandos, their ultimate fate seemed horribly uncertain as there had been repeated threats of shooting. I did my best to reassure them on this score by telling them I had myself been similarly threatened on several occasions and that Colditz was probably their final destination for the duration. This seemed most likely, especially as several of our company had come to the *Straflager* for no other reason than having raised the particular ire of the enemy. Why else would these commandos have been sent to Colditz if not to join us? It had never before been used as a transit camp.

At this stage, the Germans twigged what was going on so that Scorgie and I had to beat a hasty retreat from the window. We went straight to Daddy Stayner, told him the story and he immediately made representations to the German *Kommandant*, Oberst Prawitt, on behalf of the anxious commandos. After several days, there was still no sign of them joining us. They were kept in the cells which let off from the castle approach tunnel and later the two officers were removed to the town cells. There, several prisoners, Dominic Bruce, Dick Howe and Peter Storie-Pugh among them, were able to establish a little contact in spite of stringent German precautions against it.

At last we learned the names of the seven commando prisoners which we sent by code to the Swiss protecting power and to MI9 in London. The German military authorities were also constantly pestered about them. This fuss and airing of our knowledge of their existence and identity would, we felt sure, at least safeguard the lives of these men. It appeared that they had fought a gallant military action and had done nothing contrary to the international rules of warfare. In fact, captured documents later revealed that the commander of the German troops who fought them in Norway commended their lion-hearted spirit and gallantry. The Germans had, therefore, no justification whatsoever for the threats they were making against these lads. Their only real crime was infuriating Hitler with the audacity of their mission under the noses of the German garrison at Glomfjord.

After a few more days, the commandos disappeared from Colditz and no amount of nagging from Colonel Stayner could elicit any information about their whereabouts or fortunes. We knew from the slight contact in the town cells that they were contemplating escape, and in formulating a plan had been encouraged and helped by "old hands" like Howe, Bruce and Storie-Pugh. We were jubilant when we learned months later that the Germans had officially informed the British and Swiss authorities that all the commandos had escaped and none had been re-captured. It was assumed that they were hiding in one of the occupied countries and their families rested assured for the remainder of the war that they would eventually be reunited.

The truth was very different and did not emerge until the War Crimes Commission completed its post-war investigations. After being collected from Colditz by a detachment of the SS, the seven gallant commandos had been taken to the Reich Security Headquarters in Berlin and from there to Sachsenhausen Concentration Camp on the outskirts of the city. Before dawn on 23 October 1942, each one was shot in the back of the neck and their bodies were fed into ovens and reduced to ashes. The document relating to their execution was produced in evidence against Field Marshal Wilhelm Keitel, General Alfred Jodl and General von Falkenhorst in the war crimes trials after Germany's defeat. Real villains like Hitler and SS *Obergruppenführer* Heinrich Müller escaped the rope: Hitler by suicide and Müller, who had personally interrogated the captives, under unknown circumstances. He was last recorded in the *Führerbunker* the day after Hitler killed himself, but in the chaos of besieged Berlin was lost from sight. For many years it was believed that the USSR had used him to help administer its secret police, but the recently opened Soviet archives have disproved this theory. It is most likely that Müller was killed trying to get out of Berlin, like Martin Bormann and other top Nazis. He was the notorious Adolf Eichmann's immediate superior.

While the war was on, we prisoners in Hitler's Germany were not aware of the full extent of Nazi tyranny, brutality and genocide, but we were beginning to learn from the horrific experiences of some of the escapers who glimpsed the barbarism of the Nazi concentration camps. About this time I saw an offensive cartoon in the only German newspaper we were allowed to read—the Nazi-approved *Völkischer Beobachter*, which I felt at the time deserved some reaction. The cartoon was a rude portrayal of our King and Queen and I felt that an appropriate response was due.

In no time I had a plan and in a matter of only hours I had done all that was necessary to bring it to fruition. I knew of a French officer who had, at one time, possessed a parrot, which he kept in a large circular wire cage. Rumour had it that somebody in the extreme throes of hunger had eaten the poor bird! I am certain that story was apocryphal. Anyway, it did not take me long to barter with the Frenchman to give me the cage, especially when I hinted to him that the purpose would be to annoy our common enemy. Another strange fellow had a large rag doll—why or for what purpose or whence, I had no idea, but I soon persuaded him to let me have that as well.

I swiftly replaced the rag doll's face with an imitation of the face of Adolf Hitler whose moustache and lock of black hair hanging over his forehead was unmistakable. The doll's clothing was very easily transformed into a typical Hitler uniform with the Swastika armband and Sam Browne-type belt and shoulder strap. It was easy and I worked with feverish speed and great pleasure.

When Hitler's effigy was complete I hung it in the cage, from which I had removed the perch, dangling by the neck on a stout piece of string with a genuine hangman's noose. Fixed under the left arm of Adolf Hitler was the folded cartoon of our King and Queen. I then enlisted a small band of equally incensed conspirators who agreed to help me display the hanged German *Führer* to best advantage. I carried the cage, which stood almost hip-high, on to the next *Appell* with my greatcoat loosely covering it— more or less—and my conspirator friends surrounding me in a solid but casual phalanx. On parade I stood in the rear rank with the cage in front of me and my greatcoat over my arm almost covering it. With *Appell* over, everyone dispersed very quickly and the yard was suddenly empty except for the *Führer*, suspended by a hangman's noose in a cage.

The cage was quickly removed by German guards and we all awaited the reaction with great interest and a measure of anxiety. To our utter amazement and some relief nothing happened and nothing was even said. I admit I was greatly relieved about that because I expected considerable repercussions and there was no knowing to what length the Nazis might

Hanging Hitler in effigy.

have gone to find the culprit or force a confession with threats of mass reprisals. I can only conclude that perhaps the *Kommandant* did not dare to reveal that such a thing could have occurred under his command.

Not until some time after the war, when I read Eggers' autobiography, did I learn anything about the German reaction to my gesture. Eggers, who would have everyone believe he was no real Nazi, described the incident as "a cheap insult to our *Führer*". This is a fascinating and revealing comment from a man who pretended to us he was not an ardent Nazi. He was, however, a man who—by the time he wrote his book—must have been fully aware of the Nazi atrocities and the brutal nature of the psychopathic madman he served. Furthermore, Eggers assured his readers that they knew very well who had perpetrated the insult to their *Führer* but they could not prove it—as though he and his colleagues ever required proof. For my part, I always realised that my fingerprints must have been plastered all over the whole thing.

As time crept wearily by I made further use of the noose to control the most belligerent of our German keepers. Over the remaining years, only a very few qualified for my gesture. If a German really deserved my treatment, I would brief a chum to hold him in conversation for a few moments while I gently hooked on his back with a bent pin a neat little piece of string with a hangman's noose on the end. The victim never knew anything about it until another German would spot it and inform him that he had been selected for such recognition. There was never any reaction to this but I like to believe it gave a few of the nastier types something to think about.

Making trouble for our captors was high on Douglas Bader's list of priorities also. It was natural that he and I should have been drawn to each other, although where the wing commander was concerned, it was always implicit that he was in charge. He was an absolutely dominating character, for better or worse. At one stage two of my friends, quite independently, warned me that I was allowing Bader to use me for his own ends, but I would not listen. I admired the man so much I felt privileged.

Douglas Bader's next requirement of me was that I should send a message to MI9 by my split-photograph method. I told him of my continued security doubts and lack of a readily suitable photograph but he ignored that and immediately presented me with a screed which began with the words, "Message from Wg Cmdr Bader." I admit that I slightly resented his disregard of my misgivings but felt I must accept this as a legitimate order from a wing commander to a flying officer and I had better get on with it.

What worried me most about this was the existence of the written message in his handwriting and with his name on it. I told him I would have preferred that no message be actually written until the split photograph was ready to receive it but in his inimitable manner he scoffed at my over-cautious misgivings. I had no immediate access to a prepared and secure "hide" so I decided the safest solution was to keep his message on my person in a small wallet with a few other precious belongings, and take appropriate action if and when the need arose. At night, in bed, I kept it in the pocket of my pyjama jacket. I must admit that I felt the contents of the message hardly justified the risk of exposing the split-photograph stunt forever. The message consisted mainly of the wing commander's assessment of the effect on German morale of the increasing British bombing raids and ended with a typical Bader flourish, to wit, "Bomb these Bastards to Hell!" I felt a mite disloyal to Douglas in that I suspected its main intent was to remind everybody of his continued existence, even as a POW, and served little practical purpose otherwise. The new Commander-in-Chief of Bomber Command, "Butch" Harris, was doing an increasingly good job and did not really need exhortations from a Battle of Britain fighter boy—even one as renowned as Douglas Bader.

A few days later the worst happened. I was awakened first thing one morning by raucous German commands, "*Alles aufstehen—raus, raus*" (Everyone out of bed, get up, get up). It was the overture to an intensive search. I was not too worried about it because I knew their routine on these occasions. They would herd us all into a corner where we would be carefully watched while they ransacked the room, searched our belongings and tried to discover hides. Then at some stage they would take us individually for a personal search. Having us all in our night clothes they would not expect to find anything and, in any case, I knew if it came to the worst I must pop Bader's message into my mouth and swallow it. We all took our time about getting up—pretending still to be half asleep—and generally being uncooperative.

By this time we could hear that the rest of Colditz was coming to life and there were already prisoners' voices down in the yard beneath the open window near my bed. I knew everyone would have quickly realised that the British quarters were about to be searched and by now a few stalwart friends, certainly some of our Dutch pals, would be standing by to snatch up and run off with any contraband chucked out of our windows. It had become a normal and effective ploy which, so far, the Germans had not cottoned on to. I thought this would be a better idea than trying to swallow the message which I would first have to remove from the wallet in my pyjama pocket. Well, I could hardly swallow the whole damned wallet, could I? And they would be watching us for any skulduggery.

I feigned a very slow recovery from my deep sleep and pretended to be only half awake as I yawned and blinked my way out from my top bunk. As I passed the window I pretended to yawn again and as I stretched my arms I slipped the little wallet out of my top pyjama pocket and tossed it out of the window. Great! Nobody saw it go. My luck then deserted me. A German officer happened to come by at that precise moment. My wallet bounced off his shoulder, fell at his feet and he picked it up. I was told later that it was Eggers, of all people.

Then the poo really hit the fan! A few days later Douglas Bader was driven off to Leipzig for interrogation and I was on the mat at Colditz. I said it was a nonsense note given me by the wing commander because he thought I might be about to escape, and they couldn't really prohibit a chap to send a message home by or convey a message home as an escaper, could they?

At Leipzig Douglas Bader laughed in the face of his incensed interrogator who told him he was going to be court-martialled in Berlin for espionage. Douglas replied that they would only make fools of themselves if they tried to charge a helpless enemy prisoner, who was always in uniform, with espionage. Fortunately everything fizzled out except that the wing commander had another well-known foible. When anything went wrong it was always entirely somebody else's fault, but he got over it and our usual teamwork continued. Whatever is said about that amazing man by his rather numerous critics, Douglas Bader had one invariable saving grace. Whatever the outcome of any episode in which he was involved, whether it climaxed in success or disaster, he always recounted it with peals of laughter. This tended to increase the respect of his admirers and give more grist to the mills of his critics.

With the passage of time, though, sustaining our morale became more and more an uphill task. On my arrival at Colditz I had formed a "mess" with four other RAF prisoners, meaning that we lived together and shared our catering arrangements. They had been a keen bunch of escapers and we had much else in common. They all made good companions until I began to notice some strange reclusive moodiness in one of them and utterly outrageous exhibitionism beginning to come from another. By this time, we POWs had become accustomed to one chap or another seeming to become somewhat weird or distant for a while. It was sometimes referred to as becoming "wire happy", but most recovered as time went by and became their normal selves again. Others never did.

Don Donaldson and I began seriously to worry about our mess mate who was becoming positively morose and secretive soon after my arrival. Don eventually discovered that this young man's mother was writing to tell him that the wife he had so recently married was spending too much time gadding about with the other lads in their community, which did not surprise her because she had never approved of the marriage in the first place. That was not a very good way to cheer up your little boy in a prison camp!

Thus it was that this particular fellow was exhibiting the all too typical symptoms of prisoners who received what we somewhat jocularly, but really sadly, referred to as "Dear John" letters indicating the end of a loving relationship. Our mess mate became more and more depressed and withdrawn. At last, he tried to slash his wrists with a razor. After that was patched up, we had to take stints in keeping a twenty-four-hour watch on him but without him realising he was under constant surveillance. Even so, he managed another attempt to end his own life which was scotched in time because the lavatory in which he tried to hang himself had—like all of them—no door and he was restrained.

Eventually, the Germans were persuaded to treat this poor lad and he was taken away to hospital with another sick prisoner under guard. On the way to Colditz railway station, he managed to jump off a bridge over the River Mulde in Colditz town in a fairly obvious attempt to get the guards to shoot him. Fortunately, the guards and the other prisoner managed to get him back onto the bridge. Many months later, he was repatriated and we had no more news of him. It was a terrible pity, he was such a nice lad. I will never forget the miserable mental strain of furtively watching over suicidal friends and trying unsuccessfully to cheer them up until one began to worry about one's own mental condition. We soon came to the conclusion that suicide attempts ran in threes.

Eventually, Donaldson and I were the only two of our original mess of five left in Colditz. The other three had all been repatriated with mental problems, the second one after some spectacular displays of gymnastic brilliance up a creeper on one of the walls surrounding our yard, wearing ridiculous clothing including a hat made from an old football. Then he performed a devil-may-care breathtaking athletic escape attempt with bullets flying all round him and one wounding him. It was a wonder he survived it.

Oh the dread and dreariness of all this! It was something we tried to make light of, but we knew that all of us were vulnerable and sometimes wondered who would be next. More than anything, I dreaded a "Dear John" letter from Ann. She was worth more than my life to me. One tries to dwell only upon happier thoughts and this is how I managed to tolerate the long periods I spent in solitary confinement at Colditz. I trained my mind to take off from those cells and dwell on pleasant memories. I also imagined all sorts of travels and adventures, meeting people I used to know or inventing new ones with whom I had long interesting imaginary discussions. Hours would pass by until the bolts of my cell door rattled as a guard delivered my bowl of mid-day slop, at which point my mental absence was suddenly ended. I had not been in that cell all that time. When people asked me how I could take it for such long stretches, I told them, "It's easy—if you're not there!"

But seriously and sadly, this was the train of thought that led me to believe why it was obvious in Colditz that the preponderance of officers suffering mental breakdown—some permanent and some suicidal—were the aircrew. They were the "free spirits" rather than the stolid, stoic, severely disciplined soldiers of spit and polish, ceremony, dignity and indifference about trench warfare, or the salty, tar-encrusted, "Hearts of Oak" sailors.

The fact is that the airman's fatality rate—especially the bomber aircrewman's—was second only to that of a crewman of a German U-Boat. Postwar statistics showed that the chances of avoiding death or imprisonment were not far off fifty-fifty. His war was a series of dark plunges into extreme danger—take off, get stuck in, fight, live or die, and, with the odds against him getting away with it very many more times, land back—Phew! Then a party or two and, with luck, a few cuddles thrown in before going into battle again, two or three times a week. I concluded that prolonged misery, dreariness, confinement and boredom were harder for them to take, and that this was why, over the whole scene of wartime captivity, they were the keenest escapers and most likely to lose their marbles or become wire-happy if they didn't succeed.

During this trying period, I was fortunate to be able to fall back upon the finest friendship I have ever had the privilege of enjoying, one that lasted a lifetime. Bear Kruimink and I first expressed our friendship by knocking the daylights out of each other shortly after I arrived at Colditz. I was a boxer in my earlier youth and he was a jujitsu expert and we exchanged instruction in those martial arts. Bear felt the same as I did about the enemy, but I believe I was more demonstrative and he, in the end, more pragmatic. In fact, one of his expressed concerns was that I would get myself shot. Well, the Germans had talked about it enough and had a good try after my Spangenberg escape. I was certainly not unaware of that particular danger.

After the war, we saw each other again on only three or four occasions, but kept in touch with letters and phone calls. But still, if anyone asks me who was my best friend ever, the only answer would be Bear Kruimink. He retired from the Netherlands Navy as a Vice-Admiral and became the head of Dutch Intelligence and National Security. He wrote me many pages of a very long letter in short stages over a period of several weeks. In it are all the accolades that I never received from anywhere else, and they are worth as much, or more, to me than any others ever could be.

Because my contact with Ann seemed more and more difficult and remote, I was finding it harder to keep enthusiasm going for anything. I wrote to close friends at home, asking them if they could allay my anxieties, but nobody would commit themselves to factual answers. I even wrote to Ann's mother and had a strange reply, which amounted to her hope that I was "not becoming a bookworm"! In fairness to her, I obviously could not write openly about my anti-German activities in my letters to England. Thus, all communications had to be very reserved and stilted, and all one could possibly write about was what books one was reading. As for my split photographs, I did not know whether Ann was opening them first to read herself or passing them straight on to MI9 to split open themselves. She never used our code to write a secret letter back to me.

It is very difficult to keep a really close warm relationship alive when you cannot talk about your innermost thoughts and activities. It was agonisingly frustrating. At last I received my own dreaded "Dear John" letter from Ann asking for release from our engagement because she wanted to marry somebody else. What could I possibly do other than acquiesce and tell her that I loved her and wish her every happiness? It would have been impossible to convey to her or anyone else the utter misery I felt.

I am very thankful that I had Bear Kruimink to talk to quietly and without any emotional drama. He responded like the wonderfully wise and sincere friend he had become. He volunteered me no advice or sympathy. He was just *there*, my friend in abject dejection. I made little mention of my problem to anyone else, especially not to Douglas Bader because he would have come up with a solution like "good air discipline". One day about then, I was walking round the yard with Douglas and he was chatting away to me when I suddenly realised that I could hear his words but not follow his conversation. This was frightening. I broke away from him as quickly as possible without seeming too rude, found Bear and confided the problem to him. He tried to be helpful, but the problem persisted and we agreed that I should report to our new senior medical officer, Lieutenant-Colonel Bull. I talked to the doctor at some length about my state and had a long sympathetic session with him. The outcome of this was his opinion that there would be only one solution to my problem and that would be "the end of the war". In the meantime, he suggested I would just have to somehow pull myself together and get on with it.

I told nobody else about my misery, pulled myself together and got on with it! I sometimes felt I had suffered a complete meltdown and had been poured into a different mould. At no time did I have any thoughts about suicide, but I did not care very much about the outcome of my resolution to make life as difficult as possible for our enemy. It became my one aim and I felt comfortable about the fact that it was in accordance with my official brief from MI9 about duty as a POW, and that it afforded my companions some relief in laughter.

All ordeals do, eventually, come to an end, and after D-Day, we knew that it was finally in sight. The bogging down of the Allied offensive in the Ardennes forest in the winter of 1944/45 was a disappointment—some of us had hoped that our eternal prediction of "home by Christmas" might come true at last, but with the return of better weather, the Allied juggernaut on both the Western and Eastern fronts became unstoppable. My memories of the last grey weeks (or was it months) in Colditz remain scattered: vivid cameos of reality in the long fitful nightmare of my last couple of years in custody. Most of that time I was in solitary confinement, but strangely I cannot remember in which cellblock. I know that towards the end I was in an unusual cell with its heavily barred window directly below another like it in one of the British quarters. My friends knew I was there and positioned a gramophone just inside their window where I could hear it. A record had just arrived from some kindly organisation in Switzerland of music from the show *Oklahoma!* and it was played over and over again. I absorbed the songs like a magic salve, especially the lines "Oh what a beautiful day, I've got a wonderful feeling everything's going my way." Oh, the promise in that song! Soon I, too, would enjoy beautiful days of freedom tinged with a touch of sadness about what had NOT gone my way. Even now, nearly seventy years later, I cannot hear that music completely dry-eyed. It promised so much I had longed for, for so long. I would soon sit blissfully again by that quiet secret lake, and as for the heartbreak—hope springs eternal! Nobody had confirmed Ann's marriage.

I do not remember being released from that cell, which is strange because it must have been one of the greatest moments of my life. I believe the American, Colonel Schaeffer, was let out of solitary at the same time, along with a few others. Everything in the castle was then in a state of flux and chaos. Thousands of inmates from prison camps about to be overrun by the advancing Allies, especially the Russians from the east, were being moved by forced marches westwards. Hundreds of them were suddenly packed into Colditz. The newcomers were mainly French, and what a scruffy, half-starved lot those poor blighters were. They reminded me of the tramps of my boyhood days travelling between workhouses for a night's shelter. They had acquired such things as perambulators to convey their belongings or had made little trolleys they called "*chariots*" (pronounced sharry-oh). To make room for the influx, we were crammed into rooms in the southwest wing of the castle above the cellars.

Conversation among us, the British, centred almost entirely upon liberation and there was considerable discussion about the likelihood and hazards of a forced march. Apart from certain exhaustion, hunger and exposure, marching columns were liable to be strafed by Allied fighter bombers, mistaking them for enemy troop movements. Sadly, this had actually occurred.

My own feeling about all this was that, whatever happened, it would be a damn sight easier to break away and do one's own thing, and that was what I intended to do—if we were moved out. To hell with remaining a captive of guards with rifles! Opinions were mixed about this and there was one army officer who for some reason seemed horrified about the prospect of a forced march. He harped on and on about it after lights out, to the extent of trying the patience of most of us. "If only we could make *chariots* like the French, I'd give anything for one of those things."

"Right!" I thought. There was an obvious way to shut him up. Next morning, I visited the French and almost immediately obtained a *chariot* in exchange for a pack of twenty cigarettes. That evening, I waited for the tiresome Pongo to start his inevitable moan. "Did you say you would give £300 for a *chariot*?" I asked him.

"Oh yes—I would. I would," he said.

"Okay," I replied. "Well, here's one for a packet of twenty cigarettes!"

At this stage, we now know secret negotiations were going on between the German *Kommandant*, Oberstleutnant Prawitt and Colonel Tod, together with Brigadier Davies, a latecomer to Colditz who, on arrival, was still suffering from serious wounds, and Colonel Duke who represented a small American contingent. When the discussions affected the French, they were represented by their senior officer. Simplifying the negotiations, it came to this: the Wehrmacht was telling Prawitt to do one thing and our people were telling him he'd better not or they would see that he paid for it with his head.

Day by day the battle was raging and the nearest American force, commanded by Colonel Leo Shaughnessy, was coming ever closer. It was obvious to everybody, including Prawitt, that it was only a matter of days, or even hours, before Prawitt and his men would be the prisoners. Our negotiators won some and lost some. Prawitt was persuaded to ignore his orders to move us out on a forced march. Some of us were released from solitary confinement.

Then there were some very serious discussions about the fate of the Prominente. An order had come to Prawitt from Heinrich Himmler to move them out to an area less immediately threatened by liberation by Allied Forces. Our delegation threatened Prawitt that his head would be on the block if any harm came to them, which it would be anyway if an order from Himmler was disobeyed—the SS would see to that. A compromise was reached whereby it was agreed that Hauptmann Eggers would go with them, and return with a letter signed by them all confirming their new location and general welfare. This worked out satisfactorily.

Negotiations with Prawitt were bedevilled by another factor. There was a strong SS presence in the locality and we had been made aware they were a threat to the prisoners of Colditz, especially if the *Kommandant* appeared to be failing in his duty to the Reich or the *Führer*. This would be equally dangerous for Prawitt or any of his staff. It was understood that in the event of failure on the part of Prawitt's garrison, the SS would move in to liquidate the prisoners, who were all considered by them to be *Deutschfeindlich*, although only a few, like myself, were officially so designated. The already well-known record of the SS, quite apart from post-war revelations, could leave no doubt about the reality of this threat.

Thus it was that when Prawitt was eventually persuaded, in return for "safe conduct" pledges, to surrender the keys of the castle to us, it was necessary for all concerned—Germans and prisoners—to ensure that there were no obvious outward indications that this had happened. The SS would have been in like a shot and that would probably have meant curtains for us all. They were utterly ruthless.

For this reason, no flags or white sheets could be draped from our windows to inform the advancing Americans who we were. A few shells hit the castle and Douglas Bader was knocked off his tin legs, but unhurt. The Germans tried to blow up the bridge over the River Mulde in Colditz town, but made a hash of it. A large "POW" ground-to-air sign made with bedding was laid out in the courtyard which could be seen only from above by the American Thunderbolt pilots who were strafing ground targets with apparently no Luftwaffe opposition. In order that Prawitt's surrender should not be obvious to the SS, his German guards were ordered to remain at their posts, but armed with empty rifles.

Preparations for liberty were feverish. It was said the Frogs were looking up girl friends' telephone numbers in their little black books; the more religious people like the Roman Catholic Poles held a service of thanksgiving; and the British, especially the Pongoes, shone their boots and polished their buttons. Everyone was sorting out meagre belongings to see what should be taken home and what left behind.

I had scrounged a tatty old suitcase from somewhere and packed some clothing, especially a uniform which had, at my request by "split photograph", been sent to me by MI9. It was a Luftwaffe officer's uniform disguised as an RAF uniform. The Germans had spotted the ruse when it arrived and confiscated it for their museum in the *Kommandantur*. I plundered the museum to recover it and grabbed some other confiscated memorabilia which I brought back with papers relative to my five courts martial and my letters from Ann.

My most prized possession was a Spanish guitar with its case which I had been able to purchase from Switzerland thorough some welfare organisation with *Lagergeld*. A Dutch officer had taught me to play it well enough to perform in his "Hawaiian Band" and to amuse myself. I had really enjoyed playing my guitar.

Eventually, among all these blurred disjointed memories, the moment of liberation arrived, the moment we had all lived for, some for more than five years—the moment that everyone had conjured up in his mind as a really grand finale to a miserable dark chapter in his life. How would it be?

Perhaps the gate would open, and there would be standing a senior officer of the liberation force—say, a Guards Colonel at least—he would salute and we would all salute back. "Gentlemen," he would say. "Your days of durance vile are at an end. You are free! God save the King!" Lusty cheers and celebrations would follow.

Well, it wasn't quite like that!

On 16 April 1945, the gate did open and there stood a single American GI who had not shaved for some days. His helmet was askew, his chinstraps were dangling and he was chewing gum. His person was adorned with ammunition magazines and a couple of grenades. Snuggled in the crook of his arm was a tommy gun which he obviously knew very well how to use. It was immediately apparent that he was taken aback, slightly horrified at the sight of the wide-eyed, highly animated mob facing him, and when the ever-passionate Frenchmen surged towards him, I thought for a ghastly moment he was going to defend himself with a burst from the tommy gun. "*Vive les Américains!*" they shouted as they surged forward and overwhelmed him with embraces and attempts to kiss him on both cheeks. And, at last, we heard those long-anticipated first words of our gallant liberator.

"Aw—quit mawlin' me, will ya?"

We were now fully under the command of our own senior officers and not the Germans. Orders were given about who could and who could not leave the castle, for what reason and how long they could go. Under the circumstances it was all entirely reasonable and acceptable. We now had our own guards on the gate. The German sentries who, for appearance's sake since Prawitt's surrender, had been required to remain on duty with empty magazines in their rifles, were no longer permitted to do so.

The Colditz glider was revealed to full public gaze from its clandestine walled-off section of the attics. The Germans gaped at it, flabbergasted that such a thing could have been created under their very noses. American journalists appeared and one such, a woman, took a photograph of the glider which is the only one in existence—and even that did not surface until several years later. Some of the more newsworthy or important people, like Douglas Bader, were whisked away for their publicity value and were gone.

A message from the War Office was circulated asking for volunteers among officer POWs who could speak some German to remain behind to assist in the organisation and repatriation of the thousands of POWs. I offered to do this, pointing out that "my domestic urgency was less than for many other officers with wives, children and mothers anxiously awaiting their return whereas I had no such ties of immediate importance". I had recently heard that even my father had at last remarried and moved home to the wilds of South Wales with a dear old intellectual soulmate in a wheelchair whom I had never met. There was not really all that much needing or attracting me. In the event my services were not required. None of us remained behind.

Then ensued the most exciting, wildly anticipated, arrangements of all—our repatriation to England. We were to be driven in open American trucks to an airfield at Kölleda, quite a distance away, where we would be loaded into American Air Force DC3s (Dakotas) for a flight to England. What an ultimate joy!

Dick Howe, our erstwhile escape officer and the man from whom I had been taking operational instructions for the past three years or so, approached me. Dick told me the Americans had accepted his offer to ride a German BMW motorbike as a vanguard for our unescorted trucks in case we ran into any pockets of die-hard resistance which the American advance had by-passed and which they suspected might still exist, manned by SS fanatics or *Hitlerjugend* death-or-glory boys.

Dick also mentioned that the Americans had recommended that some of us on the open trucks arm ourselves in order to return fire if we ran into any such pockets of resistance. He asked me to do something about this and I agreed to do so. I briefed a few others and went off in search of a German rifle and ammunition. It meant I would have to abandon my guitar, but it was a small price to pay under the circumstances.

We were eventually loaded onto those American open trucks, all driven by black American soldiers. Hauptmann Püpcke, now a POW, was loaded onto our truck and shoved up to the front where I had the Mauser rifle resting on the driver's cab roof as requested by the Americans. When Püpcke saw me his sad, strained face broke into a wan smile. He said, "*Jetzt sind* Sie mein *Posten!*" (Now *you* are *my* guard!). I felt deeply touched by the pathos of it all. I put my hand on his shoulder and said, "Nein, nein, Herr Hauptmann," and added in my best German, "If I could make it so, you would now go home to your family. I have no wish for you the misery that is just ending for us. The war is over, now we must try to become friends." I was aware that Püpcke's eyes and mine were moist. I have always been too damned soft for comfort.

Püpcke spent three years or so as a prisoner of the Russians which could not have been much of a picnic considering what the Russians had suffered at the hands of the Germans, especially the murderous special SS Units, and as POWs. I was subsequently told that Püpcke's health was badly affected and I was sorry to hear it.

We drove to Kölleda encountering only one enemy roadblock which Dick Howe approached with due caution and found deserted. There was no further incident. I brought the Mauser rifle home as a souvenir and still have it to this day but, alas, no guitar!

On 20 April—Hitler's birthday, the last one he was ever to see—we arrived at Kölleda and were fed lavishly on American rations. Eventually, we were herded into lots for our final flight to England. My particular pals of the Colditz contingent stuck together. Without undue fuss, we were loaded into DC3s, twin-engined Dakotas, the famous American aerial workhorse.

As we embarked for the final leg home, I had a sudden cheeky inspiration. Instead of taking a seat in the normal passenger compartment, I made my way for'ard and plonked myself down on the jump seat in the cockpit. The First Officer (or "second pilot") was a cheery young lad, Second Lieutenant J. Hughes, who took his seat on the right and then the Captain, a more mature man, First Lieutenant D.F. Mondt, arrived. He nodded pleasantly to me, strapped himself into the left hand seat, went through the pre-flight rigmarole with his copilot, and we took off.

With perfect honesty, I said to him, "This is a great moment for me. I haven't been airborne for nearly five years." He looked at me and probably recognised my RAF pilot's wings badge. He smiled broadly and said, "Ya haven't? Well, git in here an' drive!" My saucy ploy had paid off far beyond I ever imagined it would. It was not a crazily irresponsible thing for Lieutenant Mondt to do because his "second dickey" was sitting there in the right hand seat and could have forestalled any imminent calamity.

I settled into the Captain's seat on the port side and it seemed like only yesterday that I had last flown. Flying is like swimming or riding a bike. Once you can do it, you never forget how. Only the new-fangled gadgets, instruments and procedures were strange. Lieutenant Mondt pointed to the ADF (Automatic Direction Finder) and asked, "D'ya know how this thing works?"

"No, I don't," I replied, "never seen it before."

"It's easy," and he showed me how to stay on course on a radio bearing to a beacon.

"Got it?" he asked.

"Got it!" I said, and indeed it was very simple. The weather was pleasant and flying the Dakota was a piece of wonderful refreshing cake.

The Skipper then went aft to talk to the boys. A couple of times, he came back onto the flight deck, gave me a slap on the shoulder and said, "How're ya doin', Doc?" Then he returned to continue his conversation with the passengers. I was told afterwards that he said to some of them, "Your pal Pete's up there doin' the drivin'," to which a typical response was, "Holy Mackerel! How the hell can we get out of this bloody thing?"

When we eventually crossed the White Cliffs of Dover, I was back in the cabin. Our chaps were looking down, stony faces hiding the deep emotions within, and I noticed at least one of the American crewmen was surreptitiously wiping a tear. I remember thinking how human beings can be so very nice sometimes—it's amazing how nasty they can be at others! We landed at RAF Westcot, not far from Oxford, at five minutes past eight that same evening of 20 April 1945.

We disembarked from the aircraft and were directed to the side entrance of one of the hangars. It was as well we were not expecting anything like a heroes' welcome home. There was no band, nor cheering crowd. The only ritual in the welcoming process occurred as I passed through the hangar's side door. An army medical orderly said, "Excuse me, sir," pulled open the top of my trousers and puffed a large dose of DDT powder down into my nether quarters. He was kind and courteous enough to do up my trousers for me afterwards which I really appreciated! Then a nice old dolly in Salvation Army uniform gave me a bun and a mug of tea—and that was it.

Immediately this welcoming ritual was completed, we were directed to a line of card tables in the almost empty hangar. Behind each table sat an army officer, three of whom were women, so I picked the best-looking one, made a beeline for her, and sat down on the empty chair facing her.

They were intelligence officers and this was our debriefing. It was a pleasant experience to be talking to a real live woman again after five years of deprivation. She was charming, but very brusque. Obviously, they knew the ex-prisoners would be longing to get going for home and loved ones, and were considerate and anxious to minimise the delay. She had a form in front of her and filled it in as I answered her questions. Name? Rank? Service number? Squadron? Station? When captured? Where? Which prison camps?

And suddenly she stopped and looked at me curiously. Then she said, "I'm from MI9. Aren't you the one who sent messages to us inside photographs?" I told her, yes, I was, and she beamed and the whole thing became much more personal. The form was forgotten and she asked me how I had done this, that and the other. "We were so thrilled to get them," she said. "It was quite exciting."

And then we got on with the business in hand.

Afterword

Grasmere, my old home in the village of Orsett in Essex, was no longer "home." Our housekeeper, Edith Attrill, who I once called "mummy", had become the mistress of Grasmere and was very kind and welcoming but she now had her own circle of friends with whom I had very little in common. There is no doubt about her devotion to me as an infant and she had dutifully organised such parcels as could be sent to POWs through the Red Cross. I have always been aware of the debt of gratitude I owed her, but she tended to think I ought to belong within her sphere and I simply did not. We had grown far apart.

Furthermore, Ann was living at her old home, the very next house to Grasmere about a quarter of a mile away. Her husband was serving overseas and I went to see Ann only once. Her mother was at home. We went to the summer house where I first kissed her when we were in our teens. We spoke for a very short time. I told her I still loved her and was there for her if ever she needed me. She thought I should return her letters to her, which I subsequently did. I kissed her once on the forehead and that was that. I never saw her again. I felt Grasmere could not be my home. It was too close to hers. For a short while I felt I did not want to live anywhere much.

My brother Geoff was married and living in London which I would have hated. My dear sister Lucy, who had two children, was having a really rough time. Her Scottish husband, Willy Lindsay, had died of cancer while still a young man, and now Lucy was, as it turned out, terminally ill with mitral stenosis. She and her children had left their farm and were living with Willy's married sister. My visits to Lucy's bedside, sometimes with amusing chums, cheered her up considerably, but it was a lost cause. She, too, died young.

I made a brief call on my retired father who had remarried and moved to a tiny sort of flat adjoining a disused chapel in a small village in South Wales. His wife was a gentle old lady confined to a wheelchair. He waited on her hand and foot. It was obvious that she afforded him the intellectual companionship he had so missed since my mother died a few days after my birth. They did not possess even a spare bedroom and I had to spend a couple of nights as a boarder in the village.

The RAF insisted that we have six weeks' home leave and this infuriated me. What the hell could I do with it? The Service was my home and I wanted to get back to it. Above all, I wanted to get back to flying and, if possible, into action against the Japanese. I felt I had unfinished business and things to prove. I even visited the Air Ministry to plead my case and was virtually laughed at. "Good God! We have thousands of redundant aircrew. Why should we bother to train ex-POWs?"

I had six weeks of storming around London with a Canadian Lancaster crew awaiting repatriation to Canada. Their flight engineer, the only Englishman in the crew, was a distant relative of mine. We wined (heavily) and dined and danced and the girls were extraordinarily generous to us, especially ex-POWs.

But all the time I was contacting old commanding officers—now with Air Rank—who promised to pull strings for me. Eventually I was allowed to fly aeroplanes, but NOT solo. Nobody would believe we were not a bit round the bend and perhaps they were right.

At last I contacted Douglas Bader who had become a group captain commanding the Fighter Leaders' School at Tangmere. I flew down to him in a Miles Master on 3 July 1945 with a safety pilot and Dougie arranged a quick test flight for me with a qualified RAF flying instructor. He then signed a note, which is still in my old RAF pilot's log book, stating that I was fit to fly solo. That did the trick. Only three of all those hundreds of RAF POWs were allowed back to flying: Flight Lieutenant "Abdul" Abbott, DSO, DFM; Flight Lieutenant Tim Thomas—a dashing fighter boy—and me. Others followed later after proving that, although perhaps still a bit round the bend, they could still fly.

Furthermore, Abdul and I pulled more strings and were promised by the famous Sir Gus Walker a place in "Tiger Force", the Bomber Command unit which was gearing up to bomb Japan. I still have the nice letter of acceptance from Gus Walker. Perhaps "everything was going my way" at last! Or was it? By the time we were less than halfway through our very

Return to the air: PDT performing pre-flight checks on a
heavy bomber after the war.

thorough training as bomber pilots (I had never had such training before
Ops in 1940), the American atom bomb ended the Japanese war.

I saw nothing more of my crew until after the war, and then only
Murdock and Brock. Later I heard that my Irish Observer/Air Gunner,
Sergeant Mike Joyce, had become a traitor! His American-born cousin,
William Joyce, was a leading British fascist who, when hostilities began
against Germany, had disappeared and emerged in Berlin. An infamous
broadcaster of Nazi propaganda to Britain throughout the war, his sinister
diatribes always began with the words, "Germany calling, Germany
calling." His cynical and contemptuous style earned him the nick-name
"Lord Haw Haw", but most listeners regarded him more as a joke than a
menace. After the war he was tried for treason and hanged at Wandsworth
Prison in London.

Serving with the RAF in 1940, Mike Joyce naturally kept very quiet
about his fascist relative. As a POW in Germany, however, he was favoured
and kept for a long time on the "permanent prisoner staff" at Dulag Luft.

There he became friendly with a congenial young German intelligence officer named Eberhard, who was one of the smooth interrogators who worked on me as a new arrival. Eberhard persuaded Joyce to become a stool pigeon for the Germans and help them gather information from aircrew newly landed "in the bag". By the sound of things, not much persuasion was necessary—Joyce rapidly decided that Germany was bound to win the war and decided to clamber on the bandwagon before it was too late. He then progressed with his new masters who, at his request ("because he was bored") moved him to Derna in North Africa where he again sucked information out of new prisoners, sometimes wearing his own RAF gear and sometimes a Luftwaffe uniform, as one Willi Schneider. There was nothing too unusual about a German *Dolmetscher* (interpreter) speaking perfect, even colloquial, English or American. Many German nationals who had grown up in Britain or the USA fled back to serve the Fatherland shortly before war was declared so as to avoid being interned for the duration in their host country.

Sergeant Joyce must have won the full confidence of the Germans because he was eventually offered the chance to pose as a newly shot-down RAF aircrew member, and seek out and request the assistance of a secret Franco-Belgian Resistance organisation which was sheltering Allied aircrew shot down over occupied countries. These brave people smuggled aircrews, code-named "parcels", to freedom via unoccupied southern France, then over the Pyrenees into Spain and thence into British territory at Gibraltar. From Gibraltar, escaped POWs were conveyed back to England to acclaim and glory.

The German deal offered to Joyce was that he would undertake to "blow" the identity of the Resistance operatives who would then be rounded up and shot by the Gestapo. Joyce accepted the deal but decided to see how far he got with the Resistance. He thought he was a winner either way: either he would get back to Allied territory and be hailed as an escaping hero, or would be stopped *en route* by the Germans, in which case he could betray those who had helped him and win points with his *Abwehr* masters. In the event, he made it all the way to Gibraltar and was flown back to Britain. He was immediately awarded the Military Medal (equivalent of the Military Cross for officers), and was subsequently commissioned. He ended the war

Sketch by PDT of his nerve-racking "exercise" after
the Spangenberg escape. (See p. 208)

with the RAF rank of flying officer, the same as my own when I was captain
of his bomber in 1940.

Alas for Joyce, at the end of the war the records of Dulag Luft fell into
Allied hands. My former observer was promptly interrogated by detectives
of the RAF Special Investigation Branch and ultimately confessed his
treachery. A very tiny and discreet press notice announced the withdrawal
of Joyce's Military Medal after he "resigned" his commission. The
extraordinary end to this story is that, although William Joyce had dangled
on a rope, his RAF traitor cousin was told to get the hell out of it back to
Ireland and keep his mouth shut—which he did. Maybe that saved British
Intelligence from egg on a few red faces.

Mike Joyce married, fathered seven children and died in 1976, shortly
after helping to organise the re-interment of cousin William's remains
from his villain's grave in Wandsworth Prison to Galway in the Republic

of Ireland. One wonders which cousin was more deserving of the rope. At least it was claimed that William was not really a British subject and certainly not a member of the RAF!

Did I ever suspect Joyce of anything untoward or stranger than just being your average, friendly Irish joker? The answer is an emphatic, no, never! But in 1940, RAF aircrews were not on the chummy first-name terms— the pubbing together, close-knit brotherhood—of the later Lancaster bomber era. By that time, a typical captain of a bomber aircraft, even if a commissioned officer, would rarely be addressed by his NCO crew as "sir". He had become "skipper" or just "skip", and off camp they socialised together as closely as they died together. There was nothing wrong with that as a wartime phenomenon. Things were more formal in my day, and in any case, my crew and I simply didn't have enough time together to develop that kind of relationship before we were captured and separated. While I'm on the subject of decorations, however, there's a rich irony in the fact that my observer received the fourth-highest award for gallantry, in respect of an "escape" that was actually a put-up job by the German intelligence network.

My service career continued during peacetime. I became a flight commander on 50 Squadron with Lancasters and then commanded 101 Squadron with Lincolns at RAF Binbrook. Later on, after my retirement from the RAF, I had a spell in commercial flying.

While a POW at Colditz, the director of our theatre productions, Teddy Barton, once asked me what I intended to do after the war and I said I hoped to continue my flying career. He suggested that I might turn to acting. Years later, aged 59, having won a few amateur dramatic awards in my new home, South Africa, I did just that. I became a professional actor on live stage, television, radio and films, but the seed was sown years earlier in Colditz.

I also married. My first marriage wasn't a success and didn't last very long. We weren't truly compatible, but it's also the case that I had been more deeply affected by my years in prison camp than at the time I was prepared to admit, even to myself. After the break-up, when I was at a low ebb, came the best piece of luck I ever had. I met and married another beautiful young woman named Ann. There aren't sufficient words to

On the set: a publicity photo of PDT as a film actor in the 1980s.

express what she meant and continues to mean to me: suffice it to say that she is, and will always remain, the light of my life.

I've had an unusually long, mostly healthy, and—despite some of the harrowing experiences described in this book—rich and rewarding time on this earth. I'm immensely grateful for the blessings I've received, most of all for my wife and children. Yet I know, three-quarters of a century after the war, how profound an imprint that experience has left upon me. During those more than seventy years, hardly a day has gone by when I have not relived those times, most of all that fateful last flight that led to our capture. I do not believe in wallowing in self-pity, or in useless regrets. But neither is there any point in denying reality. I emerged from the war a changed man, and those changes have been lasting. It was a truly dreadful time, filled with horrors, fear, frustration and death. It was also filled with intense comradeship, generosity, unselfishness and sense of purpose. Trying somehow to reconcile within myself these conflicting emotions has been the task of a lifetime. It isn't finished yet.

I'm a bit concerned, though, about the fact that, as we who were there pass from the scene, a misleading impression of who we were and what we were trying to do has begun to take a hold. For the current generation in particular, the Allied bombing offensive, of which I was a part, has come to stand out as a black mark against the war effort as a whole. I understand those sentiments and what lies behind them. But I also firmly believe that they are based on deep misconceptions about the period of history through which I lived, and the job that my comrades and I had to do.

As you, the reader, will know by now, I am under no illusions whatever about just how blunt an instrument was the British bomber force in the Second World War. By their nature, bombs are more or less indiscriminate weapons, no matter how precisely they're targeted. Whoever happens to be standing underneath is in the firing line. We ourselves were all too aware of that. Inadequately trained; sent off in the dark and in all weathers in aircraft whose shockingly primitive equipment more often than not didn't work; and opposed every step of the way by people trying very hard and with great ingenuity to kill us; it's miraculous that we sometimes got as close to our intended targets as we did. And an appalling number of us died in the attempt. As late as 1941, the total number of British aircrew killed while bombing Germany was greater than the total number of Germans killed by our bombs.

Later on, the technology and training improved, though not to a spectacular degree. Whereas once we had sometimes struggled to identify the correct country, by 1943 and 1944 we were able to bomb cities, at any rate, with reasonable confidence. But with rare exceptions like the Dambusters' raid—from which nearly half the attacking force failed to return—hitting precision targets was still far beyond our capabilities. Even the Americans, who tried hardest of all with their suicidally brave daylight raids, never achieved better than an average bombing error of more than two miles.

The choice we ultimately faced, then, was to attack Germany's cities or not to have a bomber offensive at all. But not bombing simply wasn't an option. After our armies were defeated in France in the summer of 1940, there was no conceivable, or even inconceivable, way of defeating the Nazis that didn't involve air attacks. Nothing else we could do stood the faintest chance of diminishing Germany's war-making capacity. The Royal Navy and Fighter Command might prevent us from losing the war—for a time. But they could not win it. Nor could what was left of our army, all of whose equipment had been left behind on the beaches of Dunkirk. Bombing was, quite literally, our only hope. To refrain from it was to acknowledge that the war was over; that Germany had won; and that hundreds of millions of Europeans must now be left to Hitler's tender mercies.

This, I think, is where today's critics of the bomber offensive miss the mark. They know that the Germans were going to invade the Soviet Union in June 1941. They know that the Americans were going to join us the following December. They know that the great Nazi offensives in the East in 1941 and 1942 were going to fail in the long run, and that from the beginning of 1943 Germany would be continuously on the retreat. They know that the D-Day landings were going to be a success. Above all, they know that the Allies rather than the Germans were going to win the race to develop the first atomic bomb. For them, it's a matter of using hindsight to decide what was the most efficient, or most humanitarian, means of achieving a victory that was never in question.

We, though, knew none of these things. Nor could we count on them occurring. When I began my operational career in earnest in the summer of 1940, there was every good reason to believe that the lifespan of Great Britain as an independent country might be measured in weeks. (That, after all, was the calculation of Sergeant Mike Joyce, and even in retrospect it's hard to argue that my observer didn't have some basis for it.) At that time, we were clinging on desperately, hoping against hope that we could somehow hold out until the autumnal gales would make a German seaborne invasion too risky a proposition. The bombing offensive into which my comrades and I were hurled to try and buy us a few more weeks of time was Winston Churchill's last throw of the dice.

By the grace of God we did hold out; Hitler did turn his attentions to the Soviet Union; and the Americans did come to help us. Even then, though, this was a war we could so easily have lost. More than once the Red Army was on the brink of defeat. We had no way of knowing that Stalin, shaken by his grievous losses, would not cut a deal with Hitler as he had already done in the past and, as we now know, he more than once seriously contemplated doing. A negotiated peace on the Eastern Front would have left Germany in a much more dominant position even than the one she enjoyed in 1940, and without Soviet assistance, all the might of the United States would probably not have been enough to dislodge her.

We had no way of knowing, then, that we were sure to win. Indeed, it was impossible to tell that we were engaged in a conflict whose outcome would be decided in four or five years. To many of us at the time, it seemed as though Europe might be heading into a renewed version of the Thirty Years' War of the seventeenth century—or perhaps even the Hundred Years' War of the fourteenth and fifteenth.

There, though, was the rub. Hitler's victims didn't have thirty or a hundred years to spare for us to come up with as yet undreamed-of ways of humanely and painlessly defeating him. As I say, we didn't know how many weeks or months our own battered and isolated country, reeling from the Blitz and pushed to the brink of starvation by the U-Boat campaign, was capable of holding out. Quite apart from that, the people under the control of Hitler and his allies were not just facing physical hardship or danger. They were facing imminent extinction.

What people nowadays fail to understand is how greatly we at the time were oppressed—I might almost say haunted—by an all-pervading sense of urgency. Time was not on our side. We did not fully understand just how unimaginably brutal and murderous our enemies truly were, but we knew enough to realise that behind the scenes appalling things were happening to the oppressed peoples of Europe: massacre, expulsion, torture, starvation. They were looking desperately to us for deliverance. And they couldn't afford to wait. Not for years. Not for minutes.

In fact, the war would last for more than 2,000 days. *On each and every one of those days, an average of 25,000 people were killed.* This was the horrific calculus that faced us. If we took just one additional day to defeat the Axis powers—there's 25,000 more corpses, the great majority of them innocent civilians butchered by our enemies. A week's delay? 175,000 dead. Let the war drag on for just one additional month? Three quarters of a million. As a point of information, that's actually a higher number than those who died in the Allied bombing of Germany.

I took no pleasure in those deaths, nor, with the rarest exceptions, did any of the aircrew with whom I served. More than others, we saw for ourselves the true ugliness of war. Nobody wanted to see an end to it more than we did. A few of us may have been embittered and wanted to see Germany suffer. The great majority didn't. But we all understood then, as people have forgotten now, that there was a moral dimension to our inaction, as well as to our actions. By refraining from bombing Germany, we might have spared German civilian lives. But at what cost to the millions of Jews, Poles, Russians, Greeks, Yugoslavs and others who were being systematically wiped out while we dithered about the ethics of warfare? What was our responsibility to them? Were we justified in valuing German lives over theirs—especially if, for every German spared, ten or twenty or thirty of the Nazis' victims were sacrificed to Hitler's genocidal agenda?

For we who were there at that time, the answer seemed clear. And I am bound to say that three-quarters of a century later, it still does. The future of humanity, and for that matter the interests of the German people themselves, required us to do everything we could, using every instrument at our disposal, to defeat the Nazis as quickly and as comprehensively as possible. The Allied bombing offensive was a necessary part of that goal. Lord knows it was far from ideal. It didn't, and couldn't, win the war by itself. But even its most stringent critics concede that it shortened the conflict and, I am convinced, saved perhaps millions of innocent lives that would otherwise have been lost. As long as the war contined, the gas chambers and crematoria of Auschwitz, Treblinka, Sobibor and elsewhere would continue with the extermination of women and children on an industrial scale. It was a terrible thing that the Nazis, in effect, should have put a cordon of their own women and children around these killing factories and dared us to shoot—or bomb—our way through so that we could rescue those victims. But that is the only choice they gave us.

What, then, can I say about all this, from the vantage point of my ninety-five years, to today's generation? I would tell you that it is too late, once the bands stop playing and the shooting starts, to look for a painless or bloodless way of fighting an armed conflict. The realities of total war mean that there is not, and cannot, be any such thing. Instead, even the most ethical leaders and strategists will infallibly find themselves confronted with a series of horrific Hobson's Choices, in which people will suffer and die no matter what they do. That is why it is so vital to work to ensure that things never get to that stage. Blessed are the peacemakers.

But blessed too are those who recognise that the freedom they enjoy was secured at a price. As soon as the war ended, the sacrifices the bomber crews had made to bring about the victory were quickly forgotten. We became something of an embarrassment, ignored by politicians and, until very recently, un-commemorated. It is now, sadly, too late to do justice to most of us. Let future generations ensure that the same thing does not happen to our memory.

Index

Index